C0-BEF-185

WHAT MAKES TEHRAN TICK:
ISLAMIST IDEOLOGY AND HEGEMONIC INTERESTS

Iran Policy Committee

3 JAN 10

A WHITE PAPER

Greame Wood;
Thanks for
your interest!
Raymond

IRAN POLICY COMMITTEE

Washington, DC

Iran Policy Committee
Alban Towers, Suite L-34
3700 Massachusetts Ave. NW
Washington, DC 20016

Phone: 202-249-1142
Fax: 202-249-1143
Email: info@iranpolicy.org
Web: www.iranpolicy.org

Copyright © 2006 by Iran Policy Committee

All rights reserved. Published in Washington,
DC by the Iran Policy Committee. No part of this
publication may be reproduced or transmitted
in any form or by any means, electronic or
mechanical, including photocopy, recording,
or any information storage or retrieval system,
without permission in writing from the publisher.

*Contributions payable to the Iran Policy
Committee (IPC) are tax-deductible to the
extent permitted by law. The Committee is a
§501(c)(3) not-for-profit organization and is
publicly supported as described in 509(a)(1) of
the Internal Revenue Code. The Committee's IRS
identification number is 20-2883425*

ISBN 1-59975-298-3

*Library of Congress Cataloging in
Publication Data:*
A CIP catalogue record for this book can be
obtained from the Library of Congress

Printed in the United States of America by Good
Printers, Inc., Bridgewater, VA.

First Edition

Book and Cover Design by Angela L. Bellefeuille,
Art Director, angelab designs

For contributions to *What Makes Tehran Tick: Islamist Ideology and Hegemonic Interests*, Professor Raymond Tanter, President, Iran Policy Committee and General Thomas McInerney, Chairman, Advisory Council, Iran Policy Committee wish to thank

Allan Gerson

Clare M. Lopez

R. Bruce McColm

Captain Chuck Nash

TABLE OF CONTENTS

CHARTS AND GRAPHS

PHOTOGRAPHS AND MAPS

APPENDIX DOCUMENTS

PROFESSOR RAYMOND TANTER AND GENERAL THOMAS McINERNEY

As President of the Iran Policy Committee (IPC) and, respectively, Chairman of its Advisory Council, we are delighted to introduce the second book under the auspices of the IPC—What Makes Tehran Tick: Islamist Ideology and Hegemonic Interests. A central theme of the first IPC White Paper book is that appeasing Iran's ruling ayatollahs suppresses democracy. By contrast, this book examines the nature of the Iranian regime to evaluate the likelihood of success for U.S. and Israeli policy options.

The nature of the Iranian regime is reminiscent of the anecdote about the Arab-Israel dispute regarding the scorpion and the frog. The scorpion, who cannot swim across the Jordan River, asks the frog for a ride. The hesitant frog expresses his fear that the scorpion might sting him. However, the scorpion asks, "Why would I sting you? We would both drown." The frog accepts the scorpion's logic that it would not be in the scorpion's interest to sting him, and agrees to give the scorpion a ride. Half way across the river, the scorpion stings the frog and they both begin to drown. When the frog questions the scorpion as to why he would take this suicidal course, the scorpion replies, "This is the Middle East."

At the core of the story is the observation that some actors in the Middle East are driven by ideological fervor and maximalist goals that overrule what Westerners consider traditional self-interests.

Iran is no different: Just as it is in the nature of the scorpion to sting, so it is in the nature of the ayatollahs ruling Iran to establish an Islamist empire and destroy Israel. Toward these ends, the regime pursues nuclear weapons, subverts Iraq, and supplies money and arms to Islamist terrorist groups like Hezbollah, Hamas, and Palestinian Islamic Jihad.

Like the frog, realists see traditional national interests as the dominant motivation behind Tehran's decision-making. This realist interpretation dictates the diplomatic tools of either coercive sanctions or a grand strategic bargain. Those advocating coercive diplomacy believe sanctions and incentives will so raise the cost of Iran's intransigence that the regime will accede to the demands of the West. Advocates of a grand bargain believe Iran has real security concerns, and assurances of good will from the United States will make Tehran feel safer, obviating the need for its provocative activities.

Realists fail to realize what makes Tehran tick: An Islamist and expansionist ideology competing with traditional national interests in the motivations of Iran's rulers. The leverage the West has over the national interests of the regime cannot pressure or induce Iran's clerics to forgo their ideological goals.

Others, who have come to the realization that diplomacy will ultimately fail, have resigned themselves to the necessity of military strikes against Iran. But military action is difficult because of the dispersed and hidden nature of Iran's nuclear facilities, dangerous because of Iran's ability to retaliate in the form of state-sponsored terrorism, and costly in human lives for all parties.

But is it not time for the West to consider a third option?

Removing Western restrictions on the two main Iranian opposition groups—the National Council of Resistance of Iran and the Mujahedeen-e Khalq—initiates the empowerment of the Iranian people to effect regime change. Empowerment of the Iranian people begins to change the regime, moving beyond the stalled diplomatic course and postponing or perhaps avoiding military action.

EXECUTIVE SUMMARY

What Makes Tehran Tick: Islamist Ideology and Hegemonic Interests

In July 2006, a dramatic scenario began to unfold involving Iran, Israel, and the United States. As Mahmoud Ahmadinejad unleashed his terrorist proxy Hezbollah on Israel, these three nations—and the legions of nations and organizations that support them—found themselves cast in roles that recall the early days of World War II. The Mid-East crisis that arose in July 2006 shares many similarities with the foreboding political stage of 1930s Europe, where the term "Munich" began to symbolize appeasement in the face of aggression.

Those who advocate a grand diplomatic bargain with the Tehran regime are reminiscent of the appeasing Chamberlain, and those who see Ahmadinejad's actions for what they are—ideological fervor run amok—seek a Churchill to confront Iran sooner rather than later.

The advocates of a grand bargain with Iran view the situation through the lens of World War I, in which an unrestrained resort to arms led to a catastrophic cycle of violence. If confronted with failing diplomacy, they suggest that now is not the time to give up on diplomacy, nor is it the time to rush the diplomatic process. They instead insist that this is the time to make additional concessions, to do whatever is necessary to avoid war.

Those who clamor for military action see the 2006 United States offer to negotiate directly with Iran as "Munich" all over again, but worse because this time, the fascist aggresor is likely to emerge from the diplomacy of appeasement not just with territory but with nuclear weapons. They ask, "If not now, when?"

The radical ayatollahs in Iran see the American offer of direct talks as weakness, emboldening them toward more provocative action in their quest for dominance of the Middle East, destruction of Israel, and global conflict with the United States. Though this analysis of Iranian perceptions is valid, those whose first choice is military confrontation ignore a crucial political alternative for the international community that emerges from an analysis of failing diplomacy and problematic military action: Empower the Iranian people to change the regime by removing western restrictions on the main Iranian opposition groups.

After Ahmadinejad assumed the presidency of Iran in 2005, there was a sharp increase in the intensity of antagonistic rhetoric coming from the regime in Tehran. Even as Iran came under severe international criticism for its nuclear program, Ahmadinejad continued to issue threats against Israel and the

United States and promises of material assistance to Hezbollah and Hamas. He seemed to be begging for conflict with the West.

The response of the West was something akin to the reaction in Europe during the 1930s to Hitler's aggressive rhetoric against Europe's Jews. Hitler's threats were dismissed as a rhetorical tool that would never be translated into action, so long as he was appeased. A decade later, appeasement had become a dirty word, yet today, many observers dismiss the statements made by Ahmadinejad. His statement that Israel should be "wiped off the map" was interpreted as merely a verbal effort to appeal to the Muslim world and they advocated continued talks and concessions in the hopes that Ahmadinejad's words, and those of the Ayatollahs, would never manifest.

One politician who takes the fiery rhetoric of the president of Iran seriously is German Chancellor Angela Merkel. In Munich on 4 February 2006, she recalled German history in the early 1930s when the Nazis were on the rise; she remarked how many outside Germany stated that, "It's only rhetoric—don't get excited." "There were times when people could have reacted differently and, in my view, Germany is obliged to do something at the early stages," she added. "We want

to; we must prevent Iran from developing its nuclear programme."

How admirable it is for a German Chancellor to step up to be the Churchill of the 21st Century. Making the comparison of Ahmadinejad with Hitler is a sign that she correctly perceives the nature of the regime and what difference the nature makes. At issue is what Germany is prepared to do about the threat. German policy is stuck on diplomacy, but Merkel's threat perception dictates political regime change.

The deliberate initiation of war with Israel in July 2006 by Hezbollah, most probably at the direction of the Iranian regime, confirmed the worst fears about Ahmadinejad. It is the convergence of intensifying hostile rhetoric, provocative and violent actions against Israel, and accelerating pace of bombmaking that make a nuclear-armed Iran the single greatest security threat to the international community in general, and to the United States and Israel in particular.

The alarming and puzzling behavior of Iran and its terrorist proxies, Hezbollah, Hamas, and Palestinian Islamic Jihad led the Iran Policy Committee to undertake an extensive study of the motivating forces in the decision-making of Islamist regimes and to spell out implications for the United States and Israel. At issue are three questions:

- What is the nature of these regimes—Iran, Hezbollah, Hamas, and Palestinian Islamic Jihad?

- What difference does the nature of these regimes make?

- What is the international community, especially Israel and the United States, prepared to do in light of the nature of these regimes, their prior actions, and their future behavior?

First, violent Islamist ideology is the driving force behind decision-making for Iran—the mother of all state terrorist enterprises. Islamism holds that tenets of the Koran and governance of a state are inseparable. Islamists believe that because Islam addresses every aspect of life, a society cannot be devoutly Islamic unless its government embodies religious instruction, and the Islamic way of life should be forced on nonbelievers and is exportable by force of arms.

Second, the ideological nature of the Iranian regime drives it to become a terrorist state as well as to sponsor like-minded sub-national terrorist groups: Hezbollah, Hamas, and Palestinian Islamic Jihad. And a combination of ideology and traditional Persian interests act as drivers propelling Iran to exercise hegemony in the Gulf, seek to create and dominate a new Islamic Caliphate, and acquire nuclear weapons as a means to coerce the neighbors and maintain power at home.

Such a combustible mix of ideology and interests makes diplomacy, as it has been conducted for Iran, unlikely to succeed.

Third, as the international community focuses mainly on two options of diplomacy in the tradition of Chamberlain and military action in the practice of Churchill, the community ignores a third option of regime change. Regime change would produce a nuclear-armed Iran of less consequence; terminate the Iranian lifeline to Hezbollah, Hamas, and Palestinian Islamic Jihad; and help jumpstart the march toward democratic peace in the Middle East.

Conclusions about the nature of the regimes derive from a quantitative content analysis of the Iranian regime's statements about Israel and the United States from 1979 through 2005. By analyzing perception of threat and expression of hostility statements and juxtaposing these against events, researchers inferred how Iran's attitude toward Israel and the United States has evolved over the lifespan of the regime. Perception of threat refers to Iran's understanding of the danger to its interests and ideology, and expression of hostility is the articulation of how Iran views Israel and the United States.

The Iran Policy Committee conducted a companion qualitative study of statements made by the leaderships of Hezbollah and Hamas. These groups directed less rhetoric toward the United States and more toward Israel than did the Iranian regime. However, the level of hostility and the "religious" nature of their rhetoric were consistent with that of Iran.

Findings of the study reveal important insights into the nature of all three actors. Although Iran perceived little threat from Israel, its expression of hostility toward the country was extreme. The Iran Policy Committee infers that this hostility derives from Islamist ideological prerogatives more than traditional national interests.

These quantitative results are consistent with the qualitative analysis of the stated objectives of all three actors. Iran, Hezbollah, and Hamas perceive as their divine mission the destruction of Israel, resistance to cultural influences of the West, and establishment of strict Islamist governance throughout the Muslim world, a mission to which all other objectives are secondary.

The ideological goals of these groups contrast sharply with the traditional interests of nation-states. Even the ideologically-defined Soviet Union was largely motivated by material prerogatives, such as security, economics, and sovereignty. Iran, Hezbollah, Hamas, and Palestinian Islamic Jihad, however, place the promotion of their radical Islamist values above all but their retention of power.

Diplomacy with traditional states revolves around the arbitration of perceived national interests. With ideological entities whose values are diametrically opposed to those of its negotiating partners, good faith diplomacy, while it ought to be attempted, is nearly impossible. The ideology of Iran, Hezbollah, Hamas, and Palestinian Islamic Jihad is founded upon resistance to Israel and the United States. Far from being able to negotiate with Israel and the United States, Iran has sworn their destruction. Ideological goals act counter to the national interests of Iran, as they risk isolation, sanctions, and retaliatory strikes.

In its quest to destroy Israel, Iran provides the vast majority of military hardware deployed in southern Lebanon by Hezbollah, and massive financial assistance to Hamas and Palestinian Islamic Jihad, strategically enveloping

Israel. Discovery of Iranian-made weapons in the possession of Hamas members in Jordan in April 2006 indicates that Iran may be providing direct military assistance to Hamas, something it has avoided in the past. Thus, these groups use traditional nation-state tools, such as arms transfers and military force, to pursue ideological ends, such as the destruction of a country whose views contrast with their own.

The rhetoric of Iran, Hezbollah, Hamas, and Palestinian Islamic Jihad and the material assistance from Iran to its terrorist proxies are telling, but their willingness to incite war in July 2006 is alarming. Not only does this quartet of terror vocally swear to destroy Israel, but it deliberately initiates unprovoked violence against what they disparage as the "Zionist entity." The willingness of these groups to strike first with the aim of destroying Israel makes a nuclear-armed Iran unacceptable.

Because Iran, Hezbollah, Hamas, and Palestinian Islamic Jihad consider themselves in holy conflict with Israel and the United States, negotiation toward the elimination of Iran's nuclear weapons program is a nonstarter. The Iranian regime perceives acquiring nuclear weapons as a necessity for continuing its struggle against Israel and the United States to achieve a world without Zionism and the United States.

The regime in Tehran and its proxies in Lebanon and Palestine are increasingly willing to initiate violence against Israel and America; hence, a way to avoid recurring crises is to place regime change on the table. When diplomacy ultimately fails, and it shall fail, it is imperative that the regime change option be fully developed or the international community will be forced to choose between an Iran with nuclear weapons and problematic military action.

The United States can place regime change on the table without military confrontation through a policy of empowering the Iranian people to bring democracy to Iran. Empowerment can be achieved by removing from the Foreign Terrorist Organizations list the most powerful and democratic Iranian opposition groups, the National Council of Resistance of Iran and the Mujahedeen-e Khalq.

CHAPTER 1

Iran: The Nature
of the Regime

INTRODUCTION

To know "What Makes Tehran Tick," it is first necessary to understand Iran's challenging, dangerous, and what at first appears to be puzzling behavior. The Tehran regime continues its aggressive stance toward Israel and the United States, risking the enormous costs of provoking military action by them.

In so doing, the Tehran regime enables like-minded terrorist proxies, such as Hezbollah and Hamas. The aggressiveness of these two groups mirrors that of their patron, necessitating an explanation of the nature of each and the relationships among them. This chapter addresses the nature of Iran, while Chapter Two addresses its terrorist proxies—Hezbollah, Hamas, and Palestinian Islamic Jihad.

Behind the decision-making of any political entity, there is a tension between ideology and interest. This tension is similar to the dual impact of nature and nurture in the psyche of individuals. Scholars argue over the prominence of each factor, but most agree that some combination of the two is at play. For individuals, "nature" refers to the intrinsic genetic traits that shape behavior, whereas "nurture" implies the environmental conditions that explain behavior. Likewise, for states, ideology refers to the basic values that define a political entity. Traditional national interests are those material priorities that arise from the environment.

In international relations theory, realists place disproportionate weight on national interests and are thus ill-equipped to analyze the behavior of states for which ideology is a guiding motivation. Realism assumes that all states behave in essentially the same manner when exposed to the same circumstances. In their analysis of international affairs, realists "black-box" states by ignoring their internal decision-making processes and underlying principles. Realists look mainly at the opaque exterior of the state, without peering into the ideological core that guides decision-making.

Realists have a particular fondness for the realpolitik approach to foreign policy, in which decisions are reached primarily using material criteria, relatively free from the influence of ideals. This approach was embodied by Prince Klemens von Metternich, the early 19th Century Austrian Foreign Minister who sought to maximize the power of the Austrian Empire with little concern for the promotion of any underlying values.

The realpolitik approach underlies the

same calculating mentality behind Israel's Doctrine of the Periphery, as described by former Israeli Prime Minister David Ben-Gurion. This doctrine drove Israel to seek alliances with non-Arab Muslim regimes to isolate Israel's Arab enemies. Hence Israel crafted alignments with such states as Turkey, Iran under the Shah, and even the early Khomeini regime.

Both the Soviet Union and United States during the Cold War embodied a balance of traditional national interest and ideology. The Soviet Union dominated Eastern Europe in order to maintain a buffer zone between itself and NATO forces but also to promote its socialist values among those polities.

The United States promised to defend Western Europe for parallel reasons. Soviet consolidation of the European continent would have placed the United States in a permanently weak position vis-à-vis the communist bloc. But Washington also placed a high priority on the protection of democratic values for their own sake. In this case, traditional tools of statecraft were applied to the pursuit of ideological objectives.

The Iranian regime is typified by a mix of ideological imperatives and traditional national interests. Iran's desire to destroy Israel arises from a conflict of values between the two nations as opposed to a response to any perceived economic or military threat. Iran is also driven by a centuries-old imperative to reconstruct a Persian empire. Iran uses traditional means such as rhetoric, military confrontation, and pursuit of nuclear weapons toward these ideological ends.

There is a consensus of realist thinking around Iran's motivations that does not take these goals into account. An August 2006 Programme Report from Chatham House embodies this approach. Among Iran's objectives, the study lists regional hegemony, establishment of a sphere of influence, and prevention of a unified, threatening Iraq. This perception only indirectly addresses Iran's 2,500-year record of attempting to establish Persian empires, and omits the religious motivation of the Iranian regime to export its Revolution to Iraq and elsewhere via terrorist groups.[1]

Until the foreign policy establishment understands the nature of the regime in Tehran, effective foreign policy options will be elusive. Chapter Three, taking into account the nature of the regime, addresses policy alternatives for the United States and Israel.

IRAN: AN ISLAMIST, FASCIST STATE IN SEARCH OF AN EMPIRE

The Islamist version of fascism combines Islamist (radical) ideology with totalitarian government, which appeals for popular support by scapegoating minorities.[2] The Iranian regime conducts an aggressive and expansionist foreign policy based on its religious ideology, fascist state institutions, and desire for empire-building. While extreme Islam has surged forth at various points throughout history, modern Islamism first came to dominate the apparatus of a modern nation state following Ayatollah Ruhollah Khomeini's ascent to power in Iran during 1979. Khomeini thus managed to seize the Islamist initiative from the Sunnis, who had taken the lead in the 1920s with the formation of the Muslim Brotherhood in Egypt in 1928.[3] The Khomeini regime attempted to transform the Sunni dream of re-creating a global Islamic rule from an unattainable ideal to an achievable goal.

The ideology of Iran's radical Shiites "represents a virulent stream of extremist Islam, characterized by misogyny, homophobia, utter intolerance of difference even within its own religion, and a belief system rooted many several centuries past."[4]

Ayatollah Ruhollah Khomeini, Founder and Supreme Leader of the Islamic Republic of Iran, 1979-1989
Photo Credit Hulton Archive/Getty Images

To convert its goal of regional dominance into reality, Tehran provides Islamist terrorist groups worldwide financial, military, and political support. If successful, Iranian Revolutionaries would seize the initiative from the Sunnis, especially al Qaeda, to turn Tehran into the global capital of Islamists—similar to the historic relationship between

Moscow and Marxism.[5] While Moscow, in its ideological role, acted as the fountainhead of communism, Tehran, because of its nature, seeks to be the wellspring of Islamism.

Iran's bid for ideological leadership of the Islamic world has always faced long odds, simply because of Shiism's perpetual minority status in a Sunni-majority Muslim world. That bid foundered definitively after Ayatollah Khomeini failed to lend support to the 1982 Sunni uprising of the Muslim Brotherhood in Syria. Yet even for groups that reject Iranian leadership, Tehran's largesse and prominence provide benefits.

Iran uses three complementary gambits in its confrontation with the West: pursuit of nuclear weapons, interference in Iraq, and initiation of war with Israel. Tehran's interference in Iraq accompanies its nuclear gambit. Iran postures as an honest negotiating partner in nuclear talks, only to renege by dismissing every Western offer. Meanwhile, Iran funnels operatives and arms into Iraq to undermine Coalition forces there and increase the regime's leverage over the West on the nuclear issue. Then, in July 2006, Tehran oversaw the provocation of war by its terrorist proxy Hezbollah, signaling to the West that Iran could inflame the region at will and distract the international community from Iran's nuclear weapons agenda.

Iran's summer 2006 deployment of Hezbollah in Lebanon resulted in a significant enhancement of Iran's "ability to reconfigure the balance of power in the Middle East in favor of the Shia."[6] Despite the shift in favor of the Shia, Iran is not accepted as the theological leader of the Islamic world. Scoring successes in a renewed drive for hegemony, Iran sharpened the hostility between Islam and the West by rallying more Sunnis behind the Shia-led attacks on Israel.[7]

The strategic gains from war did not redound into an ideological bounce. Although the Iranian regime did not achieve ideological gains, the strategy is first to accumulate enough military power to destroy its ideological nemesis, Israel, and drive the United States from the Middle East. Only then would the regime impose its conception of Shia Islam on the Muslim world, which is its ultimate ideological goal. As of mid-2006, al Qaeda, the main Sunni jihadist organization, has been decentralized and weakened by the capture of several leaders, providing Iran's aggressive regime an opportunity to seize the initiative as leader of militant Islam's jihad against the West.

Although Iran was only indirectly involved in the 9/11 attacks, President

George W. Bush's description of the perpetrators—radical Muslims and extremists who stood on the shoulders of fascists, Nazis, and tyrants—is also applicable to the Iranian regime.[8] And in

President George W. Bush, 2000-
Photo Credit Greg Mathieson/Mai/Getty Images

an October 2005 National Endowment for Democracy address, President Bush portrayed the ideology motivating terrorists as "Islamo-fascism":

> Some call this evil Islamic radicalism; others, militant Jihadism; still others, Islamo-fascism. Whatever it's called, this ideology *is very different from the religion of Islam. This form of radicalism exploits Islam to serve a violent, political vision: the establishment, by terrorism and subversion and insurgency, of a totalitarian empire that denies all political and religious freedom.*[9]

But the September 11 attacks about which Bush spoke in his National Endowment address did not initiate global Islamist terrorism. Rather, the theocrats of Tehran fired the first shots in that war after hijacking a peoples' revolt against the Shah. On 11 February 1979, Ayatollah Khomeini assumed office in Iran, riding high on the slogan "Death to America." Repeated terrorist attacks on Americans began by a variety of like-minded co-religionists.[10]

The Khomeini revolutionary slogans are part of an Islamist-fascism package. They combine anti-American and anti-Israeli chants, Islamist theology, totalitarian government, and appeals for popular support by scapegoating ethnic minorities.[11] Khomeini's Iran became the quintessence of Islamist-fascism: a political entity organized in the Western state structure, yet embodying all the features of a state ruled by an exclusive, repressive few. In this sense, Iran is organized like traditional Western fascism. Religious ideas drive the Iranian regime's ideology more than they did European fascism. Tehran's political repression and tyranny are intended to impose its own brand of radical Islam on the Muslim world. It is in the nature of the Islamic Republic of Iran to combine a radical brand of religious jurisprudence with reclaiming what its theocrats consider their rightful position at the center of the Muslim world.

In Nazi Germany, Hitler got away with murder by harnessing a pseudo-mythical Christianity to racist chauvinism; he bolstered his support within Germany by blaming ethnic groups, such as Jews, Gypsies, and other minorities for Germany's socio-economic woes. Hitler's fascist counterpart, Mussolini, enhanced his popularity by demanding a rebirth of the Roman Empire through colonialist and racist expansion.

By using blatant appeals to popular religiosity, Milosevic took an approach similar to that of his fascist predecessors, faulting ethnic Albanians for difficulties faced by Orthodox Christian Serbs in Kosovo. With even more emphasis on

Benito Mussolini and Adolf Hitler, 1 Sep 1937
Photo Credit Luce, Hulton Archive/ Getty Images

Portrait of Yugoslav Federation President Slobodan Milosevic, 29 Aug 1991
Photo Credit Francois Xavier Marit, AFP /Getty Images

religion, Khomeini used radical rhetoric against real and created enemies to consolidate his hold on power. He targeted the traditional Shiite clerical structure; religious and ethnic minorities, such as Iran's Arabs, Azeris, Baha'is, and Kurds; as well as political groups, such as the Mujahedeen-e Khalq (MEK).[12]

Despite a pseudo-reform movement from 1997 to 2005, in fact a straight line links Ayatollah Khomeini to President Ahmadinejad. Ideologically, the extreme anti-Israeli, anti-Western rhetoric that characterized Khomeini's preaching reverberates in Ahmadinejad's speeches. Strategically, the same ultimate desire to wipe Israel off the map led to Tehran's July 2006 deployment of its terrorist proxy, Hezbollah, against Israel.

Unforeseen events between 1979 and 2005 effectively stymied Khomeini's dream of exporting the Iranian Revolution. During the Iran-Iraq War, 1980 to 1988, Saddam Hussein's Iraq was a bulwark against Khomeini's expansionist objectives. Khomeini's death in 1989, shortly after the end of that war, ushered in a long period of internal political jockeying before Supreme Leader Khomeini's successor, Ali Khamenei, could fully consolidate his power with the installation of the ideologically compatible Mahmoud

Ahmadinejad as President in 2005. Once Ahmadinejad and his cohort of embittered Islamic Revolutionary Guards Corps war veterans seized control of Iran's power centers, the regime returned to its earlier, incomplete program of violent expansionism.

Official Iranian support for terrorism, development of weapons of mass destruction, and subversion of Iraq's fragile democratic process occurred in tandem with Iran's unprecedented green light to Hezbollah to trigger a war with Israel on Lebanese soil. Together, these actions signal a renewed commitment by Tehran's radical clerics to violent, even military confrontation with the West. Each of these endeavors represents one aspect of Iran's ultimate ideological objective and desire for regional hegemony. Iran wants, as many Persian empires have in the past, to expand control over the region as far as possible and will use religious ideology or whatever else comes to hand to accomplish it.

The spike in rhetoric from Tehran during 2006, and Iran's determination to foment conflict with the West, raise the issue of whether Iran's revolutionary clock ticks even louder under Khomeini, Khamenei, and Ahmadinejad than under Rafsanjani and Khatami.[13] To address such issues,

President Mahmoud Ahmadinejad and Supreme Leader Ayatollah Ali Khamenei Speak before a Photograph of Ayatollah Khomeini, 16 April 2006
Photo Credit Luce, Hulton Archive/ Getty Images

researchers collected almost 3,000 statements by the Iranian leadership from 1979-2005, performed a quantitative content analysis of these statements, and conducted a qualitative assessment of comparable statements made during 2006. For samples of these statements, see Appendix A.

While Iran's ideological rhetoric becomes louder and leads to unprovoked cross-border aggression, Iran's nuclear timetable speeds ahead. It is this convergence of an expansionist nature and accelerating pace of bombmaking that foreshadows a nuclear-armed Islamist Iran of tomorrow.

Particularly after Hezbollah launched a premeditated, Iranian-coordinated assault on Israel in July 2006, the international community became particularly aware

of how far Tehran is willing to go to impose its values, dominate the region, and distract the international community from its pursuit of nuclear weapons. With good reason, the world pays more attention to the Iranian clerics of today than to Tehran's tyrants of yesterday.

Iran's behavior reflects the ideology of the clerical regime focused on the 1979 Revolution and the perpetual struggle against the enemies of its particular brand of Shiite Islam. In this connection, the regime faces two interrelated but distinct conflicts. One is within the world of Islam; the other is with the West.

First, the leadership of Iran sought to leverage the 1979 Revolution and *Velayat-e Faqih* (rule of the Supreme Religious Jurisprudent) ideology into a leadership role within the entire Muslim world. That ideological quest quickly proved unappealing to most Muslims. But by focusing instead on such political issues as opposition to Israel and the United States, Iran hoped to achieve some measure of acceptance and influence at least among its regional neighbors of the Arab world.

Second, the Iranian leadership— convinced that only a return to its interpretation of Islam's early values can lead the Muslim world to a position of pre-eminence—believes it is locked in an ideological battle against the encroaching forces of modernization, secularization, and democratization. Because Israel and the United States embody these three trends, the allies are bound to come in conflict with a radical Islamist Iran.

Faced with conflicts within the Islamic world and with the two Satans outside of it, Israel and America, Iran quickens its quest to get the bomb for several reasons: 1) to provide a nuclear umbrella under which third-party terrorist proxies can operate; 2) to consolidate the rule of the clerics before a democratic opposition can emerge; and 3) to deter the United States from using conventional military arms to force regime change in Tehran. But Iran is simultaneously faced with opposition from the West in developing

nuclear weapons and achieving these three advantages.

Based on an examination of thousands of statements of the Iranian leadership, a portion of which are in Appendix A, it is clear that Tehran's heightened enmity is "renewed" rather than "new." The animosity reflects the clerical leadership's attempt to recapture a level of revolutionary and ideological fervor rarely seen in Iran since the termination of the Iran-Iraq war in 1988. With the Middle East in tumult in the wake of the U.S. response to 9/11, Tehran's strategy is to revive that fervor to exploit the region's instability. This window is Iran's first real opportunity since the 1980s to pursue its strategic ambitions of realigning the balance of power in the Middle East in favor of Khomeini's Shiism.

The heightened rhetoric of Iranian leaders so evident in the 2005-2006 time frame also represents a bid to provoke international, and especially Arab/Muslim, condemnation of Washington for its unwavering support of Israel. The July 2006 Hezbollah attack on Israel also served to divert world attention from Iran's own contentious nuclear issues with the United Nations nuclear watchdog, the International Atomic Energy Agency, and the UN Security Council. Iran may also have hoped to wring concessions out of the United States in ongoing negotiations over Iraq.[14]

Because there is no unified Arab Sunni response to the threat from Iran, the presence of U.S. ground forces in Iraq and Afghanistan plus U.S. naval and air forces in the Persian Gulf constitute the most important obstacles to Iran's drive for regional power.[15]

Several domestic factors have led the Iranian regime to be concerned about its grip on power: a deteriorating economy, the rising cost of imported refined petroleum products, a restless youth population, ethnic unrest, and declining public dedication to the values of the Revolution. The gathering pressures on the clerical regime are evident in March 2006 comments made by Ali Larijani, the secretary of Iran's Supreme National Security Council and its top nuclear negotiator, to a closed-door session of Iran's Parliament:

> ...the preservation of the regime has the highest priority and the Supreme Leader has placed the safeguarding of the regime at the top of Iran's foreign policy strategy in the nuclear issue.[16]

Extensive research based on the regime's rhetoric and actions suggests that Iran's leadership perceives a closing window of opportunity in which to take action to

preserve and project power. To maintain power, the Iranian leadership tries to revive its ideology but perceives such efforts as inadequate; indeed, regime survival is a principal reason for Tehran's resort to an accelerated program of militarization, including development of nuclear weapons and enhancement of existing conventional weapons systems. The regime seeks to prop itself up by creating conflict with the West; appealing to the Muslim population in the region on technological and military advancement; and supporting anti-Israeli forces.

In the mindset of Iran's clerical and Revolutionary Guards leadership, its nuclear weapons program has become a pivotal tool for the realization of its ideological and regional strategic goals. Therefore, no conceivable package of economic or even security concessions from the outside world can possibly prevail upon Iran to give up its quest for nuclear weapons status. Furthermore, given the West's opposition to Iran's nuclear program, the regime cannot abandon it without appearing to surrender to Western threats, jeopardizing both its domestic credibility and aspirations to leadership within the broader radical Islamic world.

The 2005 ascendance of Mahmoud Ahmadinejad to the presidency marked a break with the domestic and foreign policy themes of the Khatami years (1997-2005). Gone is the "Dialogue of Civilizations" that characterized Khatami's rhetoric, especially in the early years of his presidency. In its place is a far more militant and strident rhetoric that challenges the world to confront Tehran's accelerated nuclear weapons development program. This same regime supports terrorists across the Middle East and beyond, incites Shiite unrest across the Persian Gulf, and sends its agents to run interference in Iraq. Iran's apparent direction of Hezbollah's July 2006 ambush in northern Israel demonstrated with shocking clarity the kind of regional role it intends to pursue during Ahmadinejad's tenure.

Khatami provided the "reformist" public face of Iran from 1997 to 2005, all the while proceeding apace with a covert nuclear program. Ahmadinejad is much more open about his promotion of Supreme Leader Ayatollah Ali Khamenei's radical objectives and his country's pursuit of nuclear weapons. Understanding their motivations is the key to deriving an accurate threat assessment of the danger Iran poses to Israeli and American national security interests, as well as to stability in the Middle East.

Some members of Tehran's leadership seem to welcome apocalyptic visions of the return of Islam's "Hidden Imam." All strains of Islam believe in the eventual return of the *Mahdi*, also known as the 12th Imam or Shiite Messiah, after a period of great destruction. Once the forces of evil are defeated, the 12th Imam will reign over a period of great prosperity. President Ahmadinejad's selection of 22 August 2006 as the date for his decision regarding the United Nations incentives package offered in exchange for a cessation of uranium enrichment in Iran is indicative of these beliefs. In the Islamic calendar, 22 August is the date on which the Prophet Muhammad rode his steed from Jerusalem to heaven and back, and is often associated with traditions related to the apocalyptic return of the Hidden Imam.[17] It is also the date on which Saladin conquered Jerusalem, giving the day both religious and political import.

Ahmadinejad's speech at the United Nations 14 September 2005 is disturbing. At the end of his remarks, the Iranian President implored God to "hasten the emergence of your last repository, the Promised One, that perfect and pure human being, the one that will fill this world with justice and peace." After his speech, Ahmadinejad said of those in the General Assembly who listened to him

President of Iran Mahmoud Ahmadinejad, 2005-
Photo Credit Getty Images

mismanagement of either domestic or regional affairs could spell the end of their regime. Domestically, thousands of anti-government demonstrations, protests, and strikes by the students, teachers, and workers have been alarming to Ahmadinejad's cabinet, dominated by the Islamic Revolutionary Guards Corps. Geo-strategically, the implacable push for democracy, modernity, and a globalized liberal consumerist culture (as personified by the United States and its local ally, Israel) threaten the very foundations of Iran's 1979 Islamic Revolution.

Ahmadinejad and his war-age-cohort of veterans from the Iran-Iraq War, including the powerful Revolutionary Guards, were tapped to be at the leading edge of the clerics' campaign, combining as they do both revolutionary fervor and a military mindset. It is their mission to lead Tehran's new offensive that manifests itself as a two-front struggle: the struggle for leadership of the Islamic world and a struggle of civilizations against modernization, secularization, and democratization, which are embodied in the United States and Israel.

In short, Iran combines Islamist ideology with totalitarian militarism and appeals for popular support through scapegoating minorities. The Iranian regime conducts an aggressive and expansionist foreign

that the hand of God "held them there and made them sit. It had opened their eyes and ears for the message of the Islamic Republic."[18] President Ahmadinejad, more than most, believes the return of the Mahdi is close it hand. He may believe that by initiating cataclysmic destruction, Iran can hasten the return of the Hidden Imam and the millennium of prosperity for devout Muslims.

At the same time Iran aggressively exports its conception of Islam, the regime in Tehran perceives itself threatened in the geostrategic sphere. Iran's radical clerics are well aware that policy based on its religious ideology and fascist state institutions.

REGIME IDEOLOGY: SHAPED BY THE IRAN-IRAQ WAR

The eight-year war between Iran and Iraq was a searing experience for those who lived through it. The repercussions continue to unfold long after the 1988 ceasefire because the leadership of the Iranian regime that took power following the 2005 presidential elections in large part is comprised of veterans of the Iran-Iraq War.

For a number of years prior to the ascension of President Mahmoud Ahmadinejad, the power of the Revolutionary Guards grew with their assigned responsibility for Iran's ostensibly "civilian" nuclear program. By early 2006, Ahmadinejad had succeeded to a great extent in consolidating power on behalf of Supreme Leader Khamenei and in filling many top Iranian regime positions with comrades from the Revolutionary Guards.[19] Ahmadinejad himself is a commander of the Guards and former member of the *Bassij*, a division of the Revolutionary Guards responsible for suppressing political dissent inside Iran.[20]

Khomeini's ability to characterize the Iran-Iraq war as a battle between the pure

Islamic ideals of his young revolutionaries and the secular *Ba'athist* philosophy of the pan-Arabists was based on imbuing Iranian society with "themes of solidarity, sacrifice, self-reliance, and commitment." His success in doing so enabled his regime to consolidate its hold on power and, in the psyches of the generation that fought the war and saved the nation, fused the ideology of the regime and the Revolution with concepts of patriotism and loyalty to the nation-state itself.[21]

Khomeini embraced the Iran-Iraq War in 1980 as the war of Islam against the infidels (Saddam Hussein and his American, Israeli, and Arab supporters). Khomeini termed the war "a divine gift bestowed upon us by God," making the best of an unanticipated and nearly disastrous military situation. He quickly marshaled the country's defenses and turned a psychological defeat for the Iranian people into a political gain for him and his clerical followers. In other words, he used war to consolidate his power domestically, as he had done with the 1979 Revolution.

Ayatollah Khomeini issued a *fatwa*— religious edict—to kill British author Salman Rushdie for publishing a blasphemous book, *Satanic Verses*, in 1989. Khomeini was again reinforcing the religious zeal of the Revolution.

With the termination of the war against Iraq, Khomeini used Rushdie's book as a tool for mobilizing support behind his ideology. He gained experience in rekindling religious fervor by labeling the Unites States the "Great Satan," and Israel as the "Little Satan."

This fusion of ideology and patriotism is the disturbing dynamic that ought to alarm the world as it listens with growing concern to the religious zealotry of the Iranian president. Despite the defeat of Saddam Hussein, Ahmadinejad still harbors a visceral hatred for the Western powers that armed and supported Iraq. In his view, the West is hypocritical for having chosen sides in the Iran-Iraq War in which Saddam Hussein used chemical weapons and yet pronouncing support for international treaties and prohibition of weapons of mass destruction. The tacit or explicit support of most of Iran's Arab neighbors for Iraq during the war is not forgotten either, and feeds Ahmadinejad's mistrust and suspicion of the world around him.

Domestically, the easy transition of a new generation of Iranian youth to peacetime pursuits, such as Western pop culture, angers Ahmadinejad and devout revolutionaries who bitterly nurse their grievance at a nation insufficiently grateful for their sacrifices.[22] What

is galling to Ahmadinejad and the Revolutionary Guards is that the Iran-Iraq War extinguished much of the zeal of the Revolution among ordinary Iranians, while being responsible for Iran's survival.[23]

Now that Iran's war generation has enhanced its power, it is determined to drag society back to the radical, politicized Islamism that so inspired the Islamic Republic's earlier years. By reviving the moral cohesion and discipline that drove the Revolution of Khomeini, the Supreme Leader Khamenei and President Ahmadinejad hope to bolster their hold on power, when many Iranians have moved beyond the Revolutionary philosophy.

Based on their formative experiences in the Iran-Iraq War, Ahmadinejad and the Revolutionary Guards cadre he has installed in power are convinced that Iran has the right to, as well as a need for, regional hegemony. The way to ensure such an outcome is to resuscitate Khomeini's Islamist ideology, link it to a larger network of Islamists and Muslim populations in the region, and set out to take on the international community.

If the radical rhetoric of the Ahmadinejad regime were not sufficient to arouse the alarm of Iran's Arab neighbors, Hezbollah's deliberate instigation of

Destruction of Southern Beirut after Weeks of Bombing, 17 Aug 2006
Photo Credit Spencer Platt/Getty Images

an international conflict, fought on Lebanese soil, abruptly eliminated any remaining complacency. Suddenly, the clerical regime in Tehran became ready and willing to cross the line from inflammatory speech to military action.

Ahmadinejad's apocalyptic vision, limited world experience, and contempt for Western prowess and culture derive from his experiences in the Iran-Iraq War and are shared by Revolutionary Guards veterans. This worldview is alarming by itself, but the possibility that the Supreme Leader and the rest of Iran's clerical leadership may share such an outlook is even more worrisome.

VELAYAT-E FAQIH—IDEOLOGY OF THE REVOLUTION

Ayatollah Khomeini's *Velayat-e Faqih* (Rule of the Supreme Religious Jurisprudent) ideology was first developed in a series of lectures he delivered to his theological students while in exile in the holy city of Najaf, Iraq. Its basic theme is the necessity of imposing moral, Islamic behavior on society to create an atmosphere in which Muslims are able to live devoutly, in compliance with the demands of Allah. Khomeini and other extremist Shiite clergy believe that Allah already has handed down in the *Sharia* all the laws required to order

human existence, and all that is left is for Muslims to implement it through the dominance of an Islamic state.

In March 2006, an editorial writer of the Iranian weekly newspaper "Partow' eh Sokhan," considered the mouthpiece of the Ayatollah Yazdi, expressed contempt for democratic principles in describing *Velayat-e Faqih*:

> People have no rights and count for nothing in an Islamic rule; it is God that reveals his commandments to the supreme leader, Imams and Ayatollahs in order for them to carry out...The measure of the legitimacy and authority of the Islamic rule is not in the majority vote of the people; in general, people are too stupid to be involved in a process for which they are simply not qualified.[24]

Such arrogation by the Iranian Shiite clergy of the sole prerogative to govern in an Islamic society is without precedent in Shiite or Sunni thought and practice. Although a number of Shia ayatollahs had been writing and speaking about a system similar to *Velayat-e Faqih* since the mid-1960s, their concepts were geared to a systematization of theological issues that would eliminate the arbitrariness of individual spiritual leaders. Their thinking was intended for application to the religious sphere, but Khomeini applied the ideas to actual governance of a state, a departure from Shiite tradition.

Of particular concern to the leading Grand Ayatollahs at the time of Iran's 1979 Revolution was Khomeini's insistence on the infallibility of the *fiqh* (himself) in matters pertaining to imposition of *Velayat-e Faqih* and on closure of theological debate. Such ideas are utterly contrary to centuries of Shiite jurisprudence. Unlike its Sunni counterpart, Shiite Islam has long prided itself on a lively atmosphere of debate within the seminary *howzas* (or circles).

Shiite tradition, unlike Sunni Islam, holds a special place for *ijtihad*, the practice of interpretation of the Koran and the *Hadiths* (exegesis of the Koran that has become standard religious text) by respected, senior religious clerical figures. Khomeini's innovations, however, took Iran's Shia clergy into day-to-day governance of a nation state. For the first time, the clergy played a decisive role in an Islamist movement and then proceeded to establish a religious monopoly over the entire society.[25]

In many ways, Khomeini's system shares more in common with other totalitarian-isms of the 20th century, such as fascism and communism, than it does with anything traditionally Islamic. The absolute power of the *Velayat-e Faqih* structure in society is the functional equivalent of communism's Leading Role of the Party. In Khomeini's Iran, the Komiteh acts as a "morality police" much in the same way the Soviet KGB brutally suppressed any deviance from the Communist party line.

The parallel hierarchies of ideological and state organizations, with the unvarying supremacy of the former over the latter, also follow the communist model. The Iranian regime's ideological hierarchy, despite a constitution that proclaims the rights of the electorate, is entirely un-elected: The Supreme Leader is assisted by a Guardian Council with the power to veto laws and exclude presidential and parliamentary candidates, and an Islamic judiciary, completely beyond the electoral influence of the people.

The state institutions, as defined by the Iranian Constitution, might seem more democratic than the clerical establishment in that officials are "elected," but they are actually selected by the Guardian Council before being presented to the electorate. Iran's electoral process is merely a chimera or a facade of genuine civil society: The conservative clergy of the ideological infrastructure controls every aspect of popular participation in their government. In practice, thousands of would-be candidates for the Majlis (Iran's parliament) can be disqualified at the whim of the clerics, all the national media are state-controlled, and street gangs such as the *Bassij* militia intimidate voters. For these and other reasons, the vast majority of the Iranian electorate (some 85-90% in the last election) has repeatedly chosen to boycott elections despite Iran's policy of mandatory voting.

The party line in a communist or fascist party state could be found in the pages and on the channels of the state-controlled media organs, such as Pravda or Tass, and it is not different in Iran's Islamist-fascist state. There, the ruling clergy's line comes down to the people in sermons at the weekly Friday mosque services.[26]

Khomeini's insistence that *Velayat-e Faqih* take precedence over the Koran and the Hadiths, his subordination of *Sharia* law to the Iranian Constitution, and his iconoclastic treatment of the centuries-old role of the clergy in Shiite tradition de-legitimizes the theological underpinnings of his own Revolution. Khomeini's radical departure from reliance on *Sharia* as the sole foundation for the judicial norm, ironically, gives Iran a secular model of government. Behind the trappings of secular institutions,

Khomeini has installed a radical version of Islamist governance unique in the Muslim world.

Purely political exigencies of the post-Khomeini succession elevated to national leadership a supreme leader (Khamenei) who, far from holding the highest position within the clerical institution, was not an ayatollah but merely a middle-ranking *hojjat al-islam* at the time of his hasty designation.[27] So lacking in proper moral authority was Khamenei, in fact, that he was stripped of his ability to issue fatwas in Iran. The stature of the Supreme Leader, thus, has been discredited, even within the contrived parameters of *Velayat-e Faqih*.

As soon as the outlines of Khomeini's political intentions became obvious in the early 1980s, *Velayat-e Faqih* was rejected by the majority of the then-living grand ayatollahs. The Revolution itself was carried along on the zealotry of Khomeini's former theology students, not through the conviction of its Shiite establishment. By contrast, the "quietist" and Sufi currents—of which the Ayatollah Ali al-Sistani (Iranian-born but living in Iraq for many decades) is a prominent representative—have been far more common. During Iran's revolutionary period, the "quietist" current had small chance of

Commemorating the 25th Anniversary of the Islamic Revolution,
Iranian Women Burn a U.S. Flag, 3 Nov 2004
Photo Credit Majid/Getty Images

predominating, not least because it had become demonized as a "pro-Shah" position; in such an atmosphere, only radical political activism was acceptable.

Paradoxically, Khomeini further corrupted the clerical institution by promoting to positions of political power clerics who fulfilled criteria of political allegiance rather than those with the highest religious rank. Khomeini actually turned on respected senior Shiite clerics, and forcibly submitted to the Special Clerical Courts those who openly opposed his dictatorial style. His 1981 repudiation of the Ayatollah Kazem Shariatmadari essentially undermined the religious basis of Velayat-e Faqih and turned the Iranian Revolution into just another power grab.[28]

Though ostensibly intended to establish Islamic morality, Khomeini's Velayat-e Faqih has created a clerical establishment so beholden to the political system that it has betrayed its own religious principles and undermined its goal of attracting adherents elsewhere in the Ummah—the Muslim world.

IRAN'S QUEST TO LEAD THE MUSLIM WORLD AND DOMINATE THE REGION

When the regime in Tehran came to power on the wave of the 1979 Iranian Revolution, the Ayatollah Khomeini and his ideological cohorts intended not only to take political and religious control, but they also expected the ideology of Velayat-e Faqih to lead the Islamic revival of the late 20th century. Thus, the very nature of the regime was based on ideological export.

> We have a huge position in the Islamic world. No country other than Iran can lead the Islamic world; this is a historical position.
>
> — Muhammad-Javad Larijani, 7 August 1989, principal foreign policy advisor to President Rafsanjani[29]

When circumstances inside Iran converged in the 1970s to forge an unprecedented alliance between a radical intelligentsia and an Islamist clergy, the Pahlavi dynasty collapsed and a violently anti-Western collection of religious extremists took power.

The guiding ideology, Velayat-e Faqih (Rule of the Jurisprudent), was conceived by the Ayatollah Khomeini during his years of exile in Najaf, Iraq. As stated, this ideology breaks with centuries of

Shiite tradition in its demand that the clergy not only exert influence on society, but actually participate in and dominate the governance of society. According to this vision, until the return of the Mahdi can usher in a period of just rule on earth, a suitable representative must govern in his place.

That representative is defined by *Velayat-e Faqih* as a senior member of the Shiite clergy who has achieved the supreme status of *marja'al-taqlid* (worthy of emulation, object of imitation). The regime was further discredited when they eliminated that criterion in order to install Khamenei as Supreme Leader.

In the wedding of the Shiite clergy to the political leadership of a nation state (and especially through the creation of such structures as the Assembly of Experts, the Guardian Council, the Expediency Council, and the Clerical Courts), Khomeini and his radical clerical supporters imparted a territorial dimension to the Iranian Revolution, which was perceived by Arab and other neighboring countries to be as much a grab for regional hegemony as a vehicle for the global expansion of Islam. Iran's geographical location at the center of the Muslim world—in the middle of Arabs, Turks, Central, and South Asians—easily evokes memories of Persian empires past

that spanned much of this territory.

The true velayat-e-faqih is in Iran. This velayat is responsible for the entire Islamic world.

—Muhammad-Javad Larijani, 7 August 1989, principal foreign policy advisor to President Rafsanjani[30]

Sunni neighbors in the Gulf saw Iran's move to export the ideology of its Revolution as a typical case of national aggression by an upstart, would-be hegemon. In fact, Iran applied traditional national security tools of military domination to impose its religious principles. This reach was resisted by Saudi and other financing from rich, and frightened, Gulf sheikhdoms. Iran's aggression was also met head-on by a complete refusal to condemn Saddam's invasion of Iran in 1980 and, indeed, an active backing for it.

Following a hiatus in militaristic efforts to dominate its region, Iran's coordination of Hezbollah's July 2006 strike into Israeli territory signaled a distinct shift in foreign policy strategy for Tehran. Hezbollah's initiative followed nearly a year of stepped-up support to Iran's proxy militias, such as Moqtada al-Sadr's *Mahdi Army* inside Iraq. The expanding influence of Revolutionary Guards and intelligence elements throughout most

Israeli Policemen Inspect Buildings Bombed by Hezbollah, Northern Israel, 11 Aug 2006
Photo Credit Roni Schutzer, AFP/Getty Images

of Iraq spearheaded the expansion of its Shiite ambitions there, even as its simultaneous support for Sunni terrorists ignited expanding sectarian strife. Once again, Iran simultaneously sought regional hegemony and ideological expansion.

The Drive for Regional Hegemony

The resurgence of Iranian hegemonic designs under the Khamenei-Ahmadinejad regime in the Persian Gulf, Caucasus, and Central Asia contains both ideological and geostrategic aspects. Historically, Persian Empires have spanned huge swathes of these regions: The greatest of these, under storied kings Cyrus and Darius, stretched from Egypt in the west far into Central Asia, Pakistan, and India in the east, and from as far north as Greece and Turkey to the coast of today's Arabian Sea.

Later, during the first millennium C.E. (A.D.), the domain of the Persian Sassanid Empire eventually encompassed not only modern day Iran and Iraq, but also the greater part of Central Asia and the Near East, including at times the regions corresponding to present-day Israel, Turkey, and Egypt. The Safavid Empire, which ruled Persia from 1502-1736, originated among a militant Sufi order centered among Turkish people living west of the Caspian Sea and eventually included much of the Caucasus and Mesopotamia.

During the reign of the Shah Mohammad Reza Pahlavi (1953-1979), Iran experienced a revival of historical pride in its Persian culture, which led to expansionist policies in the Gulf. During 1971, Iranian forces occupied the Persian Gulf islands of Abu Musa, Tunb al Kubra

(Greater Tumb), and Tunb as Sughra (Lesser Tumb), located at the mouth of the gulf between Iran and the United Arab Emirates (UAE).[31] The Iranians were reasserting historic claims to the islands, although they had been dislodged from these islands by the British in the late 19th century.[32]

Periodically, Iran has laid claim to Bahrain, based on its 17th-century defeat of the Portuguese and subsequent occupation of the Bahrain archipelago. Even though Arabs pushed the Iranians out of Bahrain in 1780, the Shah attempted to raise the Bahrain question again when the British withdrew from areas east of Suez, but dropped his claim after a 1970 United Nations-sponsored plebiscite showed that Bahrainis "overwhelmingly preferred independence to Iranian hegemony."[33]

While the Shah's territorial ambitions were meant to enhance the traditional national interests of Iran by enhancing security, the Iranian Revolution of 1979 introduced an ideological element to Iranian irredentism. This new imperative was a threat to stability in the Persian Gulf, as Khomeini's Islamist clerics made clear their intentions to spread the revolutionary ideology throughout the region. The small Arab nations of the Persian Gulf with their large Shia populations were seen as primary targets

by Tehran. The radical regime there soon began to provide Persian Gulf Islamist organizations with funding, weapons, logistics, and terrorist training.

One of the most visible and dramatic developments to result from this policy was the 1981 failed coup d'etat in Bahrain, as the clerics once again attempted to revive Iran's claim to that country on the grounds that the majority of Bahrainis were Shia Muslims. Operating through an Iranian-based Islamist group called The Islamic Front for the Liberation of Bahrain, Iran plotted the assassination of Bahrain's leadership in an effort to spark a popular uprising of Bahraini Shia and engineer the ultimate installation of a theocratic government in Manama, Bahrain's capital. The Tehran coup plotters had even selected an Iranian-based Iraqi cleric, Hojjat ol-Eslam Hadi al-Modarresi, who was to have been put in power as supreme leader of a government of clerics. The coup was foiled when Bahraini security forces were alerted to impending events.

Iran's regime was also responsible for numerous attacks in Kuwait during the 1980s. On 12 December 1983, local Islamist extremists backed by Tehran launched six suicide attacks against targets in Kuwait; the most deadly of these was a bomb-laden truck assault against the

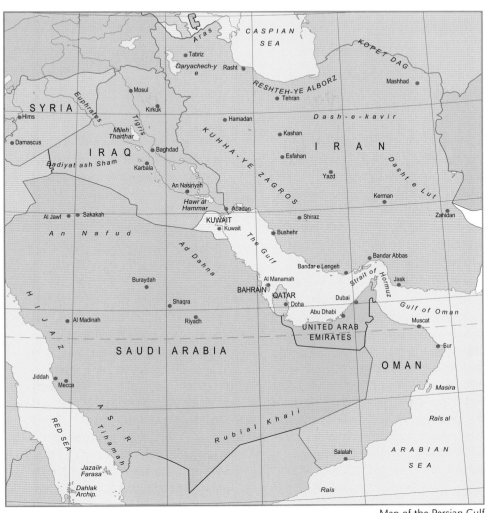

Map of the Persian Gulf

American Embassy in Kuwait City, which killed five people and injured 62 others. The French Embassy and several Kuwaiti installations also were destroyed that day. Jabir al-Ahmad al-Sabah, the emir of Kuwait, fought back against the Islamists, instituting a tough anti-terrorism bill and imposing emergency measures. More attacks followed, including the hijacking of a Kuwaiti airliner, an attack against the emir's motorcade, bombings of Kuwaiti cafes, assassination of a newspaper editor, and sabotage of Kuwait's oil facilities.[34]

In a defensive response to the dangers posed by the Iran-Iraq War and the political violence associated with Iran's Revolution, the six Persian Gulf states of the Arabian Peninsula—Bahrain, Kuwait, Oman, Qatar, Saudi Arabia, and the UAE—formed the Gulf Cooperation Council (GCC) in 1981. Although security was not explicitly addressed among the initial provisions of the pact, managing common security challenges collectively has developed over the years into a key objective.[35] Unfortunately, the collective capabilities and resolve of the Gulf Cooperation Council members pales next to that of Iran.

With the rise of Revolutionary Iran, the Persian Gulf policy of the United States became one of balance of power. Designed to protect Saudi Arabia, U.S. policy maintained a rough balance of power between Iran and Iraq. Except for the covert supply of American arms to Iran in the Iran-Contra case during the mid-1980s, U.S. assistance to Iraq far exceeded support for Iran. In June 1987, after Iran had begun targeting Arab oil tankers with missile attacks, the United States took the exceptional step of reflagging eleven Kuwaiti oil tankers with the Stars and Stripes to protect the flow of Persian Gulf oil.

The U.S. failure to overthrow Saddam Hussein during the First Gulf War preserved a rough balance of power in the Gulf region. Subsequent sanctions, intrusive International Atomic Energy Agency inspection program, and establishment of northern and southern no-fly zones in Iraq seriously weakened the Iraqi side of that balance. Small Gulf states found themselves confronted with a relatively strengthened Iran and, following the lead of Saudi Arabia, took the steps they felt they needed to maintain their sovereignty. The sentiment expressed by Qatar's Foreign Minister Shaykh Hamad bin Jasim is illustrative: "...we cannot afford to have enemies in the region."[36]

When Khatami was elected president of Iran in 1997, the West and Iran's Arab neighbors hoped that Iran's regional policy had changed. Former Iranian president Rafsanjani was received in Bahrain quite warmly in March 1998. Qatar received a constant stream of high level visitors from Iran and even accepted visits of Iranian warships, and Omani officials spoke out against the U.S. policy of isolating Iran. Even Kuwait, which more closely supported U.S. policy in the region, was more amenable to dealing with Iran; Kuwait perceived as necessary a strong Iran to balance the threat from Baghdad.[37]

Bahrain's skepticism about Iranian designs was illustrated by a joking comment made by Crown Prince Shaykh Hamad bin 'Isa, who was quoted in 1998 as telling a U.S. official, "In Iran you have three people in charge: You have

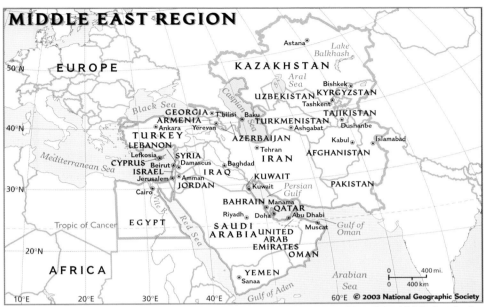

Map of the Middle East Region

Khamenei, who is in charge of religion and terrorism. You have Rafsanjani, and he is in charge of business and terrorism. And then you have Khatami, and he is in charge of internal politics, moderation, and terrorism."[38]

Iran's neighbors were concerned following the ouster of Saddam Hussein in March 2003 and the rise of former Revolutionary Guards commander Mahmoud Ahmadinejad as President of Iran in August 2005. Since then, Gulf countries have feared that a nuclear-armed Iran would be powerful enough to dominate its neighbors. These anxieties are exacerbated by Iran's defiance of the European Union, the International Atomic Energy Agency, and the UN Security Council over its nuclear weapons program.

Iran's resurgent ambitions extend well beyond the Persian Gulf. The Iran-

Iraq War and United States policy of dual containment prevented Iran from achieving local dominance during the 1980s. Iran's attempt to champion the cause of its favored Afghan warlords during their war against the Soviet Union was headed off by funding from Saudi Arabia to the broader Mujahedeen movement that eventually triumphed. Tehran's leadership since 2005 is an ideological throwback to the Khomeini years, fixated on expanding Iran's influence as widely as possible.

The collapse of the Soviet Union opened up across Central Asia and the Caucasus a new version of Rudyard Kipling's late 19th century Great Game, in which European powers competed for territory. In the 21st century, this competition is focused on the area's huge oil and natural gas resources. The contest for economic and political influence includes three major powers—Russia, China, and the United States. Also competing are the Central Asian states and countries on the periphery of the Caspian Basin, including Iran.

Multinational oil companies, such as Exxon-Mobil, Dutch Shell, Russia's Gasprom and Transneft, France's Total and Elf, Britain's BP, and various Chinese firms, are all vying for the enormous profits anticipated from the opening up of the region. The competition for oil and gas pipeline routes is intense, and organized crime bosses, corrupt government officials, and the militaries of a dozen countries are among the players.

Iran is making a play for an ambitious program of trade and infrastructure investment in Central Asia and the Caucasus, in response to U.S. attempts to isolate it geopolitically. Tehran focuses most of its attention on areas with which it shares strong ties of culture and history, such as Tajikistan and western Afghanistan. Among Iran's initiatives are large road, rail, tunnel, and hydroelectric projects in Tajikistan, Turkmenistan, Uzbekistan, and Afghanistan. Iran's Caspian Oil Company is pursuing development of its offshore oil fields in competition with other countries bordering the Caspian.[39]

The Shanghai Cooperation Organization (SCO) is another forum in which Tehran attempts to expand its influence in Central Asia. This six-member security alliance includes Russia, China, Kazakhstan, Kyrgyzstan, Tajikistan, and Uzbekistan. Iran, along with Mongolia and Pakistan, has observer status at the SCO but is seeking to upgrade to membership status and has offered an expanded Eurasian energy partnership with Moscow in an effort to make its case.[40]

Iran's relationship with Afghanistan has been a complex and shifting one. Information obtained from a high-level Taliban detainee's tribunal session in Guantanamo Bay, Cuba shed new light on Iran's relationships in Afghanistan. This information alleges that Iran secretly agreed to assist the Taliban in its war against U.S. forces in October 2001. The Pentagon released a transcript of the session on 3 March 2006 that includes an admission by the official (identified as the former governor of Herat Province in Afghanistan) that he participated in a meeting between Taliban and Iranian officials. An Iranian pledge of support is alleged to have been provided.[41]

Regime changes in Kabul and Baghdad have changed the balance of power around Iran. The U.S. ouster of the

Taliban and *Ba'athist* regimes placed these territories into play. The United States intends to exploit this vacuum for the expansion of democratic rule, but the Khamenei-Ahmadinejad regime in Tehran plans to spread Iran's influence. After the United States, Iran is now the strongest presence in Afghanistan and, according to a Chatham House report, has surpassed the United States as the dominant influence in Iraq.[42] By turning Syria and Lebanon into military outposts, "for the first time since the seventh century, Iran is militarily present on the coast of the Mediterranean."[43]

A 14 November 2005 confidential strategic accord signed between Iran and Syria was intended to preempt possible international punitive measures against either party. It includes a sensitive section "dealing with co-operation and mutual aid during times of international sanctions, or scenarios of military confrontation with the West." Diplomatic sources say the agreement "includes Syria's commitment to allow Iran to safely store weapons, sensitive equipment or even hazardous materials on Syrian soil should Iran need such help in a time of crisis."[44]

Ahmadinejad's bid for control of the Arab confrontation with Israel flared into military hostilities in the Israel-Hezbollah War of 2006. Tehran's efforts to dominate the Palestinian movement are not likely to end, despite a nationalist-minded Hamas that sometimes resists Iranian influence and an al Qaeda effort to influence Palestinian terrorist leaders.

Reactions of the Sunni Arab States

Saudi reactions to Iran's Islamic Revolution, as described earlier, have swung wildly over the years, reflecting the complex interplay of economic, ideological, and geopolitical elements in the relationship between Saudi monarchs and Iranian clerics. Saudi rulers reacted with initial alarm to the Iranian Revolution on both an ideological and political level. Saudi reaction to Khomeini's efforts to export his Revolution was especially acute because of the heavy concentration of Saudi Arabia's minority Shia population in its Eastern province, where they constitute up to 33 percent of the population. Saudi Arabia's Shia are situated along the Persian Gulf, which is also the location of most of the country's major oil fields. Iranian subversion among this Shia population naturally provoked serious concern in the Kingdom, where strict adherence to the Islamist Wahhabi strain of Sunni Islam forms one of the pillars of Saudi rule.[45]

The Saudi response to the Iranian Shia challenge included massive funding for Wahhabi missionary and mosque construction activities around the world, as well as diplomatic, financial, and logistical support to the mujahedeen fighting the Soviet invasion of Afghanistan. Saudi Arabia, along with most of the Arab Middle East, also supported Saddam Hussein's Iraq in its bitter 1980-1988 war with Iran. The Arab states supported Iraq to preserve an Arab, Sunni-controlled buffer zone to counterbalance the aggressive Shia offensive coming out of Tehran.

The Saudi-Iranian rivalry subsided during the 1990s, as Saudi Arabia reexamined its policy of containing Iran. Crown Prince 'Abdallah bin 'Abd al-Aziz took over the day-to-day running of the Kingdom's affairs after a November 1995 stroke sidelined his half-brother, King Fahd. Abdullah's efforts to improve regional relationships led to a real rapprochement between Tehran and Riyadh. The 1997 election of the supposedly moderate president Khatami in Iran and the December 1997 Organization of the Islamic Conference (OIC) summit in Tehran ushered in something of a honeymoon period for the two states.

President Ahmadinejad's incendiary rhetoric is causing yet another reevaluation of regional relations among Middle East, Caucasus, and Central Asian countries. Iran's Revolutionary Guards commander, Yahya Rahim Safavi, led naval war games in the Persian Gulf in early April 2006, during which Iran tested several new weapons systems. Safavi's comments to Iranian state television defined Iran's expanding regional ambitions: "The Americans should accept Iran as a great regional power..."[46]

Similar comments by Iran's supreme leader Khamenei aired on Iranian state television on 25 March 2006: "The depth of our nation's strategy and revolution has reached Islamic countries of the region, Palestine, North Africa, the Middle East, Central Asia, and the Indian subcontinent."[47]

Barely veiled Iranian threats about shutting off the flow of oil through the Straits of Hormuz, which links the Persian Gulf with the Gulf of Oman, alarm the oil producers in the region. Saudi Arabia is reported to be considering the acquisition of nuclear weapons from Pakistan if Iran achieves nuclear weapons status. During 2006, Pakistan and Saudi Arabia completed two rounds of high-level defense cooperation talks. They reportedly "signed a strategic defense agreement that could pave the way for Islamabad to help Riyadh launch a

Supreme Leader Ayatollah Ali Khamenei Speaks before Iranians, 25 Mar 2006
Photo Credit AFP/Getty Images

nuclear program."[48]

A member of Saudi Arabia's *Shura Council* (consultative council) expressed concerns felt by the entire Gulf region: "As a Gulf area, we don't want to see Iran as the major power in the area. And we don't want to see Iran having this nuclear weapon, where it will be a major threat to the stability of the Gulf area and even to the Arab world altogether."[49] The Saudi leadership is acutely aware of its country's status as the sole remaining bulwark to Iranian expansionism in the Persian Gulf. However, the Kingdom's ability to contain Iran is questionable.

King Abdullah II of Jordan voiced his concerns regarding Iranian interference in Iraq in a December 2004 interview: "If Iraq goes Islamic republic, then, yes, we've opened ourselves to a whole set of new problems that will not be limited to the borders of Iraq. I'm looking at the glass half-full, and let's hope that's not the case. But strategic planners around the world have got to be aware that is a possibility."[50]

Abdullah is keenly aware of the maximalist aims that are part of Iran's ideological, expansionist nature. A state adhering to the pursuit of traditional national interests would be expected to intervene and extend its influence if a neighboring state were destabilized. But even if Tehran were able to mold an Islamist ally out of Iraq, it would not be satisfied. Abdullah goes on to raise the prospect of a "Shiite crescent," stretching from Iran, through Iraq, to southern Lebanon, that would seek to drive the United States from the region, destroy Israel, and ultimately confront the majority Sunni states in the Middle East.[51]

Following the Hezbollah ambush of Israeli forces and kidnapping of two soldiers on 12 July 2006, the vast majority of Arab states spoke out against the actions of Hezbollah, but did not name Iran directly. The Saudi government took the lead, saying, "A difference should be drawn between legitimate resistance and rash adventures carried out by elements inside the state and those behind them." By "those behind them," the Saudis no doubt meant Iran and Syria.

The entire Arab League agreed with this position. Saudi Foreign Minister Al-Faisal issued a statement on behalf of the League calling the attacks "unexpected, inappropriate, and irresponsible." There is no better vantage point from which to observe Iranian expansionist designs than from those states directly threatened by them.

In April 2006, Ahmadinejad welcomed visiting Sudanese President Omar al-Bashir to Tehran in another attempt to expand Tehran's reach into a sympathetic Arab capital at a time when both Iran and Sudan faced mounting international pressure: Iran is criticized over its nuclear weapons program, and Sudan over Arab genocide against black African villagers in Sudan's Darfur region. Ahmadinejad referred to their shared status as global pariahs at a joint press conference: "The Iranian and Sudanese nations and governments have a joint enemy that is constantly creating obstacles in the way of their advancement, and hatch plots against them."[52]

The Iranian regime's tendency to hegemonic behavior is nothing new. What alarmed the Middle East and the international community in the summer of 2006 was the willingness of the Tehran regime to spark a major offensive against Israel, using its terrorist proxy, Hezbollah. Ever since the most extremist elements took over the top civilian positions in Iran during 2005, Tehran's foreign policy pronouncements have been increasingly bellicose. When Iran's radical leadership actually turned words into action and unleashed Hezbollah in a deliberate, cross-border attack on Israel on 12 July 2006, a new phase began in radical Islam's war against the West. In light of Iran's drive to acquire nuclear weapons, subvert Iraq, and support Islamist terrorism, such aggression and the maximalist, ideological goals it serves threaten to inflame conflicts both near and far from Tehran.

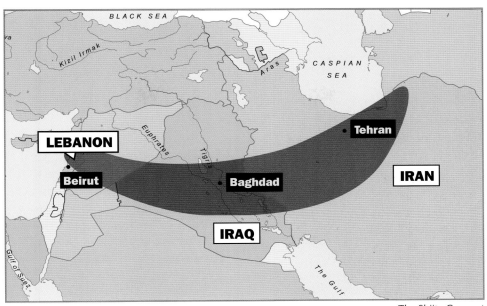

The Shiite Crescent

THE DOMESTIC IDEOLOGICAL REVOLUTION

The Tehran regime's clash with the West plays out on two stages: domestic and international. In both arenas, the Supreme Leader assigned the Revolutionary Guards the task of reviving the ideology and imposing strictures on a reluctant Iranian population. On the international front, the Guards have the duty of exporting the Revolution to Muslim groups in general and Shiite populations in particular. In support of the domestic mission, the Guards repress internal dissent. The international mission is carried out by the Islamic Revolutionary Guards Corps *Qods Force*, which maintains close links with a rogues' gallery of terrorist movements.

The extreme ideological viewpoint of the Supreme Leader Ayatollah Ali Khamenei and his selected executive, President Ahmadinejad, is a throwback to a Shiite splinter position discredited and rejected by influential Sunni and Shiite thinkers long ago, both at home and abroad. Indeed, from their earliest inception, Khomeini's political and theological opinions were at odds with those of the ranking Islamic scholars of his day. Because of his scholarly eminence in the mid-20th century, Ayatollah Hossein Borujerdi was recognized as the sole *marja'* (model for emulation) of his time. He found Khomeini's insistence on a political role for religious clerics so objectionable that he actually placed Khomeini under virtual house arrest for some time during the 1950s.[53] Borujerdi's death in the early 1960s opened the way for Khomeini to develop his philosophy of Islamic government that led eventually to the *Velayat-e Faqih* ideology.

As expounded and implemented by Khomeini after Iran's 1979 Revolution, *Velayat-e Faqih* diverged sharply from centuries of Shiite clerical tradition. The most offensive elements were its forcible closure of debate over the interpretation of Islamic law, and concentration of juridical authority in a single individual. This role was filled by Khomeini, while he lived, and his successor as Supreme Leader, Ali Khamenei. This unorthodox arrogation of unassailable theological authority by an individual Muslim cleric, and designation of clerical authority from above rather than below, created a religious hierarchy more akin to the Catholic faith than the Islamic one.

Such divergence from long-established Shiite traditions naturally provoked intense opposition from among leading religious scholars and authorities, in Iran and elsewhere in the Shiite world. During his rule, Khomeini dealt ruthlessly with such challenges, first bypassing the objections of the most senior Iranian Ayatollahs in the early days of the Revolution, and later through raw repression; he discredited and ultimately defrocked the widely respected Ayatollah Kazem Shariatmadari. Because Khomeini's successor as Supreme Leader, Ayatollah Ali Khamenei, lacked Khomeini's prestige and was held to

be considerably inferior in his religious scholarship, he faced much greater difficulty exerting his authority over theological challenges from seminary circles. In response, Khamenei formed the "Special Clergy Court" in 1987 to intimidate and try members of the clergy. The number of high-profile cases brought before this court attests to the intensity and quality of the opposition to the uniquely Iranian institution of the jurist-ruler.[54]

THE QUEST FOR LEGITIMACY AND SUPPRESSION OF DISSENT

In spite of such opposition, and driven by the imperative to hang on to political power, Tehran's ruling clerics seek to impose a renewed revolutionary fervor on the whole of the domestic population by means of brutally repressive policies. Understanding that the value system of the 1979 Revolution is engaged in an existential conflict with a Western culture that is more attractive to Iranian youth, Tehran uses every tool of oppression at its disposal to restrict Western influence spread by the technologies of global communication. Since the ascension of Ahmadinejad to the presidency in August 2005, there has been a renewed campaign to confiscate satellite dishes, jam broadcasts from abroad, and limit access to the Internet.

Iranian Police Suppress Students Protesting Previous Night's Brutality when Iranian Security Forces Clashed with Student Protestors Opposed to Tehran's New Press Restrictions
Photo Credit Atta Kenare, AFP/Getty Images

The administration cracks down on journalists, writers, students, Internet bloggers, labor leaders, and women who rally for freedom of speech. The harsh revival of *Sharia* social strictures and punishments across Iran is evidence of the regime's failure to inspire its people; incessant demonstrations, rebellions, and uprisings are evidence that even coercion has its limits. However, domestic repression in Iran will increase in intensity and brutality as its leaders become more desperate to head off the natural attraction to democratic freedoms.

The early rejection among the traditional Iranian Shiite clergy of the ideology of Iran's Revolution presented Khomeini and his remaining supporters with a dilemma: The unity of the successful revolutionary forces rapidly began to come apart as the various factions each demanded implementation of its own vision for post-Shah Iran. These visions ranged from the strict Islamic regime that Khomeini planned, to liberal secular ideas about social democracy, to socialism and communism. Khomeini recognized the danger fragmentation posed to the stability of Iran, and moved swiftly to consolidate physical control over the country and impose Islamist structures over society. This consolidation ensured his own personal authority based on the doctrine of the Rule of the Jurisprudent.

Although the theological opposition movement remains distinct from broader societal demands for political freedoms, there is a point of convergence between the two on the issue of the people's role and right to input in an Islamic system.

In both traditional Shiite and modern democratic thinking, mechanisms for grassroots to have input from the governed constitute an essential element; the roughshod trampling of such long-established traditions by Khomeini and his successors is a particular affront to both clerical and lay constituencies.

In 1979, a hasty national referendum was held on the question of whether Iran should be an Islamic republic based on *Velayat-e Faqih*. The presidential elections of January 1980 brought Abol Hassan Bani-Sadr into a civilian government; however, this development was only a temporary and duplicitous façade for Khomeini's real intentions, which were never about sharing power with others. Bani-Sadr was soon impeached, and fanatic supporters of the most radical clerics were organized into military forces tasked with implementing a crackdown on any and all opposition to Khomeini's emerging rule. The following two years were marked by extensive violence as groups vied for power; the regime responded by carrying out mass arrests and executions, many of the latter staged in public. On some days, the total number executed exceeded 100 persons.[55]

The Islamic Revolutionary Guards Corps, the shock troops of the regime, were assigned to defend the Revolution from both foreign and domestic enemies. The Guards were unleashed upon Khomeini's domestic opponents. They played a key role in meeting the onslaught of Saddam Hussein's armies in 1980 and also bore the brunt of the fighting. The *Qods Force* (Jerusalem Force) was formed as the training arm of the Revolutionary Guards and quickly began establishing terrorist training camps and other outposts in Iran's near abroad.

Terrorism has been a key instrument of Tehran's policy of exporting its Revolution, and the *Qods Force* maintains links with such terrorist organizations as Hamas, the Palestinian Islamic Jihad, the Lebanese and other Hezbollah groups, and al Qaeda. Revolutionary Guards hit squads have been responsible for dozens of assassinations of regime dissidents and opponents in the decades since the 1979 Revolution. In July 2006, Revolutionary Guards training and liaison units posted in southern Lebanon supported Hezbollah's assault against Israel.

The Revolutionary Guards were prohibited by the Ayatollah Khomeini before his death in 1989 from becoming actively involved in politics; in addition, the Iranian Constitution prohibits members of the armed forces from direct engagement in politics.[56] However,

The Islamic Revolutionary Guards Corps (IRGC) Parades before President Ahmadinejad, 22 Sep 2003
Photo Credit Scott Peterson/ Getty Images

since the 2005 ascendancy of Mahmoud Ahmadinejad to the presidency, that taboo has been broken. The rise to power in Iran of the generation of Revolutionary Guards members who survived the crucible of the Iran-Iraq War brought to the top echelons of government a group of individuals who yearn to resurrect the ideological fervor of the war years to expand Iran's ideological hegemony throughout the Middle East region.

The *Bassiji Mostazafan* (Mobilization of the Oppressed) forces were created by Khomeini in 1979. This mass movement and volunteer militia consisted mostly of underage youth and older men who were militarized under the command of the Revolutionary Guards after the war with Iraq began in September 1980. During that war, hundreds of thousands of *Bassij* child-volunteers marched in human wave formations to their deaths across the minefields, clearing a pathway for the regular Iranian armed forces, with a plastic "key to Paradise" hung from their necks.

Since the end of hostilities with Iraq in 1988, the *Bassij* has grown both in numbers and influence and has been deployed as a vice squad to enforce religious law in Iran.[57] *Bassij* and other vigilante militias, backed by the regular police forces, invaded the student dorms in Tehran and other universities in 1999, beating, arresting, and killing students to crush their democratic reform movement.[58]

By the August 2005 ascension of Ahmadinejad to the Iranian presidency, *Bassij* forces were assigned an expanded mission as Revolutionary Guards "enforcers" of renewed piety in the domestic sphere and were dispatched across the border into southern Iraq to attempt the same imposition there. In 2006, it was announced that the *Bassij* would be assigned an unprecedented oversight role in the Iranian electoral process, with authority to vet potential candidates for public office.

Ahmadinejad reportedly served as a *Bassij* instructor during the Iran-Iraq War and, like many Iranian veterans of that conflict, was profoundly affected by his experiences.[59] In public, Ahmadinejad often wears the black-and-white *Bassij* scarf, and makes frequent references to "*Bassij* culture" and "*Bassij* power," as if propelled by a righteous belief that those who defended the Revolution are entitled to impose their ideology on the rest of society.

There is nostalgia for this Revolutionary heritage, which springs from a recognition of, and disappointment in, the fading allure of the ideology that captivated participants in the heady days of the Revolution. In 1994, radicals like Ahmadinejad, having been unable to impose an effective model of Islamic economy and society or to successfully export and establish such a model abroad, could only fight a "rearguard action."[60] Bassij forces often are drawn from the poorest segments of Iranian society, and the simple piety of such village boys is used and manipulated rather easily by Tehran's more cynical leadership figures.

The influence of the martyr complex in Iran has extended beyond the war years to form the ideological underpinnings for the cult of the suicide bomber, integral to contemporary terrorist operations.

Tehran announced in 2005 and 2006 the formation across Iran of suicide brigades that are reportedly attracting thousands of volunteers ready to attack American, Israeli, British, and other Western interests around the world.

Veneration of the revered figures of early Shiite Islam and an abiding belief in the ultimate return of the vanished 12th Imam demonstrate the power of the regime's deeply rooted beliefs. This ideology plays out in Iran's propaganda efforts to repress some members of an outwardly modern population, and its initiatives to export Khomeini's Revolution abroad.

A Bassiji Soldier Demonstrates Iranian Prowess Against America, 11 Feb 2000
Photo Credit Henghameh Fahimi, AFP/ Getty Images

CONCLUSION

The nature of the Iranian regime is Islamist and expansionist. The very foundations of the state as established in the Iranian Constitution dictate the export of a radical Islamist ideology. This imperative was manifest in the efforts of Khomeini to foment unrest in Bahrain and Kuwait during the 1980s, and is present again in Ahmadinejad's support for insurgent groups in Iraq, Hezbollah in Lebanon, and Hamas and Palestinian Islamic Jihad in Palestine.

Realists fail to give this ideological motivation and aggressive expansionist nature its proper weight. They try to find the source of Tehran's hostility toward the United States and Israel in its security concerns, which is given the presence of U.S. forces and anarchy in the neighborhood. With the fall of Saddam

Hussein and the Taliban, Iran should feel less threatened than it was in the past. In fact, Tehran views the presence of U.S. forces in Iraq more as an opportunity than a threat, with senior Iranian officials identifying Americans as potential hostages. Since the fall of the Taliban and Saddam, Tehran's behavior has only grown more provocative. This chapter concludes that Tehran's provocations derive mainly from an ideological predisposition to export its version of Islam and create an empire.

For the clerical decision-makers who run Iran, the "nature" instilled in the state by Khomeini far outweighs the peripheral ("nurture") conditions of Iran's neighborhood. This worldview has serious consequences, as the environment can be shaped and changed, while the intrinsic qualities of the state are intractable.

ENDNOTES

[1] Chatham House, "Iran, Its Neighbours and the Regional Crises." August 2006; available from http://www.chathamhouse.org.uk/pdf/research/mep/Iran0806.pdf

[2] Christopher Hitchens is one of the first to use the term "fascism with an Islamic face." *The Nation*, 8 October 2001; available from http://www.thenation.com/doc/20011008/hitchens20010924
> Walter Mead describes the post-9/11 threat of Islamist militancy as "Arabian fascism," although Islamists advocate religious rather than ethnic solidarity. See Mead in *Power, Terror, Peace, and War: America's Grand Strategy in a World at Risk* (New York: Knopf Publishing Group, 2004).

[3] Richard P. Mitchell, *The Society of the Muslim Brothers* (London: Oxford University Press, 1969).

[4] "A Question of Values." *Times Online*, 1 August 2006; available from http://www.timesonline.co.uk/article/0,,542-2293701,00.html

[5] Mohammad Mohaddessin, *Islamic Fundamentalism: The New Global Threat* (Washington, DC: Seven Locks Press, 1993 and 2001).

[6] "Implications of a Shaky Ceasefire." *Stratfor*, 15 August 2006.

[7] Also see Vali Nasr, *The Shia Revival* (New York: W.W. Norton & Company, 2006).

[8] George W. Bush, "Address of the President to the Joint Session of Congress and the American People." (Washington, DC: White House, 20 September 2001); available from http://www.whitehouse.gov/news/releases/2001/09/20010920-8.html

[9] "President George W. Bush Discusses War on Terror at National Endowment for Democracy." (Washington, DC: White House, 6 October 2005); available from http://www.whitehouse.gov/news/releases/2005/10/20051006-3.html
> Although President Bush uses the term Islamo-fascism in the context of individual terrorists, such as Osama bin Laden, this book considers the Government of Iran as presiding over an Islamo-fascist state.

[10] Daniel Pipes, "Death to America." *New York Post*, 8 September 2002.

[11] Amir Taheri, "Iran: Ethnic Woes." *New York Post*, 6 February 2006. Available at: www.benadorassociates.com/article/19305

[12] Eric Rouleau, "Iranian left and right slugging it out in chaotic fighting body," *The New York Times*, 14 June 1980, P. 2, "... tens of thousands of militants in sympathy with the People's Mujahideen were standing in line outside the stadium...Khomeini supporters from the Party of God, known as the Hezbollahi, approached calling for "Death to Massoud Rajavi!"..."there is only one party," they chanted, "the Party of God, and one chief, Ayatollah Khomeini."..."Do you hear?" Mr. Rajavi asked as he addressed himself to the Hezbollahi. "We are neither Communists nor pro-Soviet as you claim. We are fighting for the total freedom and independence of Iran."

[13] Ali Akbar Hashemi Rafsanjani served two terms as the fourth President of Iran from 1989 to 1997, lost on the second round ballot to Tehran Mayor Mahmoud Ahmadinejad in the 2005 Iranian presidential election, and serves as Chairman of the Expediency Council of Iran, which resolves legislative issues between the Parliament and the Council of Guardians and advises the Supreme Leader Ali Khamenei on matters of national policy.

[14] "Iran: Threatening Israel to Get to the United States?" *Stratfor*, 18 August 2004.

[15] "Iran's Bid for Regional Power: Assets and Liabilities." *Power and Interest News Report (PINR)*, 6 September 2004.

[16] "Desperate Clerical Measures." *U.S. Alliance for Democratic Iran (USADI) Dispatch*, Volume II, No. 6, 24 March 2006.

[17] Bernard Lewis, "August 22: Does Iran Have Something in Store." *Wall Street Journal*, 8 August 2006.

[18] Anton La Guardia, "'Divine mission' driving Iran's new leader." *Telegraph*, 14 January 2006; available from http://www.telegraph.co.uk/news/main.jhtml?xml=/news/2006/01/14/wiran14.xml&sSheet=/news/2006/01/14/ixworld.html

[19] For instance, 13 out of 21 of Ahmadinejad's Cabinet Ministers hail from the Revolutionary Guards. See "18 of 21 new ministers hail from Revolutionary Guards, secret police" and "Revolutionary Guards and allies sweep Iran's new cabinet." *Iran Focus*, 14 August 2005.

[20] Matthias Kuntzel, "A Child of the Revolution Takes Over." *The New Republic*, 24 April 2006.

[21] Ray Takeyh, "A Profile in Defiance." *The National Interest*, Spring 2006.

[22] *Ibid.*

[23] Roger Hardy, "The Iran-Iraq war: 25 years on." *BBC News*, 22 September 2005; available from http://news.bbc.co.uk/1/hi/world/middle_east/4260420.stm

[24] "The only way is to set their entire world on fire." *Iran Press News*, 6 March 2006; available from http://www.iranpressnews.com/english/source/011275.html

[25] Olivier Roy, *The Failure of Political Islam* (Cambridge, Massachusetts: Harvard University Press, 1994).

[26] Timothy Garton Ash, "Soldiers of the Hidden Imam." *The New York Review of Books*, Volume 52, Number 17 (3 November 2005).

[27] *Ibid.*

[28] *Ibid.*

[29] Mohammad Mohaddessin, *Islamic Fundamentalism: The New Global Threat* (Washington DC: Seven Locks Press, 1993 and 2001).

[30] *Ibid.*

[31] "Abu Musa Island." *GlobalSecurity.org*, 28 April 2005; available from http://www.globalsecurity.org/wmd/world/iran/abu-musa.htm

[32] "Territorial Disputes." *U.S Library of Congress*; available from http://countrystudies.us/persian-gulf-states/94.htm

[33] *Ibid.*

[34] Daniel Pipes, "Kuwait's Terrorism Policy Sets an Example." *Wall Street Journal*, 18 November 1986.

[35] "Collective Security under the Gulf Cooperation Council." *U.S. Library of Congress*; available from http://countrystudies.us/persian-gulf-states/96.htm

[36] Joshua Teitelbaum, "The Gulf States and the End of Dual Containment." *MERIA Journal*, September 1998 (Volume 2, No. 3).

[37] *Ibid.*

[38] *Ibid.*

[39] Joshua Kucera, "Iran Expanding Ties with Central Asian States to Counterbalance US Geopolitical Pressure." *Eurasia Insight, Eurasianet.org*, 13 April 2006; available from http://www.eurasianet.org/departments/insight/articles/eav041305b_pr.shtml

[40] "Official Visiting Moscow Says Iran to Join Shanghai Body Summer 06." *Itar-Tass,* 14 April 2006.

[41] Thomas Joscelyn, "The Iran-Taliban Affair." *Weekly Standard*, 9 March 2006.

[42] Amir Taheri, "The Frightening Truth of Why Iran Wants a Bomb." *Telegraph*, 16 April 2006; available from http://www.telegraph.co.uk/opinion/main.jhtml?xml=/opinion/2006/04/16/do1609.xml

[43] Robin Hughes, "Iran and Syria Sign Mutual Assistance Accord." *Jane's Defense Weekly*, 21 December 2005.

[44] Helen Chapin Metz, ed. *Saudi Arabia: A Country Study* (Washington: Federal Research Division, Library of Congress, 1993); available from http://rs6.loc.gov/frd/cs/satoc.html

[45] "Iran says military threats not in US interests." *Reuters*, 5 April 2006.

[46] "Supreme leader: Iran's ideology spans N. Africa to India." *Iran Focus*, 25 March 2006.

[47] "Saudis consider nukes to achieve 'balance of terror' with Iran." *World Tribune*, 17 April 2006.

[48] Allister Heath, "Ahmadinejad's Iran: A Monster of Our Own Making." *The Spectator*, 9 February 2006.

[49] Robin Wright and Peter Baker, "Iraq, Jordan See Threat To Election From Iran." *Washington Post*, 8 December 2004; available from http://www.washingtonpost.com/wp-dyn/articles/A43980-2004Dec7.html

[50] *Ibid.*

[51] "Arab-parast president: Iran and Sudan two pillars of the arabs' culture." *Iran News*, 24 April 2006.

[52] Charles Kurzman, "Critics Within Islamic Scholars' Protests Against the Islamic State in Iran." *International Journal of Politics, Culture and Society*, Volume 15, No. 2, Winter 2001.

[53] *Ibid.*

[54] "Terror and Repression, Country Studies, Iran." *U.S. Library of Congress;* available from http://countrystudies.us/iran/26.htm
See also "The Iranian Revolution: History;" available from www.fsmitha.com

[55] Kamal Nazer Yasin, "Iran's Revolutionary Guards Making a Bid for Increased Power." *Eurasianet.org,* 19 May 2004; available from www.eurasianet.org

[56] Matthias Kuntzel, "A Child of the Revolution Takes Over: Ahmadinejad's Dreams." *The New Republic,* 14 April 2006.

[57] Special Report from Iran, the Middle East Research and Information Project (MERIP), 15 July 1999; see also Foundation for Freedom in Iran, July 9, 1999; available from http://www.iran.org/humanrights/students.htm
"Iran Hopes." *Committee of Correspondence,* 13 July 2005; available from http://www.angelfire.com/ky/kentuckydan/CommitteesofCorrespondance/index.blog?from=20050713

[58] Kuntzel, "A Child of the Revolution Takes Over," *The New Republic,* 24 April 2006.

[59] Dilip Hiro, *The Iranian Labyrinth* (New York: Nation Books, 2005).

CHAPTER 2

Why the Nature of
the Regime Matters

INTRODUCTION

Decision-making in Tehran is based on both ideological imperatives and traditional national interests. The Iranian regime's desire to destroy Israel arises mainly from incompatibility of values more than perceived economic or military threats. The regime is also driven to reconstruct a Persian empire, an imperative stretching back over 2,500 years. Tehran uses traditional means, such as rhetoric, empowerment of terrorist proxies, and pursuit of nuclear weapons toward these ideological ends. Given the aggressive, expansionist nature of the Iranian regime, at issue is what difference that nature makes for the international community, in general, and the United States and Israel, in particular.

One hypothesis is that Iran's bellicose stance results from living in a "tough neighborhood" and feeling threatened by neighbors. Data collected and analyzed in this chapter, however, indicate that Iran does not fear for its security as much as it fears the encroaching influence of Western civilization in contradiction to the Islamic Republic's revolutionary beliefs, and that its hostile rhetoric is a result of its ingrained values. Since Ahmadinejad's ascendancy to the presidency, the regime has stepped up its rhetoric in an attempt to generate popular support in its battle against the West.

To destroy its ideological enemies, Iran empowers a host of terrorist groups. The three most important groups are Hezbollah, Hamas, and Palestinian Islamic Jihad. These three groups adhere to Islamist beliefs, receive Iranian support, and intend to destroy Israel.

Sheik Hassan Nasrallah, political leader of the Shiite Hezbollah has pledged his loyalty to the Supreme Leader of Iran, Ali Khamenei. The Sunni Hamas, since their electoral success in 2006, has sought Iranian material support to compensate for funds denied by Israel, Europe, and the United States. Palestinian Islamic Jihad split from the Muslim Brotherhood in Egypt and became the first Sunni terrorist group to use Khomeini's Revolution as an Islamist model.

In addition to supporting terrorist proxies, Tehran is accelerating its pursuit of nuclear weapons, which its leaders believe to be the *sine qua non* for regime survival. The confluence of two disturbing trends—vitriolic posturing and increased nuclear bombmaking—makes Iran the greatest threat to the international community. The Khamenei-Ahmadinejad regime is determined to acquire nuclear weapons because it understands that the bomb is the regime's ultimate defense against the encroaching forces of democracy, secularization, and modernization.

Understood in the context of ambitions that are both geostrategic and ideological, Iran's behavior poses a serious threat to American, Israeli, and international interests. The Tehran regime intends to impose a "religious empire" across the Middle East, in the words of Israeli Deputy Prime Minister Shimon Peres.[1] Toward this end, Iran's rulers pursue nuclear weapons. Therefore, an Islamist-fascist regime with nuclear weapons is unacceptable.

IRAN'S PERCEPTION OF THREAT AND EXPRESSION OF HOSTILITY

Recall the questions that guide this inquiry: First, what is the nature of the regime in Iran? Second, what difference does its character make? Third, what is the international community prepared to do in light of the nature of the regime?

With respect to the second question regarding what difference an Islamist fascist regime makes, consider the following: Because the regime is Islamist-fascist in nature, it expresses and justifies hostility by claiming that it is the target of perceived threats.

To test whether perception of threat and expression of hostility move in tandem as expected, this inquiry collected perception and expression statements, applied content analysis, and used the results to draw inferences about the role of ideology as a driver in the Iranian regime's decision making. The purpose of content analysis is to "infer the characteristics and intentions of sources from inspection of the messages they produce." [2]

This book draws upon prior work by the Stanford University Studies in International Conflict and Integration. Those researchers describe content analysis as "a scientific way to measure attitudinal variables in international conflict, when personal interviews, questionnaires and direct observations of the decision makers in action are unavailable." [3]

Because the ayatollahs of Iran are unlikely to submit to western psychological screening anytime soon, it is left to scholars to infer their cognitive preferences from available information, namely their public discourse. Given the deep cultural differences between western and eastern thought processes and behavioral patterns, examination of the public discourse of Iranian leaders has its limits. While acknowledging such limits, however, this study finds content analysis methodology a valuable tool with which to gauge the motivation and intent of the Iranian regime.

The overall aim of the content analysis study is to analyze how and why Iran's attitudes toward Israel and the United States evolved over time. A first goal was to determine the relative degree of threat Iran perceived from Israel and the United States and how those perceptions of threat changed over time. A second purpose was to determine how Iran expressed hostility and to trace the relative intensity of its expression of hostility over the duration of the regime. And a third aim was to determine the role of ideology in explaining why perception and expression correlate across time.

The methodology measures consistency and variability of perception of threat and expression of hostility statements. A principal research issue is whether or not there is a correlation between Iran's perception of threat and expression of hostility. The study of regime statements and related events seeks to determine to what extent Iran's perception of threat from Israel and from the United States drives the hostility toward each since the Iranian Revolution of 1979.

Researchers collected an extensive set of public statements by the top leadership of the Tehran regime, placed the statements into a large database, and sorted them into two major categories: perception of threat and expression of hostility. Coders also created historical event timelines to provide a control data set of actual events that occurred from 1979-2006. Mapping perception, hostility, and events facilitates making inferences about the future behavior of the Iranian regime.

At issue is how to determine to what degree pragmatic national interest considerations and Iran's ideological motivations each drive Iranian hostility. If regime statements correspond to events and there were a correlation between perception of threat and expression of hostility, it would seem reasonable that Tehran's foreign policy vis-à-vis the United States and Israel was based on pragmatic considerations. If Iranian hostility does not correspond to events, however, it would demonstrate a predominance of ideology.

An assumption underlying the research is that officially-expressed Iranian hostility not identified as a response to perceived threat derives from the influence of ideology. The ideology in question is the Islamist basis of the Revolution and the innate drive for regional hegemony. Such ideas have served as the blueprint of the clerical regime in Tehran since the Ayatollah Khomeini first imposed its harsh strictures on the Iranian people.

Analysis of the collected data indicates that the public rhetoric of the Iranian regime vis-à-vis the United States remains consistently intense with respect to the perception of threat and hostility over the period under review. At issue is why such rhetoric changes so little during periods when Iranian regime actions imply sensitivity to geopolitical circumstances. An hypothesis of this study is that regime statement consistency is a reflection of Tehran's ideological character.

Iran's collusion with Hezbollah to attack Israel in July 2006, addresses the issue of perception of threat, or lack thereof, as a catalyst to aggressive actions. In other words, as events of July 2006 carried Iranian regime hostility toward Israel well beyond the realm of rhetoric, perhaps it was the lack of a perceived, credible threat from either the United States or Israel that emboldened Iran to approve the attack of 12 July 2006. Iran signed off on a conflict because it did not perceive a deterrent threat. Therefore, its expressions of hostility and claims of threat are likely based on ideological predispositions rather than security concerns.

Principal Queries

Researchers performed content analysis on an extensive database of Tehran leadership statements collected from the period of 1979-2005. This study formulated three principal queries for analysis:

- To what extent does Iran's perception of threat from the United States and Israel drive the hostility that has characterized the Iranian regime's attitude toward these two countries since 1979?

- To what extent does the Iranian regime's ideology drive Iranian expressions of hostility?

- To what extent does ideology explain the correlation between Iranian perception of threat and expression of hostility?

Scholarly Literature

Content analysis has been an important component of international relations scholarship since the 1960s. Robert North describes its scientific basis in his groundbreaking book *Content Analysis: A Handbook with Applications for the Study of International Crisis*: "The central decision-making functions include *the cognitive interpretation of incoming information*—what is it and what are its dimensions and what are its characteristics and properties; its affective evaluation—is it good or bad, supportive or threatening? The formulation and explication of intention or policy; and the affective ordering of preference." [4]

This study builds upon previous content analyses in historical significance and magnitude. The first of two benchmark content analysis studies was conducted by Robert North in 1967 and titled "Perception and Action in the 1914 Crisis." The other was authored by Edward Azar and titled "Conflict Escalation and Conflict Reduction in an International Crisis: Suez, 1956."

This study followed the same academic processes as these studies, and closely resembles them in size and scope. However, the present inquiry is unique. Rather than relegating content analysis to historical study of past circumstances, this analysis sheds light on matters of pressing concern to the international community.

Data Collection

The study addressed the reliability and validity of the data set. Reliability is the consistency with which individual(s) collected and coded statements. Validity is the degree to which indicators measure the underlying concept. Based upon tests, the data appear to be both reliable and valid.

To ensure the reliability of data, coders collected a large number of data points from Iranian regime sources; the final number of statements collected exceeded 2,400. By way of comparison, the two benchmark studies of Azar and North collected 835 and 5,000 statements respectively.

Rather than collecting the universe of statements from the Iranian regime from 1979-2005, the research team engaged in targeted sampling. The team selected statements from the two weeks surrounding three different dates: Embassy Takeover Day (4 November), Jerusalem Day (the last Friday of the Muslim holy month of Ramadan), and May Day (1 May). Embassy Takeover Day is a yearly celebration of the 1979 seizure of the U.S. embassy in Tehran. Jerusalem Day is a holiday created by Ayatollah Khomeini to call attention to Israel's claim of sovereignty over a united Jerusalem. May Day is a neutral control date to ensure validity.

North suggests in the book *Content Analysis* that for a sample to be statistically significant, it should include at least 25 statements. This study went above and beyond that requirement, collecting an average of 25 statements for each of the three time periods each year, yielding a total of over 75 statements per year.

Sources

To keep sample size manageable and content consistent, researches collected from two databases: the Foreign Broadcast Information Service (FBIS) and the BBC International Monitoring Reports. FBIS microfiche archives were accessed first to obtain the requisite 25 statements from each date set for each year. FBIS materials after 1997 are available through the Internet-based World News Connection, while BBC International Monitoring Reports were obtained via Lexis-Nexis.

All relevant archives were personally searched by research staff rather than merely using search engines, so as to avoid any technical exclusion programs or biased search techniques. Researchers used a tiered priority system for gathering statements most closely related to the regime power structure. Statements from the supreme leader, president, and leading clerics were the top priority, followed by important ayatollahs and major government officials. Secondary sources included minor government officials and state-controlled media outlets.

Coding

The definition of a statement is a slightly modified version of the definition of a signal by Azar in "Conflict Escalation and Conflict Reduction in an International Crisis: Suez, 1956." He defines signals as "a verbal or physical event on a specific date, by a specific actor, directed toward a specific target, regarding an issue of mutual concern."[5] The IPC project focused on statements that expressed Iran's perception of threat emanating from the United States or from Israel; likewise, all statements describing any, or in some cases, an absence of hostility, inclusive of value judgments of policy actions, were designated as expressions of hostility.

All statements were coded by topic, for either the United States or Israel, and then coded as a perception of threat or an expression of hostility.

All collected statements were then broken down into their component parts and coded according to their intensity.

The breakdown of each statement's components is as follows:

1) Citation: Full citation including source document number.

2) Quotation: Whole sentence(s).

3) Perceiver: This is almost invariably the author of the statement; usually it is the name of the author, but if not specific, perceiver was referred to as a state agency or, if a lesser person, Iranian official or Iran, the country.

4) Perceived: The perceived is the actor described in the statement. That which is perceived is a country or person, not an action or ideal. Sorting perceiver and perceived also allowed researchers to sort the data for analysis. The perceived is synonymous with the subject of the sentence.

5) Target: Whatever the perceived affects; that is, the direct object of the subject.

6) Descriptive Connector: Language that describes the connection between the perceived and the target. The purpose was to isolate the key phrase in the statement that demonstrates the intensity of either threat perceived, or hostility expressed. The descriptive connector is used to rank each statement in intensity of feeling expressed.

Each statement was then ranked relative to the other statements for intensity of feeling expressed (either perception of threat or expression of hostility), as specified by the Azar and North studies. In conformity with principles established by North, each statement was ranked from 1-9 relative to the other statements, and then they were ordered on a normal distribution curve. When assigning a 1-9 value to each statement, two independent coders were used, so as to ensure consistency. By using two independent coders, higher reliability was also attainable.

Forcing the statement magnitudes into a normal distribution allows for a measure of variation in intensity over time. The 1-9 scale does not measure the absolute intensity of the statements, but only how the statements compare with one another across time. The average of all statements collected for any actor would be 5, regardless of how intense the actor's rhetoric was in an absolute sense. This type of distribution allows for comparative conclusions, e.g., "Rhetoric was more intense in time period A than in time period B." The normal distribution method would not allow for an absolute conclusion, e.g., "Rhetoric is very intense." To analyze the absolute level of intensity, researchers applied their own qualitative sensitivities.

Hypotheses

Entering into this study of Iranian regime statements about Israel and the United States, the task was to find whether the clerical regime's commitment to its Revolutionary ideology would prove a constant or variable factor in the regime's perception of threat and expression of hostility over the entire time period from 1979-2005.

Researchers were to determine if events exert a correspondingly significant impact on the Iranian regime's external outlook, as measured by perception of threat and expression of hostility. The answer to this question would shed light on whether Ayatollah Khomeini and his successors are driven more by ideological concerns or by the pragmatic, flexible behavior more commonly associated with other nation states. This premise was an important one because of its implications for the formulation of U.S. foreign policy vis-à-vis Iran: If the usual carrot and stick approaches were deemed ineffectual because of the Iranian regime's single-minded pursuit of its ideologically-motivated objectives, then a very different policy strategy would be in order.

Initial research results indicated that perception of threat and expression of hostility were closely correlated, and seemed to trend similarly in almost every year. The question then became whether the linkage between these two factors was because a) perception of threat drove expression of hostility, or b) both perception of threat and expression of hostility were ideological characteristics of the regime.

Essentially, are expression of hostility and perception of threat merely two facets of the same phenomenon, a phenomenon driven ultimately by the regime's hostile ideology? To examine this possibility, the study constructed a number of event timelines against which to compare the trend lines for perception of threat and expression of hostility. Results showed an inconsistent pattern: The Iranian regime sometimes but not always issued official leadership statements reflecting perception of threat and expression of hostility in relation to actual events in the Middle East region, and especially in the Persian Gulf neighborhood of Iran.

Although Iranian expression of hostility and perception of threat did vary somewhat from year to year, they oscillated only in the narrow band between intensity values of 4-6 on a scale of 1-9. Despite the fact that Iran and the United States have had enormous changes in their relationship over the course of the last 27 years, Iran's perception of threat and expression of hostility did not move from this narrow band. This tight pattern suggested the possibility that Iran's attitudes toward the United States were relatively fixed, and that its attitudes were based more on judgments about the nature of the regime and the nature of the United States than on direct security threats posed by the United States.

It became apparent with these comparisons that, while clearly reacting upon occasion to definite events in the region with statements that indicated a perception of threat and expression of hostility, the Iranian regime was not always reacting with alarm or hostility to events that posed a direct threat to its own well-being or survival.

Instead, the Tehran regime seemed to be reacting on numerous occasions to events related specifically to the Arab-Israel conflict; the regime's perception of threat statements more accurately reflected its perception about Israel's threat to Arab or Palestinian interests, rather than to the regime's own immediate concerns. In the same vein, the Iranian regime's expressions of hostility regularly were directed at Israel, even though Israel had not elicited such expressions by any of its own statements or actions directed offensively at Iran.

The final working hypothesis suggested that Iran's particular ideology does form the basis for much regime behavior, including many of its statements reflecting perception of threat and expression of hostility. The environment, in which Iran operates, however, is multifaceted and involves far more than only Israel and the United States. Most importantly, Iran is waging struggles on two major fronts—against the West and within the Islamic World. Its focus

of hostility vis-à-vis Israel is only one subordinate element.

Iran's clerics intended to seize leadership of the Islamic revival with its 1979 Revolution; they believed that establishment of an Islamic regime in Tehran coupled with aggressive expansion throughout the region would achieve that end. As the inevitable regional and international backlash to Iranian Shiite plans, however, Tehran found itself blocked and opposed by Sunni-led regimes on multiple fronts around the world. Moreover, one of the direct consequences of that Sunni pushback was massive funding by Saudi Arabia for the export and spread of radical Wahhabi Islamism.

The international *jihad* movement benefited from a generalized awakening of radical Muslim elements that the Iranian Revolution and Soviet invasion of Afghanistan encouraged. Nevertheless, these events also sharpened the sectarian animosities that have spurred Sunni-Shiite conflict for centuries. The ongoing frustration inherent in this conflict is one major source of the clerical regime's perception of threat, although that particular threat emanates from the Sunni Muslim world rather than the United States or Israel.

In addition to the conflict within Islam, the second major front on which Iran's leadership has been engaged since launching the Revolution is the one that pits radical Islamism in general against the West as a whole and the United States in particular. In this battle, Iran views Israel as a local proxy for its protector and sponsor, the United States. Israel represents for Islamist Iran the leading edge of a much broader, vastly more threatening cultural challenge from the Western world. Appendix A contains statements by Iranian leaders that demonstrate their linking the United States and Israel.

The study hypothesized that Iran's leadership perceives an indirect threat in the State of Israel, although Tehran's true enemy is Washington. Incapable of taking on the world's superpower directly, Iran instead channels some of its leadership's most inflammatory statements about threat and hostility toward Israel. Alarmingly, as the Hezbollah war with Israel during the summer of 2006 demonstrates, under the Khamenei-Ahmadinejad regime, Tehran is more than ready to act out its threatening and hostile statements directed toward Israel.

IRAN'S PERCEPTION OF AND HOSTILITY TOWARD THE UNITED STATES

I tell you what it is that Americans want to uproot: the nation's wish to be independent, Islam which makes this nation reject tyranny, the spirit of struggle which is buried deep in the heart of every individual in this nation and the spirit of not surrendering to force.

— Supreme Leader, Ayatollah Ali Khamenei, 1997

Ayatollah Khamenei's 1997 statement about the U.S. threat to independence and Islam reflects the dual nature of national interest and ideology underlying his perceptions. Throughout this study of statements made during 1979-2005, Iran perceived a steady and high level of threat from the United States and expressed hostility with the same consistency and intensity. The study shows a high correlation between perception of threat and expression of hostility over time.

As Figure I indicates, Iran's perception of threat and its expression of hostility declined consistently from 1979 to 1986. The Tehran regime's hostility toward the United States pre-dated the Revolution and forms part of the Khomeini clerics' antipathy to the West

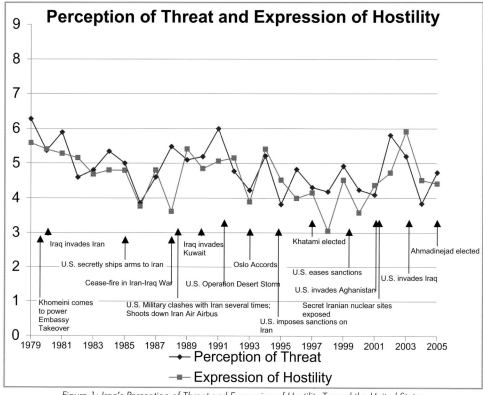

Figure 1: Iran's Perception of Threat and Expression of Hostility Toward the United States

in general. Resentment toward the United States for its support of the Shah (as well as its leadership of globalization, secularization, and democratization) exploded into the Embassy takeover and subsequent hostage crisis of 1979-81. United States support for the reviled Shah is responsible for the peak in expression of hostility and perception of threat in 1979. While Iranian perception of threat never exceeded the level of 1979, it reached similar heights during the Gulf War and buildup to the invasion of Afghanistan. The growing regional influence of the United States at these two points explains the high levels of

Iran's perception of threat and expression of hostility.

Iran did not anticipate the overwhelming American response that the 9/11 attacks brought to the Middle East. The influx of U.S. troops, first into Afghanistan and then into Iraq, with accompanying naval assets in the Persian Gulf, by 2003 had encircled Iran. Supreme Leader Khamenei had listened to President George W. Bush's January 2002 State of the Union address, in which he labeled Iran part of an "axis of evil." The spike in perception of threat values demonstrates Tehran's alarmed initial reaction to the U.S. campaign against the Taliban. The

Iranian Perception of Threat From the United States

Year	Value	Year	Value	Year	Value
1979	6.28	1988	5.48	1997	4.31
1980	5.36	1989	5.1	1998	4.19
1981	5.89	1990	5.19	1999	4.92
1982	4.6	1991	6	2000	4.24
1983	4.81	1992	4.78	2001	4.1
1984	5.34	1993	4.23	2002	5.81
1985	5	1994	5.21	2003	5.2
1986	3.86	1995	3.82	2004	3.84
1987	4.61	1996	4.83	2005	4.74

Figure 2: Average Iranian Perception of threat from the United States

precipitous dive in both threat perception and expression of hostility that followed indicates that either the regime's anxieties calmed somewhat as the United States became increasingly bogged down in Iraq, or that the regime deliberately toned down its rhetoric as it came under fire for its nuclear program.

The values corresponding to Iranian perception of threat from the United States were lower during years in which U.S. interests were struck heavy blows by terrorist attacks than in previous or following years: 1986 (Khobar Towers attack); 1993 (first World Trade Tower attack); and 1998 (Nairobi and Dar Es Salaam Embassy attacks). Iran may have perceived the United States to be less of a direct threat in these years because American power was shown to be vulnerable.

The polynomial "best fit" line in figure 3 demonstrates how closely the trends in Iran's expression of hostility and perception of threat correlate. One potential inference from this fact is that perception of threat has a significant influence on Iran's expression of hostility. Another possibility is that perception of threat and expression of hostility are viewed through the regime's tinted ideological lens, and that they reinforce each other.

Consider the following: If any given leadership were unable to ascertain or respond to external events and made statements based only on its ideological nature, one would expect that, over time their rhetoric would remain relatively constant. Thus, that leadership's relative average perception of threat each year would remain constant at a value of "5." If, however, we could hypothesize a leader who was completely free from past biases or ideology, and responded purely to events and real threats, then the yearly score would fluctuate from 1-9 as the relative level of threat increased or declined.

Given the volatile nature of Iran's neighborhood, one would expect large fluctuations in intensity of rhetoric over a 27-year period. However, Iran's statements are confined to a very narrow band of intensity near "5."

U.S. and Saudi Military Personnel Assess Damage after Khobar Towers Bombing
Photo Credit Getty Image

What the data indicate is that Iran is responding to world events, but that ideology contributes to the unexpected consistency in perception of threat. This uniform intensity is a result of the Iranian leadership's pre-existing ideological opposition to basic western values of democracy and liberty.

At times, Iran's perception of threat appears disconnected from events. From 2002-2004 as the United States invaded Afghanistan and Iraq, the regime's perception of threat from the United States actually fell. In the year leading up to the ceasefire in the Iran-Iraq War, the regime's perception of threat actually rose and continued to rise slightly over the next five years even after the cessation of hostilities. The disconnect between events and Iran's perception of threat also indicates that ideology might be driving its perception of threat.

Low variation from year to year in the regime's perception of threat, coupled with the persistently high levels of threat that it perceived (even in times of relative quiet or even rapprochement with the United States) indicated strongly that the regime believes its ideological interests were in conflict with the values of the United States.

As noted above, even the rather consistently hostile relationship between Iran and the United States after the 1979 Revolution has had its high and low points. American overtures to Iran in the

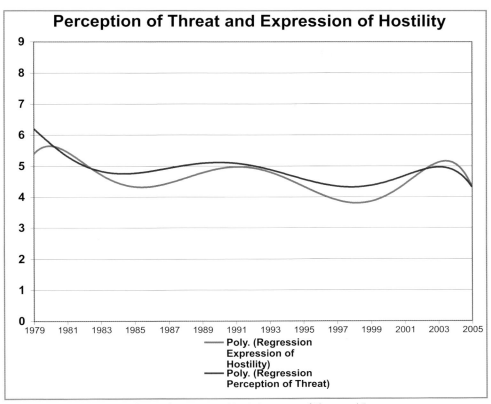

Perception of Threat and Expression of Hostility

— Poly. (Regression Expression of Hostility)
— Poly. (Regression Perception of Threat)

Figure 3: Polynomial Regression of Iran's Perception of Threat and Expression of Hostility Toward the United States and Israel

1980s, intended to secure the release of kidnapped hostages, eventually included back channel dialogue and the provision of U.S. weapons to the Tehran regime (at a time when official U.S. policy was backing Saddam Hussein's Iraq).

In the lead-up to the March 2003 launch of Operation Iraqi Freedom, more back channel discussions between U.S. military forces and the Tehran regime were intended to secure an agreement from Iran to refrain from stirring up Shiite populations in southern Iraq following the toppling of the Iraqi Ba'athist regime, in return for a U.S. pledge to back off

from pressuring Iran over its nuclear weapons program.[6]

Then, in December 2003, U.S. military cargo planes airlifted over 150,000 pounds of emergency medical supplies in the wake of the devastating Bam earthquake.[7] In April 2006, however, another U.S. offer of humanitarian aid to Iran after another earthquake was met with refusal. And yet, with one apparent dip (during the early years of the Khatami presidency), Iranian rhetoric remained unremittingly hostile toward the United States, in seeming contradiction to the actual bilateral discussions, exchanges, and even

Iranian Expression of Hostility Toward the United States

Year	Value	Year	Value	Year	Value
1979	5.588	1988	3.613	1997	4.159
1980	5.4	1989	5.407	1998	3.054
1981	5.28	1990	4.852	1999	4.526
1982	5.154	1991	5.061	2000	3.579
1983	4.684	1992	5.152	2001	4.375
1984	4.803	1993	3.893	2002	4.731
1985	4.8	1994	5.407	2003	5.912
1986	3.76	1995	4.522	2004	4.514
1987	4.804	1996	4	2005	4.417

Figure 4: Iranian Expression of Hostility Toward the United States

cooperation, that were taking place.

Figure 4 demonstrates a lower magnitude for Iranian expression of hostility toward the United States in those years when U.S. interests were attacked around the world by Islamist terrorists, some of them supported by Iran: 1983 (U.S. Beirut Embassy and Marine Barracks bombings); 1986 (Khobar Towers bombing); 1993 (first World Trade Center bombing); and 1998 (Nairobi and Dar Es Salaam Embassy bombings). As with the perception of threat displayed in Figure 2 above, such a pattern may indicate just how shrewdly the Iranian regime assesses the ebb and flow of U.S. power and vulnerability.

The data suggest that the clerical regime in Tehran functions simultaneously on a number of levels that can leave Western analysts confused. The inherently hostile nature of the Iranian Revolution and its radical ideology of Velayat-e Faqih were known by Ayatollah Khomeini and his cohorts to be existentially threatening to the values of modern Western civilization. From that deliberately hostile starting point, then, Tehran's clerical

regime also takes into account threats to and opportunities for its traditional national interests.

Thus, the clerical regime's perception of threat and expressions of hostility vis-à-vis the United States and other Western powers acknowledge the conflict between the values of liberal democracy and those of the revolutionary Islamist regime in Tehran.

They probe every corner of the great trench that the Iranian nation has established to block the enemy's influence.

— Supreme Leader, Ayatollah Ali Khamenei, 2000

The 1979 Iranian Revolution in large part was aimed at the Westward-leaning, mostly secular monarchy of the Shah. The brutality of the Shah's notorious secret police, SAVAK, which once secured his rule, turned into a major factor that unified the population, eventually ending his rule. Corruption and economic factors played an important role, too, in the anger, frustration, and unhappiness that brought so many sectors of the population into the Shah's overthrow, but do not explain the ultimate success of the Islamist, theologically backward-looking agenda of the Khomeini faction.

If economics had been uppermost, then Communist, Tudeh, or other Marxist-socialist models might have served; indeed, Khomeini's Revolution included liberal measures of Marxist and Third World revolutionary themes. In its early phases, it also cannily manipulated popular yearnings for social justice that are common to both Third World movements and centuries of Shiite tradition. But, once in power, Khomeini showed his true colors and purged the regime from any liberal-minded and secular-leaning elements consolidating power in the hands of the clergy. It was the radical, reactionary, violent Islamist ideology that took over in the end. The clerics violently and forcibly submerged all other societal concerns beneath that ideology.[8] Iran's new president, Mahmoud Ahmadinejad, acting on point for the Supreme Leader, Ayatollah Ali Khamenei, is attempting to revive this ideology to an intensity and ferocity not seen since the early days of the Revolution.

Khomeini was fully cognizant from the start that his *Velayat-e Faqih* ideology would prove offensive, hostile, and

threatening to Israel, his Arab neighbors, and to Western civilization as a whole, with its expanding trends towards modernization and democratization. Khomeini's forces quickly created the Islamic Revolutionary Guards Corps to defend and export the Revolution. The regular Iranian army retained its territorial defense mission (including contingency responsibility for forays into the near abroad) but never was entrusted with the special mission of the Revolution itself, which was both defense and export.

Given the hostile nature of the Tehran regime's ideology and its fanatically dedicated defenders of the Revolution, a study of this regime is most useful if it analyzes that hostility toward the United States and Israel vis-à-vis the perception of external threat.

IRAN'S PERCEPTION OF HOSTILITY TOWARD ISRAEL

God is using one of Ali's descendents [Nasrallah] to confront the spiritual and physical descendents of Marhab of Khaybar [the Jews]. God is reviving the memories of early Islam - the memories of the conflict between Ali and the Jews of [the battles] of Khaybar and Khandaq. On one side stood Ali with a small number of Muslims, and on the other side stood the strong, rich, vain, and arrogant Jews. Ultimately, the sword of Ali did what had to be done, and he humiliated the people of Khaybar and the vain and arrogant Jews. Today, this descendent of Ali stands in the same position, and so do the descendents of Marhab of Khaybar, the Jews of Khaybar and Khandaq.[9]

— Ayatollah Ahmad Jannati

Although anti-Semitism abounds in the Friday Prayers in Tehran, treatment of Jews in Persia has varied greatly. But the worst expressions of anti-Semitism, including persecutions and pogroms, seem to coincide most closely with the upheavals that outside influences and conquerors brought. Anti-Semitism (or xenophobia in general) is not a trait usually associated with the indigenous Persian population or its ancient Zoroastrian faith. With the Ahmadinejad regime's rising hostility towards Israel, however, Iranian Jews faced an increasingly precarious situation.

While there is an official policy of freedom of religion, Iran's Jews are made to know in many ways that they are identified by the radically anti-Semitic regime of Ahmadinejad first and foremost with their co-religionists in Israel. Jewish schools in Iran are staffed mostly by Muslims and the Bible is taught in Farsi, not Hebrew. Radio broadcasts from Israel are often jammed.[10] Still, the Jewish community in Iran has been represented in the *Majlis* since 1997 by Maurice Motamed, an Iranian Jew whose reportedly excellent relationship with the reformist supporters of former President Khatami allowed him to champion Jewish interests in the legal and social areas.

Ironically, given Iran's extreme hostility towards Israel since 1979, ever since its modern inception, the State of Israel has shared a geostrategic position and concerns similar to those of Iran, as it has had to defend its own existence and identity against the far more numerous Muslim Arabs that surround and threaten it.

As a free market democracy during the Cold War years, Israel became an outpost of the Free World and, through its strategic alliance with the United States, a bulwark against Soviet inroads among socialist Arabs. Such commonalities in defense requirements, quite reasonably, drew Iran and Israel together in the decades before the 1979 Revolution, albeit discreetly.

This congruency of interests in an anarchic and often chaotic environment tended to supersede the obvious differences in culture and religion between

Iran and Israel and led the two countries to seek stability and security for their respective regimes within the framework of a discreet alliance that allowed a united front to oppose the multiple external threats that faced them both.[11] It was in this political climate that Iran accorded Israel recognition upon its birth in 1948, a recognition reaffirmed publicly by the Shah in 1960 (although after the Revolution that recognition was rescinded).

Aside from purely geostrategic considerations, Iran and Israel have had other reasons for maintaining a friendly bilateral relationship: Demographic and economic interests also have played an important role in their foreign policy. The historical presence of a Jewish minority in Iran dates to the Babylonian captivity, after which not all captives freed by Cyrus the Great chose to return home. There were some 100,000 Jews living in Iran when the State of Israel was formed in 1948 and their status there and ability to migrate to Israel surely affected, in some measure, the deliberations of Israel's first national leadership, which established good relations with the Shah.

In general, those Jews who remained in Iran prospered over the next quarter century; under the Shah Reza Pahlavi, Iran was a generally secularized country, oriented toward the West. This situation allowed the Jews an emancipated existence and they played an important role in the economic and cultural life of Iran during the years of his rule.[12] Indeed, when persecution of Jews in neighboring Iraq under Saddam Hussein sent thousands fleeing, many found safe haven inside Iran.

Israel's external energy needs also provided a close fit with Iran's huge petroleum resources and, under the Shah, the sale of Iranian oil to Israel was one of the most important features of the relationship. Israeli technical expertise in agricultural areas was especially well-suited to Iran's small-scale requirements and its prowess in military technology was perceived by the Shah as an important source of hardware for his plans to expand and modernize his armed forces while developing, in the process, an indigenous military-industrial base as well.

The Shah's military imperative reached a climax with a 1977 oil-for-arms agreement, under which Israel, among other things, agreed to assist Iran to develop a missile system capable of carrying nuclear warheads. Upgrades to Iran's aircraft armaments, 120 mm and 155 mm self-propelled guns, and other weapons systems were among other agreements between the two.[13]

The seeds of today's antagonism between Iran and Israel began to grow with the rapid development of a virulent anti-Semitism among Arab Muslims that had barely existed in the Middle East before the development of the Zionist movement in the late 19th century and the advent of the Israeli state in 1948. To be sure, the European and especially, Nazi, versions of anti-Semitism, were quite familiar to Arabs and nowhere more so than among the Arab population of Palestine.

The Grand Mufti of Jerusalem, Haj Amin al-Husseini, played a leading role in arousing Arab hatred of Jews in the 1920s and 1930s, and became closely identified with the wartime Nazi regime in Germany. Strains of thought from certain German political philosophers, such as Martin Heidegger, infiltrated the thinking of some Islamic clerics, including Iran's own radical Ayatollah Mesbah Yazdi. With the establishment of their own country in 1948, however, and in one fell swoop, Jews cast off their *dhimmi* status in Muslim lands, established a modern nation state on land Muslims considered their patrimony (the *Waqf*), and to make matters even worse, single-handedly defeated the combined Arab armies of five countries.

Although, as noted above, Iranians, for a variety of reasons and for the most part, did not share the new Arab enmity toward all things Jewish, the Pahlavi Dynasty had sown seeds of anger and resentment among Iran's deeply traditional Shiite clergy long before the Israeli state came into being. This antipathy among this particular group would have repercussions with enormous significance for Jews and Israelis in later years.

Iran's monarchs steadily had been curtailing the traditional power of the Shiite clergy ever since the first efforts of Reza Pahlavi Shah (1925-1941) to centralize and modernize the state. His socioeconomic reforms, while widely popular among ordinary Iranians, chipped away at many of the economic privileges long considered their due by the clergy.

On the cultural front, inspiration brought home from a 1934 trip to Turkey, led to steps to improve the status of women and otherwise institute secular changes in what had been a deeply traditional society. The resentment engendered among the Shiite clergy over such modernization smoldered and grew even more bitter with the land reform program of Mohammad Reza Shah (1941-1979) that reached its full development in his 1961 White Revolution.[14]

Khomeini's years in Najaf were formative ones, in terms of the development of his peculiar ideology. He had been raised in a deeply religious family and educated in the *Sharia*, ethics, and spiritual philosophy. Some of his earliest writing, attacking secularism, previewed his convictions, more fully developed in his later *Velayat-e Faqih* ideology, that only religious leaders were fit to ensure that Muslim society complied with *Sharia*.

Anti-Semitic motifs emerged as well, reflecting European anti-Semitic themes, but also hearkening back to early Koranic references, as well as to the teaching of Khomeini's mentor, the Ayatollah Abol-Shassem Kashani, who had opposed foreign influences in Iran in the early years of the 20th century and harbored intensely anti-Semitic sentiments as well.

The Ayatollah Muhammad Taqi Mesbah Yazdi, who sits on the influential Assembly of Experts (which elects the Supreme Leader) and is the spiritual advisor and mentor of Iranian president Mahmoud Ahmadinejad, was a student of the Ayatollah Khomeini and shares—perhaps exceeds—his hatred for Jews and invocations to violence against Israel. Khomeini's own rise to power forced more than 50,000 Jews to flee to Israel.[15]

During the early years of the 21st century, however, Jews and Israelis had new cause for concern as they watched the insidious infiltration of Iranian power centers by members of the quasi-clandestine *Hojjatieh* Society (which Yazdi heads). This is a group founded in the 1950s by Shi'ite clerics who opposed the followers of the *Ba'hai* faith. Its opposition to Khomeini's concept of *Velayat-e Faqih* (based on the belief that a functioning Islamic government would delay the return of the Twelfth Imam—the *Mahdi*) led him to ban the group in 1983.

Even before the 2005 ascendance to power of Ahmadinejad and his Revolutionary Guards cadres, however, Ayatollah Yazdi and the *Hojjatieh* began to enjoy a comeback. Concern about *Hojjatieh* influence on the president and regime leadership centers on *Hojjatieh* beliefs that an activist role that encourages earthly chaos and conflict will expedite the return of the *Mahdi*, and thus, the dominance of Islamic rule on earth.

With Iran's July 2006 instigation of open warfare between Hezbollah and Israel, concern only mounted that this Iranian regime indeed is bent on turning violent rhetoric into violent action that could engulf the entire Middle East in flames.

This conclusion was underlined when, on 10 August 2006, the website of the U.S.-based *Al-Watan* newspaper quoted the head of the Middle East Research Institute in Moscow, Dr. Yevgeny Satanovsky,

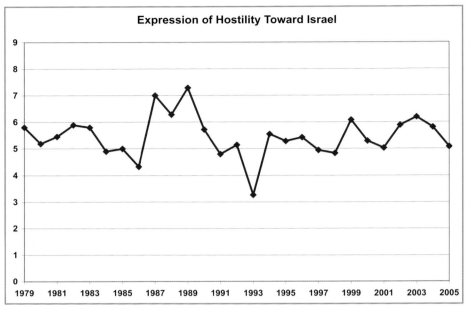

Figure 5: Iran's Expression of Hostility Toward Israel over Time

as saying: "What is happening now in Lebanon is the beginning of the first Iran-Israel war. The events in Lebanon are only a test of Iranian strength by means of its proxy, Hizbullah, before [Iran] becomes a superpower in the region... Iran will, in the near future, attain great political achievements from this crisis, and therefore it will continue to support Hizbullah."[16]

The research quantifies changes in Iran's perception of threat from Israel and the intensity of its expression of hostility toward Israel. Iranian executive, legislative, judicial, and military leadership figures quite often issue official statements reflecting perception of threat and expression of hostility that are in conflict with one another. Although it is beyond question that the Supreme Leader and the clerical leadership closest to him

wield ultimate power in Iran, other power nodes in the Expediency Council, the *Majlis*, the Revolutionary Guards, and the Shiite clerical establishment vie at lower levels for the chance to influence decisions made at higher levels.

Despite the bureaucratic politics that occur in Tehran, the research proceeds as if Iran were a unitary actor. In so doing, this assumption allows for aggregation of statements across the leadership. This approach is justified by the rigid hierarchy in the Iranian political system and the fact that the object of analysis is the change in this aggregation over time. Indeed, the regime became more hierarchical after 2005 with the election of Ahmadinejad and the closeness of the Revolutionary Guards to the clerical leadership.[17]

A good example of the multifaceted and not always straightforward aspect

Portion of Statements Expressing Hostility Toward the U.S. or Israel

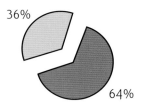

Figure 6: Percentage of Iranian Statements Expressing Hostility Toward the United States or Israel

Portion of Statements Perceiving Threat from the U.S. or Israel

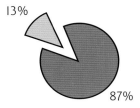

Figure 7: Percentage of Iranian Statements Perceiving Threat from the United States or Israel

☐ Israel Statements

▩ U.S. Statements

of the Iranian regime is the drumbeat of expression of hostility statements from Tehran directed toward Israel during the 1980s; such statements, at least on the surface, seemed to contradict what is now known about the rather cozy relationship between Tel Aviv and Tehran. At that time, Iran was providing Israel with a significant discount on its oil purchases, and Israel was selling hundreds of thousands of dollars worth of food, military equipment, and weapons systems to support Iran in its war against Iraq. Although this difference is a glaring example of the disparity in what Iran says and does, this analysis assumes that outside of this case there is more similarity than difference between rhetoric and action.

Figure 6 shows that out of the universe of Iranian expression of hostility statements collected by the research team, 36% (515) were directed at Israel and 64% (919) were directed at the United States. By contrast, Iran seems to perceive very little threat from Israel. The number of perception of threat statements referring

to the United States remained relatively constant (938), but only 137 statements (13% of total) assessed a threat from Israel (Figure 7).

Figure 6 and Figure 7 indicate that Iran perceives little direct threat from Israel, but Tehran nonetheless is extremely hostile toward Israel. Indeed, the number of Iranian statements reflecting perceived threat from Israel was so low that there were not enough to conduct a reliable statistical analysis of their intensity over time. The near absence from the Iranian leadership of perception of threat statements about Israel strengthens the argument that Iran's expressed hostility toward Israel reflects ideological rhetoric rather than any genuine sense of threat emanating from Israel.

Furthermore, this discrepancy led to an important and unexpected realization that emerged from the historical record. It became apparent through comparison of the perception of threat/expression of hostility trend lines with the various event timelines, that there was both more and less than met the eye with respect to Iran's relationship with Israel. During periods of time when Israel clearly posed, and was perceived by Iran to pose, absolutely no imminent threat to the regime or the country, the shrillness of Tehran's rhetoric toward Israel did not diminish. This reality initially presented a puzzle to the IPC analysts, who considered the most obvious explanation, that Iran's motivations have been driven consistently over the last decades by its radical ideology but also by a need to find issues that would bring Iran acceptance among the wider Arab and Muslim population. An aggressive anti-American, anti-Israeli stance fit the bill nicely.

Given the confluence of lowered perception of threat and attacks against U.S. and Israeli interests, Iranian support for Hezbollah's offensive against Israel in summer 2006 may demonstrate that its perception of Israeli and U.S. vulnerability correlates with decisions about timing and initiation of hostile action. One hypothesis is that when Iran's perception of threat diminishes (and thus its calculation of adversary vulnerability rises), the clerical regime judges the timing propitious to launch an attack.

While the regime's *Velayat-e Faqih* ideology is central to its view of the world, this factor fell short of explaining

Tehran's single-minded focus on the small State of Israel. In and of itself, Israel historically has projected little animosity in word or deed that posed a clear or present threat to either the Iranian regime or to the Persian people. It was only when the research team began to look at the broader context in which Iran's radical clerics had essentially thrown down a gauntlet to the entire Western world that its enmity toward Israel began to make sense. This understanding opens the possibility that Tehran's expressions of hostility toward Israel reflect hostility by proxy for the greater clash of civilizations, in which Tehran views itself as a leader.

In other words, it may be that Iran's radical, reactionary clerical regime perceived Israel as a representative outpost of the broader Western forces of democratization and modernization that, in fact, did and do pose an existential threat to Tehran's *Velayat-e Faqih* ideology in a way that Israel alone never could.

Iran shares no border with Israel, and so long as it does not threaten Israel, it would have no need to fear Israel's military. The encroachment of the ideals of democracy, liberty, and freedom of the press and speech, however, threaten the regime's grip on power. Tehran's return expressions of hostility toward Israel (and support for the Palestinians and various terrorist organizations fighting Israel) may be understood in this context to be a kind of proxy hostility, whose ultimate target in fact is the United States and the West.

The very existence of Israel is also an opportunity for the achievement of Tehran's second major ideological goal: gaining leadership in the Islamic world. The regime can portray itself as a potential leader of the radical Islamic world by taking a strong stance against Zionism and Israel. The Israel-Palestine conflict is a naturally hot button that the regime can press anytime it feels the revolutionary fervor of its people flagging, or to energize its radical base.

To understand the period of the 1980s and the empirical data collected, it is useful to place the decade in historical perspective; in this regard, the research team took particular care to capture the Iran-Israel relationship as it evolved in radically new and often contradictory directions during these ten years.

The study finds that the relationship between Iran and Israel in that context appears almost symbiotic. Iran was literally fighting for its life to repel the onslaught of Saddam Hussein's armies, which had invaded Iran in 1980; Israel had already fought four wars with its Arab neighbors to defend its own

existence and faced a continuous threat to its northern border from the forces of Yasser Arafat's Palestinian Liberation Organization (PLO), which had found safe haven in southern Lebanon.

From the Israeli perspective, the Arab threat, both personified and backed by Saddam Hussein, made Iran's survival in its defensive war against Iraq the preferred choice between two evils.

The research team analyzed the Iranian perception of threat from and expressions of hostility toward Israel and the United States since the death of Ayatollah Khomeini in 1989 and also took into consideration regional events from the 1990s forward to 2005.

Among the external events captured in the several event timelines were the First Gulf War (1991), increasingly intrusive International Atomic Energy Association (IAEA) Weapons of Mass Destruction (WMD) inspection regimes in Iraq, the Oslo Accords period followed by the outbreak of the Al-Aqsa Intifada (2000), and eventually, the sequence of events unleashed by the attacks of 11 September 2001, which brought large numbers of U.S. and other Western military troops to Afghanistan, Iraq, and the Gulf region in general.

In light of the dearth of significant perception of threat from Israel and

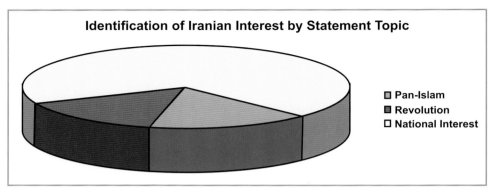

Figure 8: Percentage of Iranian Statements Perceiving Threat to Iranian Areas of Interest

Tehran's willingness to even cooperate with Israel when its own existence comes into question, it would appear that Iran's consistently bellicose rhetoric toward Israel must derive from opposition to Israel's existence rather than as a response to events in the region.

The regime's hostility toward Israel derives its momentum from Iran's existential engagement in an ideological two-front war: the war for leadership of the international Islamic revival and the war against the West. The fact that Tehran perceives no direct threat from Israel, however, does not mean its hostility should be discounted. As part of its twin quests for leadership in the Islamic world and against the forces of modernization, secularization, and democratization, war between Iran and Israel is a significant possibility.

IRAN'S USE OF RHETORIC TO PROP UP ITS GOVERNMENT

The peoples are prepared to hear the good news of unity...Islamic unity is in the benefit of Muslims and against the interests of the superpowers...

— Ayatollah Ali Khamenei, 1984

Supreme Leader Khamenei's statement suggests that he uses rhetoric against the west to drum up domestic support and portray western culture and influence as anti-Muslim. Like many other repressive regimes, Iran paints a picture of an external-internal struggle that portrays the outside world as dangerous. By manufacturing visions of existential threats to its statehood, the Revolution, and Islam, the Iranian regime redirects frustration, anger, and malaise away from itself toward external scapegoats. Tehran's appeal to a pan-Islamic ideal is also aimed at wresting leadership of the radical Islamist movement away from the Sunnis who have dominated the Muslim revival for decades.[18] Iran's backing for terrorist groups that form the leading edge of radical Islam's front against Israel is as much an attempt to shore up its

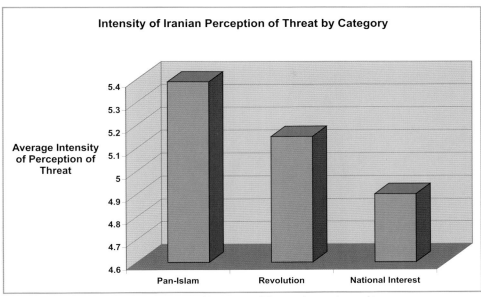

Figure 9: Average Intensity of Perception of Threat to Iranian Areas of Interest

revolutionary credentials with the broader Islamic world as with its own population. Iran relies on harsh internal repression to keep its own people under control but directs much of its violent rhetoric as well as its external military adventurism at a pan-Islamic audience.

Concerning pan-Islamic motivations of the regime in Tehran, consider Figure 8. It compares the number of statements from the Iranian leadership according to whether they reference pan-Islamic goals, revolutionary ideals, or traditional national interests.

Researchers classified regime perception of threat statements into three categories: statements that dealt with threat to Islam and Muslims, threats to the Iranian Revolution and its expansion, and traditional threats to security, economics, or the nation state. In a full 16% of its

statements, Iran identifies its interest with those of Muslims in general, and 15% of the time, the regime describes its interests in terms of the Revolution. Together, the leadership in Iran defines about one-third of the perils to its interests as dangers to religious interests, such as to Muslims in general and the Revolution in particular. By emphasizing the threat the United States poses to religion so heavily, Tehran triggers an emotional response against the West in an effort to rally people behind the regime.

In addition to the frequency of statements (the number of statements made), researchers also quantified the relative intensity of each category compared to the others. researchers also quantified the relative intensity of each category compared to the others. Not only does the regime frequently use the rhetoric of threat to religion and culture to inflame

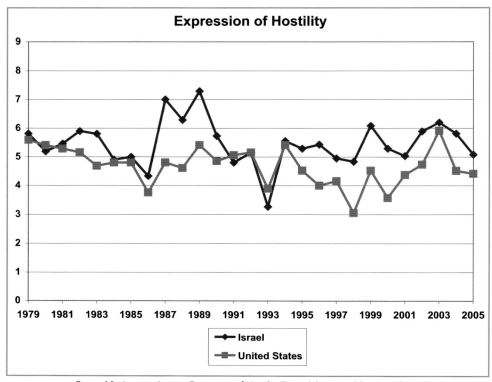

Figure 10: Average Iranian Expression of Hostility Toward the United States and Israel

public opinion against the West, it also ramps up the intensity of its rhetoric when addressing perceived Western threats to Islam or to the Revolution. Figure 9 demonstrates that the average intensity of the threat perceived to religious and revolutionary interests is higher than the regime's perceived threat to its traditional national interests.

The regime devoted the greatest number of perception of threat statements to national interests. But when Iran's leaders did speak about threats to Islam or the Revolution, they spoke with much greater intensity than when addressing national interests. Although the regime's perceived threats to Islam and the Revolution

are expressed with greater intensity than threats to national interests, the methodology does not yield conclusions regarding the absolute level of intensity for any given category.

Figure 10 tracks Tehran's expression of hostility toward both the United States and Israel. The data indicate two things about Tehran's attitude toward these two nations: Iran is consistently more hostile toward Israel than the United States, and that change in Iran's expression of hostility toward Israel and the United States trend together across time.

The fact that Tehran is consistently more hostile toward Israel despite the lack of significant perception of threat from Israel implies there is much more behind the regime's hostility toward Israel than the dynamic of threat and response. The most plausible explanation for this apparent anomaly is that the regime's attitude toward Israel is strongly influenced by Iran's ideological predispositions.

The second issue raised by comparing expression of hostility toward the United States and Israel is why Iran's hostility trends the same in nearly every year. These data reinforce the argument made earlier that Iran's hostility toward Israel may be antipathy-by-proxy from Tehran's hatred of the United States. If indeed Israel serves as a local representative of the United States and the values it embodies, it would be natural for Tehran to ramp up its rhetoric against Israel in tandem with increased antagonism toward the United States.

These data also reinforce the argument that Tehran uses bellicose rhetoric toward the United States, even in the absence of a significant perception of threat, to inflame public opinion against the West and Israel and to portray the regime as the incarnation of true Islamic faith.

IRANIAN SUPPORT FOR TERRORIST GROUPS

Iran's mission of exporting its Revolution and constructing an empire is facilitated by several terrorist groups. Indeed, the United States perennially classifies Iran as a leading state sponsor of terrorism. Consistent with Iran's ideological opposition to Israel's Western values, the regime channels most of its support to Palestinian and Lebanese groups that seek to destroy the Jewish State.

Iran employs a results-based approach when choosing which terrorist groups to support. The connection between Iran and Hezbollah is a natural one, given several factors: Iran's leading role in the creation of the group; Hezbollah's commitment to Shiism and *Velayat-e Faqih*; and Hezbollah leader Hassan Nasrallah's pledge of religious allegiance to Iran's Supreme Leader Ayatollah Ali Khamenei. Thus, most of Iran's terrorist support goes to Hezbollah in the form of rockets and money. In exchange, Iran receives a certain degree of control over Hezbollah decision-making. There is a wealth of circumstantial evidence that Iran played a part in approving Hezbollah's kidnapping of two Israeli soldiers in July 2006. Sunni-based Hamas is not as close to the Iranian regime as Shiite Hezbollah but has cooperated closely with Tehran at times. Hamas is a Sunni movement like Palestinian Islamic Jihad; but unlike, that organization Hamas was never inspired by Khomeini. In fact, for several years after the formation of Hamas in the late 1980s, the group's leaders publicly condemned Khomeini's Iran. By the mid-1990s, though, Iran had realized the effectiveness of Hamas terror operations inside Israel. For its part, Hamas came to see what Iran could offer as support, resulting in closer cooperation between the two. That cooperation was enhanced again in 2006 when Hamas won a majority of seats in the Palestinian Authority. As the West immediately denied funds to the Hamas government, the Iranian regime pledged greater funding to the Palestinians and won the allegiance of Hamas political leader Khaled Mashaal. Despite cooperation in 2006, the relationship between Iran and Hamas remains the most tenuous of the three discussed below. Some Hamas officials warn against accepting Iranian support and see Tehran's generosity as an attempt to appropriate the Palestinian cause.

Like Hamas, Palestinian Islamic Jihad is a Sunni Muslim organization. It was inspired to leave the Muslim Brotherhood by the Shiite Revolution of Ayatollah Khomeini in Iran. The group's disillusionment with the more moderate approach of Sunni Islamist organizations drove it directly into the arms of the violent Khomeini regime. Iran was eager to sponsor the group, as Palestinian Islamic Jihad was single-mindedly determined to destroy Israel and to create an Islamist Palestinian state.

The important ideological component that all these groups share is their opposition to the values that Israel represents. Their strategic interests complement their ideological commitment to destroy Israel.

Hezbollah

Islamic Jihad, Islamic Jihad for the Liberation of Palestine, Organization of the Oppressed on Earth, Party of God, Revolutionary Justice Organization, The Islamic Resistance

Hezbollah calls itself by various names and is a complex umbrella organization of radical Islamist Shiite groups based in Lebanon but with a global reach for political, social, and terrorist operations. Its allegiance and chain of command lead directly to the Supreme Leader of Iran. Hezbollah receives massive financial support as well as its philosophical identity from Iran. Until 11 September 2001, Hezbollah had murdered more Americans than any other terrorist group. Hezbollah was responsible for bombings of the U.S. Embassy Beirut that killed 63 in 1983, the marine barracks in Beirut that killed 241 Marines in 1983, and another attack at the American Embassy the following year that killed 22.

Hezbollah was formed in 1982 in response to Israel's invasion of Lebanon. A coalition of existing Lebanese Shiite groups, including the secular political movement, Amal, created Hezbollah. It was very much a design of Iran's Islamic Revolutionary Guards Corps, hundreds of whose members had arrived in Lebanon as the vanguard of Ayatollah Khomeini's Islamic Revolution with the intention of establishing an outpost of the Revolution among Lebanon's radicalized Shiite population. In many ways, Hezbollah became the international wing of the Iranian Islamic Revolution and served as a model for similar organizations in other Arab states. Its intention remains the establishment of an Islamic regime in Lebanon, but its attitude of Shiite superiority ensured that its sphere of influence has never spread much beyond the Levant and southern Iraq, where existing Shiite populations offered fertile soil for its ideology.

Hezbollah identified itself publicly for the first time in 1985, when it published its manifesto, declaring its enmity toward the West. Although hostility to Israel and the United States forms the core of Hezbollah's program, its close collaboration with Iran also serves Tehran's objectives. These goals reflect the clerical regime's determination to create a counterbalance to the socialist, pan-Arab Sunni forces that, prior to the Iranian Revolution, had led the militant, anti-Western forces in the Middle East. With the creation of Hezbollah, Iran sought to challenge these secular Arab movements and provide a powerful Islamist alternative to Nasserism—the pan-Arab movement begun by former President Gamal Abdel Nasser of Egypt. Tehran's goal was to challenge American interests in the Middle East, pose a credible threat to the conservative Sunni monarchies, and provide a religiously-based challenge to Israel. Finally, with the creation of Hezbollah, Iran succeeded in providing itself with a regional ally, which unlike Syria, was firmly under its control and unreservedly dedicated not only to the destruction of Israel, but also to the creation of a Palestinian state.[19]

Reflecting its roots among Lebanon's Shiite society, Hezbollah developed parallel political and social structures, even as it continued to increase its terrorist and guerrilla capabilities. In the mid-1980s, Hezbollah began to set up a system of Islamic courts across Beirut and southern Lebanon, which take their authority from a Supreme Shura Council (a seven-member religious council of prominent elders). Other branches of the Shura Council are responsible for oversight of financial, military, political, and social committees. Later, an executive council and a politburo were added to Hezbollah's hierarchical structure.[20] The position of clerical figures at the top of the decision-making hierarchy mirrors the *Velayat-e Faqih* structure of governance imposed by Khomeini in Iran.

As the Lebanese Civil War drew to a close in the late 1980s, Lebanon's changing political spectrum and regional politics compelled Hezbollah to expand its activities beyond the perpetual state of *jihad* against Israel. In particular, the Taif Agreement of 1989 brought Hezbollah objectives into conflict with those of its closest regional sponsor, Syria. While Syria sought to maintain its traditional policy of balancing the Lebanese factions against one another to preserve for itself the dominant role as arbiter, Hezbollah (acting on Iranian objectives) worked to spread Islamic order across as much of Lebanon as possible. The death of the

Ayatollah Khomeini in 1989 and the rise of Ayatollah Khamenei to the position of Supreme Leader and Hashemi Rafsanjani to the presidency in Iran opened the way for a pragmatic course of action, both in Iran and for Hezbollah in Lebanon.[21]

Khamenei was a major proponent of a "gradualist-pragmatic" mode and it was he who urged Hezbollah to seek a foothold within the Lebanese political system. Thus began Hezbollah's move in the early 1990s to work within Lebanon's multi-party confessional system, in which the highest offices are proportionately reserved for representatives from specific religious communities. Within this system, Hezbollah operated without backing away from its military program of exerting pressure against Israel.[22] Khamenei was willing to use the short-term tools of political participation in Lebanon to contribute to the long-term ideological goal of destroying Israel.

Hezbollah's participation in Lebanon's 1992 parliamentary elections was its first foray into mainstream Lebanese politics. That year, the party won eight seats in the 128-member legislature, and its allies won an additional four. In the 2005 elections, Hezbollah increased its parliamentary representation to 14 seats, in a voting bloc with other parties that took a total of 35. Also in 2005, for the first time, the party chose to participate in the cabinet and holds two portfolios.[23] Its extensive system of social welfare services has established a broad base of support among a Shiite population already ideologically committed to the Hezbollah-Iranian agenda. The group's battles against Israel also contribute to its popularity among a radicalized electorate.

Hezbollah's participation in partisan politics presents something of a contradiction to traditional Shiite ideology, which holds that until the return of the Disappeared 12th Imam (the *Mahdi*) no earthly political system can substitute for his rule. With Iranian approval, Hezbollah has made a commitment to a political track parallel to its military campaign, which underlines the pragmatic aspect of its strategy. In the words of Shaykh Na'im Qasim: "*We are still in our armed jihad against Israel and its designs in the region. However, when the Ta'if Agreement took place, we entered the political life because every effort carried out by committed Muslims is jihad that is within the general jihad.*"[24]

Unfortunately, Hezbollah's extensive system of schools, hospitals, and other social services in southern Lebanon has led some European and other governments to resist classifying Hezbollah as a terrorist organization,

a move that would prohibit Hezbollah from raising funds in those countries. As of 2006, only the Netherlands, Italy, and Poland consider Hezbollah a terrorist group, despite its long history of attacks against U.S. and Jewish targets in Africa, Argentina, Denmark, Sweden, Thailand, and the United Kingdom. The 1992 bombings of the Israeli Embassy in Buenos Aires and the 1994 bombing of the Jewish Cultural Center in the same city are among the most brutal; extensive investigations into both attacks imply the direct involvement of the Iranian government. Acting through its Ministry of Intelligence Services, which has responsibility for supervision of Hezbollah's international cells outside of the Levant, Tehran is the unseen hand behind its proxy.[25]

As noted earlier, Hezbollah is managed directly by the Revolutionary Guards. It provides training in guerrilla warfare, intelligence, and advanced weaponry such as the Katyusha. This training includes operation of the Fajr-3 and Fajr-5 rockets and Zelzal-2 missiles, which Hezbollah launched against Israeli civilian population centers in the July-August 2006 war involving Lebanon. The direct chain of command from Hezbollah to Iran's Supreme Leader is evident in the words of Hezbollah's leader:

Where is the force in us? What is Hizbullah's secret? The power is in the obedience to Khamenei's vilayat. The secret of our strength, growth, unity, struggle, and martyrdom is vilayat al-faqih, the spinal cord of Hizbullah.[26]

— Hassan Nasrallah

Appendix B contains additional statements made by the Hezbollah leadership regarding Israel, the United States, and Iran. Furthermore, Nasrallah demonstrated allegiance to Khamenei in a gesture full of meaning to Shia: When Nasrallah met with Iranian Supreme Leader Khamenei in 2001 and publicly kissed his hand, the Hezbollah leader acknowledged personal acceptance of the leadership of Khamenei.[27]

Iran does not exercise the same direct day-to-day control over Hezbollah that it did in the past, but as its main sponsor, Iran is involved in important political and military decisions. It has been estimated that Iran provides Hezbollah with $100-200 million each year, much of it in the form of military equipment. Iran's financial support also underwrites Hezbollah's al-Manar television station, which in December 2004, was added to the U.S. list of terrorist organizations for its inflammatory anti-Semitic programming that glorifies suicide bombing and other attacks against Jewish targets. In the wake of the summer 2006 hostilities between Hezbollah and Israel, Iran has channeled additional millions of dollars for distribution by Hezbollah in Lebanon. Hezbollah has given families displaced by Israeli bombing $300 to $400 million to cover rent and repairs to their homes, according to the Arab news agency, Elaph.[28] The Arabic language London daily *Asharq al-Awsat* reported that the Iranian government pledged $500 million to Hezbollah.[29]

Almost every Iranian government ministry, including the Ministries of Intelligence, Education, Telecommunications, Health, Welfare, and Culture and Islamic Guidance, maintains offices in Beirut. These extensions of the Tehran regime spend millions on infrastructure projects. Offices of the Iranian Supreme Leader also function as dedicated facilities for Iranian and Hezbollah intelligence services for information gathering, political and security meetings, surveillance posts, and military courts. Supported by a sophisticated propaganda machine, Tehran assists Hezbollah not only in its military confrontation with Israel, but to win over Lebanon's poor Shiite communities by convincing them of Hezbollah's ability to provide what Lebanon's own government does not.[30]

Iran's Revolutionary Guards *Qods Force* unit maintains a very close operational relationship with Hezbollah's military units. Israel hoped its withdrawal from Lebanon in May 2000 and from the Gaza Strip in August 2005 would drive Hezbollah to focus on social services and domestic politics instead of terrorist operations, but precisely the opposite occurred. Israel's territorial concessions were viewed as admissions of vulnerability and weakness. For a *jihadist* organization, such as Hezbollah, at the command of an aggressively expansionist regime in Tehran, enemy concessions led to an intensified campaign of attacks.

The September 2000 launch of the Al-Aqsa Intifada (uprising), named after the mosque in Jerusalem where rioting began, was the first riposte from the radical Islamists. During the bloody four-year course of that conflict, Iranian supported Hezbollah, Hamas, the Palestinian Islamic Jihad, and al-Aqsa Martyrs Brigade. Such support fueled and inspired the most extremist elements among the Palestinians. With sophisticated weapons, advanced training, and experience in fighting Israel, Lebanese Hezbollah increasingly sought a leading role among Palestinian terrorist groups.

Hezbollah became directly involved in military operations in the West Bank and Gaza Strip.[31]

The Iranian hand behind Hezbollah's summer 2006 attack across Israel's border shows that Tehran and its proxy continue to subscribe to a violent, confrontational mentality. This attitude leaves no room for negotiated settlement, a telltale sign of the nature of the regimes in Tehran and its terrorist proxy. In this respect, during 1992, Hezbollah's former leader, Hussein Massawi declared: "*We are not fighting so that you will offer us something. We are fighting to eliminate you.*"

A review of the sequence of events leading up to and following Hezbollah's 12 July 2006 Israeli border incursion reveals the close coordination among Hezbollah, Iran, and Syria. Iran's decision to unleash Hezbollah reflects the intensifying confrontation between Iran and the international community over its nuclear weapons program. European Union officials had given Iran that date as a deadline for a response to the West's package of incentives to suspend Iran's nuclear enrichment activities.

In the period leading up to Hezbollah's attack, Damascus hosted regular operational planning meetings among Hezbollah, Iranian and Syrian leaders, as well as chiefs of other Middle East terrorist organizations. In December 2005, Syria and Iran signed a mutual assistance accord that included provisions under which Syria pledged to store Iranian nuclear weapons and missiles should Tehran come under United Nations sanctions.[32] This accord was followed in June 2006 by an agreement for military cooperation against what they called the "common threats" posed by Israel and the United States.[33] A January 2006 conference in Damascus included Iranian president Ahmadinejad, Hezbollah Secretary General Nasrallah, and leaders of Hamas, Palestinian Islamic Jihad, Popular Front for the Liberation of Palestine-General Command, and Lebanese Amal.[34]

The night before the 2006 war began, Iranian chief nuclear negotiator Ali Larijani met with European Union foreign policy chief Javier Solana to discuss a deal in which Iran would suspend uranium enrichment in return for a package of western incentives. The results were reported as "disappointing."[35] Larajani left Europe and flew directly to Damascus that same night (although Syria is not involved in the nuclear negotiations).[36] As the crisis unfolded, Larijani remained in Damascus, closely coordinating with Hezbollah and Syrian officials about the increasing

military action between Hezbollah and Israel in Lebanon. Larajani even held a press conference with Syrian Vice-President Farouk al-Sharaa on 12 July.

To set the stage for the war, Iran stepped up its dispatch of weapons, ammunition, and missiles to Lebanon over the course of several months leading to the war. Iran's Islamic Revolutionary Guards forces, long present inside Lebanon were augmented.[37] Iranian Revolutionary Guards were reported fighting and killed in Lebanon, with their bodies secretly flown back to Iran via Damascus.[38] Israeli intelligence reported that Nasrallah was working out of a Hezbollah secret headquarters in the basement of "an embassy in Beirut," presumably the Iranian embassy.[39]

Ongoing coordination among Larijani, Hezbollah, and Syrian officials ensured that Hezbollah received continuous resupply shipments of armaments and other materiel throughout the conflict. There were rumors that even Hassan Nasrallah was in Damascus at this time to meet Larijani.[40] Advanced Iranian-made anti-ship missiles and anti-tank missiles not previously known to be in Hezbollah's possession were discovered by Israeli Defense Forces in the course of the fighting. If there were any doubt about Iran's direct military linkage with

Hezbollah remained, such doubts were dispelled on 6 August 2006 by Ali Akbar Mohtashemi-Pur, an Iranian Member of Parliament who helped found Hezbollah when he was ambassador to Damascus. He explicitly admitted that Iran supplies Hezbollah with Katyusha rockets and Zelzal-2 missiles.[41] Hezbollah commander Bastam Husayn also underlined the group's Iranian sponsorship when he declared in early August 2006, "Anything the Lebanese people have comes from the esteemed leader of the Revolution and the ever-ready government of Iran."[42]

Hezbollah, called the "A-team" of terrorist organizations by former Deputy Secretary of State Richard Armitage, has metastasized throughout Lebanese society, insinuating itself into the very fabric of that factionalized nation. Once it reached the status of "a state within a state," Hezbollah acted in the summer of 2006 as the proxy militia of another government, the terrorist regime in Tehran, to take its host country, willing or not, to war.

Despite military losses from Israel's counterstrikes, Hezbollah survived the conflict, with diplomatic and political gains. Hezbollah's survival has shifted the balance of power in the Middle East, dispelling Israel's vaunted status as the region's pre-eminent and undefeated military power and feeding Iran's growing aspirations to regional hegemony. Neighboring Arab Sunni rulers find new reason to fear an expanding "Shiite crescent" across the Middle East but hesitate to confront directly the aggressive power of a rising Tehran. Noting that the United States and traditional European powers seem weak and vacillating, Iran is encouraged to accelerate its nuclear weapons program, project power via terrorist proxies in Lebanon, Iraq, and elsewhere, and crack down even more harshly on its own domestic population.

Such a moment, when existing impressions about power relationships are in flux and outcomes are in doubt, is one fraught with danger. Only resolute action will resolve the uncertainty. If the West does not take such action, and quickly, it is beyond certain that Iran will.

Hamas

Harakat al Muqawammah al-Islammiyya, Islamic Resistance Movement

Just as Islamic Iran defends the rights of the Palestinians, we defend the rights of Islamic Iran.

— Khaled Meshaal, Hamas Leader

Hamas, whose name (which means "zeal") is an acronym formed from the Arabic "Harakat al-Muqawammah al-Islammiyya" or Islamic Resistance Movement, is a radical Islamist offshoot of the Muslim Brotherhood. It is the largest and most influential of all the Palestinian terrorist organizations, with as many as 1,000 active members and many thousands more supporters. Like the Brotherhood, Hamas is a radical Sunni religious movement that espouses violent confrontation with Israel, Arab regimes, and the encroaching influence of Western ideas and influences. Long a recipient of Iranian funding, since its January 2006 electoral victory Hamas has moved even closer to an open political alliance with Iran.

As founded by Sheikh Ahmed Yassin, Hamas predecessor organizations initially engaged in non-violent preaching, education, and charity work in the Palestinian Territories in the late 1960s. Yassin established the al-Mujamma' al-Islami (Islamic Center) during 1973 in the Gaza Strip to oversee Muslim Brotherhood activities there, but by the early 1980s, Yassin's ideology had shifted to a more radical version that called for violence against Israel. With the 1987 outbreak of the first Palestinian Intifada, Yassin established Hamas itself as a political wing for Brotherhood activities; its August

1988 official Charter openly calls for the establishment of an Islamic state on all of the land encompassing both Israel and the Palestinian Territories, thus effectively seeking the destruction of the State of Israel. According to the Hamas charter, this land has been endowed by Allah to Islam in perpetuity (a *waqf*), making it incumbent on all Muslims to seize it through violent *jihad*.[43]

Between the founding of Hamas 1988 and its January 2006 victory in Palestinian elections, the Hamas military wing, the so-called *Izz al-Din al-Qassam Brigade*, racked up a long and bloody history of suicide bombings and rocket attacks against Israeli civilians. At the same time, the political structures of Hamas were establishing a network of social services in Gaza and the West Bank that provided education, health care, and recreation facilities. These amenities were welcomed by a Palestinian population generally neglected by the corrupt administration of Yasser Arafat's Fatah party. Hamas successfully leveraged these social services and a reputation for honesty into popular support. This support translated into its January 2006 election victory over the Fatah party of the Palestinian Authority's president, Mahmoud Abbas. Despite its new leading role in the government, Hamas held fast

Hamas Wins General Parliamentary Election of Palestine, 26 January 2006
Photo Credit Ahmad Khateib/Getty Images

to its adamant refusal to compromise on its hard-line stance toward Israel.[44]

Hamas maintained a ceasefire with Israel from March 2005 until June 2006. Explosions on a Gaza beach that killed a number of Palestinian civilians were blamed on Israel, despite denials of responsibility from the Israel Defense Forces. Israel, the United States, and Europe imposed crippling economic sanctions following the electoral victory of Hamas and its refusal to recognize the State of Israel. Still, as Hamas develops into a governing political party it has shown no indication it intends to give up the use of terrorism.

Hamas would not negotiate on the road map or any other plan that talks about resistance as if it's terrorism

— Khaled Meshaal; 24 May 2006

Given the substantial funding Hamas receives from Iran and other sources, it feels less urgency over the cutting off of Western funding than it otherwise would. In the wake of its electoral victory and refusal to recognize Israel, Hamas found a new donor. Iran pledged to support the Palestinian Authority, following meetings in Tehran with Hamas leader Khaled Meshaal. Media reports indicated that Tehran had promised Meshaal about $250 million to compensate for the loss of U.S. and European aid.[45]

Iran is the one state sponsor to which

Hamas can turn that fully supports its goals to eradicate the State of Israel. By the same token, however, Hamas may be sacrificing its long-term nationalist objectives with the Palestinian people, as its alignment with Iran's radical Shiite regime alienates other principal financial supporters within the Sunni Arab world. For instance, Saudi Arabia already has delayed some $92 million it had promised the Palestinian Authority, later releasing only $20 million at the personal request of President Abbas.[46]

The annual budget of Hamas is about $70 million. According to a Council on Foreign Relations report, Iranian support amounts to some $20-30 million per year. Additional money comes to Hamas from Palestinian expatriates as well as private donors in Saudi Arabia and other oil-rich Persian Gulf states. Additionally, Hamas has organized a worldwide network of so-called "Muslim charities" in the United States, Canada, Western Europe, and elsewhere that funnel money back to Hamas coffers. In one highly-publicized event, the Bush administration in December 2001 seized the assets of the Holy Land Foundation, the largest Muslim "charity" in the United States, alleging that it was funding Hamas.[47]

Relations between Hamas and Iran were not always so close. While Iran's 1979 Islamic revolution inspired a surge of pride across the Islamic world, it was nevertheless a Shiite Revolution, and the Sunni response, led by Saudi Arabia, soon followed. A huge outpouring of Saudi funding for the spread of Wahhabist ideology through the construction of mosques and Islamic centers worldwide– and support to the *mujahedeen* fighting the Soviet Army in Afghanistan— reasserted Sunni predominance in the Islamic world. Additionally, even as Iran's fledgling regime was fighting for its life against Saddam Hussein's armies, al Qaeda, out of the battlefields of Afghanistan, seized leadership of the Islamist movement for Sunni radicals.

With the 2005 consolidation of power inside Iran by Supreme Leader Khamenei, President Mahmoud Ahmadinejad and a cohort of Iran-Iraq War veterans, Iran made its move to revive its Revolution, reassert radical Shiite ideology, and renew aggressive aspirations to regional hegemony.

During the years of the Al-Aqsa Intifada (2000-2004), Hamas developed increasingly close ties to Hezbollah, the Iranian-supported Lebanese Shiite group, which led to the provision of significant military support and financial assistance. This alliance was reinforced by the physical location of Hamas headquarters in Damascus, where senior

President of Iran Mahmoud Ahmadinejad speaks at the "World Without Zionism" conference in Tehran, 26 October 2005
Photo Credit Behrouz Mehri, AFP/ Getty Images

Hamas official Khaled Meshaal lives, thus bringing Hamas effectively into the Iran-Syria-Hezbollah axis. Hamas and Iran even exchanged "ambassadors," with Imad al-Alami, a senior Hamas military leader, becoming the first Hamas resident representative in Tehran; Hamas is represented in Tehran by Abu-Osama Abd-al-Moti. Still, Hamas has retained a certain distance from its Iranian benefactor and avoids submitting to directives from Tehran.[48]

Hamas and Tehran perceive their cooperative relationship to be beneficial, as they are united in a common hatred of Israel. A series of high-level meetings and exchanges has served to reinforce the relationship: At the "World without Zionism" conference in Tehran in October 2005, both Iranian president Mahmoud Ahmadinejad and Hamas representative in Tehran, Abu-Osama Abd-al-Moti, called for the destruction of the Jewish State. Khaled Meshaal attended Tehran's international Islamic conference in December 2005, followed by the January 2006 gathering in Damascus of Hamas, other Palestinian terror groups, as well as Hezbollah, and Amal with Ahmadinejad and Syrian president Bashar al-Assad. In April 2006, Iran held the "Support for the Palestinian Intifada" conference, chaired by the conference Secretary-General Hojatoleslam Ali-Akbar Mohtashami-Pur, who was instrumental in the formation of Hezbollah.

Material indicators of Iranian support to Hamas were uncovered with the April 2006 discovery by Jordanian officials of a Hamas cache of Iranian-made Katyusha rockets and anti-tank missiles that had been smuggled into Jordan from Syria.[49] Also in May 2006, Iran pledged 300 heavy and light vehicles to the Hamas-led government for use by municipal workers.[50]

With the Iranian decision to unleash

Hezbollah forces against Israel in July 2006, the scope of Iran's ambitions to establish radical Shiite hegemony across the region took an ominous step forward, crossing the line between extremist rhetoric to military aggression. Just how far Hamas will be willing to accompany Iran on its quest for territorial expansion remains to be seen.

Palestinian Islamic Jihad (PIJ)[51]

Harakat al-Jihad al-Islami al-Filasttini

The Palestinian Islamic Jihad is one of the many fruits on our leader Khomeini's tree.

— Ramadan Shalah, Secretary-General
22 May 2002

The acknowledgment that Palestinian Islamic Jihad is a fruit of the Iranian Revolution tree indicates ideological affinity between this terrorist proxy and its state sponsor.

Palestinian Islamic Jihad is a violent terrorist organization whose stated goal is the destruction of the Zionist entity—the State of Israel—and its replacement with an Islamist state. The group was formed in Egypt during the 1970s as an offshoot of the Egyptian Islamic Jihad, itself an offshoot of the Muslim Brotherhood. The founders of Palestinian Islamic Jihad were a group of radical Palestinians led by Fathi Shakaki, who believed that the Brotherhood movement had become too moderate and who wanted to fight for the Palestinian cause. Palestinian Islamic Jihad group is one among a number of loosely organized, highly secretive Islamic jihad movements that span the Middle East.

Although its membership is Sunni, Palestinian Islamic Jihad took inspiration from the 1979 Shiite Islamic revolution in Iran. It incorporates Shiite revolutionary thought into an ideological base that seeks a renewed Islamic unity, which it believes can only be achieved with the total annihilation of the Jewish State. In keeping with its Muslim Brotherhood roots, Palestinian Islamic Jihad's radical ideology espouses violent jihad to impose by force an Islamist form of government across the Muslim world.

Like other extremist Sunni-based movements, such as Ayman al-Zawahiri's Egyptian Islamic Jihad and al Qaeda, Palestinian Islamic Jihad pursues a campaign of spectacular terrorist attacks against Israel in the expectation that they will inspire a popular revolt.[52] The group views most of the contemporary Arab Muslim leadership as corrupt and subservient to Western interests. Its armed

Palestinian Islamic Jihad Fighters Parading as Suicide Bombers to Protest Israel, 10 April 2006
Photo Credit Saif Dahlah, AFP/Getty Images

struggle against Israel is seen as just one facet of a larger worldwide holy war, pitting Islam against hypocrites and apostates.

Palestinian Islamic Jihad's ability to operate in close coordination with Hezbollah on Lebanese soil, until its 1999 relocation to the Palestinian territories, was made possible with Syrian approval for Iran's policy of supporting terrorism against Israel.[53]

By comparison with Hamas, which split from it, Palestinian Islamic Jihad is a relatively small organization, with probably fewer than 1,000 fighters in its armed wing, the al Qods (Jerusalem) Brigades. Also unlike Hamas or Hezbollah, Palestinian Islamic Jihad does not seek to attract a mass following, engages in few social or institutional political activities, and consequently

refused to participate in the 2006 Palestinian elections that brought Hamas to power. Instead, Palestinian Islamic Jihad deliberately cultivated a hard-line image of unrelenting hostility to the State of Israel. Especially during the 2000-2004 Al-Aqsa Intifada, Palestinian Islamic Jihad took responsibility for numerous suicide bombing attacks against Israel, many of which were launched out of its operational headquarters in Jenin, West Bank. It gained notoriety for its use of women and teenagers to carry out such attacks.

After Israel cracked down hard on Palestinian Islamic Jihad's West Bank strongholds in Hebron and Jenin during Operation Defensive Shield in 2002, killing and arresting some of its key commanders, the group's power was diminished. Still, it continues to carry out attacks against Israel, one of which was in July 2006. Palestinian Islamic Jihad's founder, Fathi Shakaki, was killed in Malta in October 1995, likely by an Israeli assassination squad. Ramadan Abdullah Shallah was appointed secretary general of the Palestinian Islamic Jihad to replace him, and as of November 2005 is designated a Specially Designated Terrorist by the United States.

Palestinian Islamic Jihad is based out of the Syrian capital, Damascus, which provides the group with safe haven and substantial financial backing. The group also maintains a widespread presence outside of the Middle East for the purposes of fundraising, propaganda, and recruitment. University of South Florida computer engineering professor Dr. Sami Al-Arian was arrested on 20 February 2003 and indicted on numerous terrorism-related charges as the head of the group's North American operations. Eventually acquitted by a Florida jury of most charges against him, Dr. Al-Arian accepted a plea bargain deal in May 2006, under which he was sentenced to serve 10 additional months in federal prison before being deported.

Palestinian Islamic Jihad is almost entirely dependent on two state sponsors of terrorism: Syria, which allows its leadership under Ramadan Abdullah Shallah to operate from its territory, and Iran, which provides almost its entire operating budget. The group's relationship with Iran remains critically important to its continued ability to survive and function; it is believed that Iran provides an estimated $2 million of state-sponsored funding to the group annually. According to Matt Levitt, writing for the Middle East Intelligence Bulletin during 2002, the group's leadership openly acknowledged as early as 1993 that the group received Iranian funding and channeled it to operatives in Gaza and the West Bank.

Levitt quotes Palestinian Islamic Jihad's founding leader, Fathi Shikaki in a Newsday interview: "Iran gives us money and supports us," he said, "then we supply the money and arms to the occupied territories and support the families of our people. Just about all of it goes there because that's where most of our organization is."[54]

The most detailed evidence that Islamic Jihad leaders in Damascus have been closely involved in managing and funding Palestinian Islamic Jihad attacks against Israel was obtained by Israeli forces in documents captured from the Palestinian Authority intelligence services in the West Bank during 2002. Financial support from Iran for the group was explicitly mentioned in these documents and additional evidence points to extensive use of the Syrian banking and financial system for transfers of such funding.[55] Later, in July 2003, the Palestinian security forces claimed that they had confiscated $3 million in cash which Iran had transferred to the group.[56]

In the period following Israel's withdrawal from the Gaza Strip in 2005, Palestinian Islamic Jihad has appeared to struggle with its image and mission. Unwilling even to begin a transition into a political-military organization, the group nevertheless is reluctant to allow itself to be marginalized by Hamas' seizure of the Palestinian political initiative vis-à-vis Israel. Conflicting statements issued by the group's leadership since Hamas' electoral victory seem to indicate a crisis of identity within the group; to date, however, Palestinian Islamic Jihad clings to its offensive military role, incapable of matching the complexity of Hamas' evolving strategy.[57]

Tehran and its terrorist proxies' possession of conventional weapons is manageable. But the possibility that Iran might give nuclear weapons to its terrorist proxies or use a nuclear umbrella to cover expanded terrorist activities is unacceptable.

IRAN'S PURSUIT OF NUCLEAR WEAPONS

The terms of the Nuclear Non-Proliferation Treaty, which Iran signed and ratified in 1968, require it to submit all nuclear-related facilities and material to International Atomic Energy Agency (IAEA) inspections. The National Council of Resistance of Iran's August 2002 revelations about the regime's previously secret nuclear weapons research and production sites at Natanz and Arak blew the lid off nearly two decades of Tehran's efforts to build a nuclear weapon, hidden from international view and in violation of its treaty obligations.

Subsequent Iranian opposition revelations and an International Atomic Energy Agency inspection program that began in February 2003 confirmed that Iran had built up an extensive nuclear research, development, testing, and production infrastructure. In addition to the civilian nuclear reactor being built with Russian cooperation at Bushehr, the list of Iran's facilities grew to include as many as perhaps 300 sites, among them:

- An enormous nuclear enrichment facility at Natanz that includes a centrifuge pilot plant in operation since January 2006.[58] The two underground centrifuge cascade halls are nearly completed, which could eventually

Covert-Aboveground Nuclear Fuel Enrichment Facility at Natanz,
20 September 2002
Photo Credit IKONOS satellite image courtesy of GeoEye/SIME

house as many as 50,000 centrifuges[59]

- A heavy water production plant at Arak, operational since August 2006, and a heavy water nuclear reactor under construction capable of producing plutonium (the second route to production of nuclear weapons)[60]

- A centrifuge testing facility at the "Kalaye Electric Company" in Tehran[61]

Satellite Image Credit
www.isis-online.org/publications/iran/
kalayeelectric.html

- A nuclear facility at Lavizan-Shian that was razed to the ground to purportedly hide evidence from the IAEA[62]

- A laser enrichment facility at the Center for Readiness and New Defense Technology (known as Lavizan 2), built with equipment removed from the Lavizan-Shian site, kept off limits to the IAEA since its revelation in 2004 by the NCRI[63]

- A sprawling uranium conversion facility at Isfahan, used to convert uranium "yellowcake" into uranium hexafluoride, the feedstock for centrifuges[64]

- Extensive tunnels and hardened underground bunker sites near Tehran and elsewhere, built to hide Iran's nuclear weapons program and missiles[65]

- A widespread use of Revolutionary Guards military complexes such as Imam Hussein University for research and development[66]

- A widespread use of national universities, such as Malek-Ashtar University for nuclear weapons research and development[67]

- A secret company in Tehran producing P1 (aluminum rotor) and P2 (steel rotor) centrifuges for uranium enrichment; P2 centrifuges enrich uranium much faster than the P1; P stands for Pakistan[68]

Since the International Atomic Energy

Covert-Underground Nuclear Fuel Enrichment Plant at Natanz, 22 March 2006
Photo Credit IKONOS satellite image courtesy of GeoEye/SIME

nuclear weapons technology purchases; and the use of research centers and companies as front organizations for nuclear weapons work. All of these elements have been high-priority missions of the regime in its attempt to acquire a nuclear bomb.[69]

Agency initiated its investigations of Iran's nuclear weapons program in 2003, Iran has continued to intimidate, obfuscate, and prevaricate, only admitting to nuclear capabilities as they become publicly revealed. Iran has repeatedly failed to report to the Agency key nuclear-related activities, elements, facilities, materials, and transactions as required by the provisions of the Nuclear Non-Proliferation Treaty.

Iran expert and the author of *The Iran Threat: President Ahmadinejad and the Coming Nuclear Crisis*, Alireza Jafarzadeh, who revealed the nuclear sites of Natanz and Arak in 2002, asserts that the Iranian regime's strategy for hiding its nuclear weapons program involves several elements, including secret operations hidden within the legitimate nuclear organization; a top-secret military command that operates the clandestine weapons program, including

Tehran has concluded that only acquisition of nuclear weapons can keep it in power and that it will allow nothing, least of all treaty obligations, to deter it from attaining that objective. Indeed, even as the Security Council pressured Iran during the first half of 2006 to comply with its demands, Iran not only refused to halt its enrichment activities but also threatened to withdraw from the Nuclear Non-Proliferation Treaty if such pressure did not end. Iran's support for the 12 July 2006 Hezbollah attack across Israel's borders, which sparked more than a month of intense fighting in Lebanon, illustrated the kind of tactics Tehran's radical clerics are prepared to employ to divert world attention from its intransigence over its nuclear program. After the Security Council imposed a final deadline of 31 August 2006 for Tehran to respond to a package of incentives in return for closing down all nuclear enrichment activities, Iranian

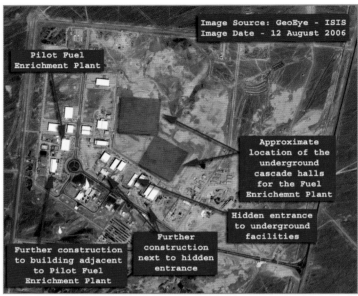

Underground Facilities at Natanz, 23 Aug 2006 (See Appendix D)

leaders responded with increasingly belligerent pronouncements that permitted scant hope that they would ever consider relinquishing their nuclear weapons program.

As the 31 August 2006 deadline passed, Iran vowed that it would never cede its right to nuclear technology and refused to comply with the Security Council demands. The regime couched this rejection in an expressed desire for more negotiations, but asserted that the nuclear issue would not be on the table.

Illustrative of Iran's contempt for and defiance of international regulatory mechanisms is the admission by Iran's former chief nuclear negotiator that Iran played "cheat and retreat" with the IAEA and the European Three (Britain, France, and Germany—the EU-3). Quoted in the state-run daily *Kayhan*, and speaking of Iran's November 2004 agreement with the EU-3 to suspend enrichment, Rowhani was quoted as saying that:

It may seem on the surface that we have accepted the suspension. But in reality, we have used the time to alleviate many of our shortcomings. We continued building centrifuges until the Paris Accord [November 2004]. After June [2004], we doubled our efforts to make up for the suspension. We have not suspended work in Isfahan, even for a second. Arak has not been suspended at any time.[70]

— Hassan Rowhani

Parallel to Iran's nuclear weapons program is its equally alarming ballistic missile program. Ballistic missiles provide Iran with the delivery system required to convert a nuclear bomb into a nuclear weapon. The Shahab-3 program consists of two tracks: a liquid-fuel medium-range ballistic missile (MRBM), the range of

Image Credit: GeoEye/Space Imaging Middle East - ISIS
Image Date 26 March 2006

Construction materials

New construction of reactor walls

Reactor stack

New structures

Construction materials and new structures

Heavy water production plant

New Construction of Arak Reactor, 26 Mar 2006 (See Appendix D)

which already has been extended to 2,000 kms., and a solid-propellant missile program designed to serve as the basis for an eventual satellite launch capability as well as an intercontinental ballistic missile (ICBM). Former Iranian Defense Minister Ali Shamkhani boasted of the Shahab-3's enhanced accuracy and range in August 2005, saying that the nuclear-capable, liquid-fueled Shahab-3 could strike any target within a 2,000 km. radius, including any Israeli or U.S. base in the Middle East.[71]

According to Jane's Defense Weekly, in late 2005 Iran bought 18 medium/intermediate range ballistic missiles from North Korea with a range of at least 2,500 kms. Major General Amos Yadlin, head of the Israeli Defense Forces Intelligence Branch, declared in April 2006 that Iran had received some of

these missiles, known in the West as BM-25s. With their 2,500 km. range, these surface-to-surface models can reach parts of Europe.[72] As these missiles are based on an older, liquid fuel technology, their acquisition by Iran puzzled analysts, who speculated that their inclusion at this time in the Iranian inventory could be intended as a stop-gap measure intended to provide an immediate capability that Iran's Shahab-3 missiles could not.[73] Why Iran should perceive a near-term need for such capability is the more ominous question.

Additionally, and as discussed in greater detail below, Iran's provision of Katyusha, Fajr 3, and Fajr 5 rockets, in addition to the Zelzal 2 missiles to Hezbollah for use in the summer 2006 war against Israel, served to eradicate the gap in Iran's current strategic reach with its Shahab

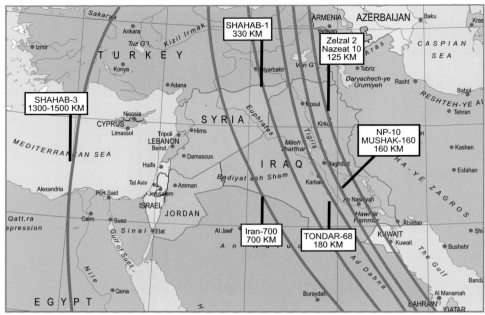

Approximate Ranges of Iranian Missiles (The range of the Shahab-3 is slightly distorted to the East in the North and to the West in the South, but completely envelopes Israel.)

missiles by placing advanced weaponry in the hands of its terrorist proxy, on the Mediterranean coast and within demonstrated range of many of Israel's population centers.

There was also new and startling information, reportedly obtained in May 2006 from Britain's MI-6 intelligence service, which suggested that Iran's fanatical clerics would share nuclear technology with terrorists. Although it has long been known that Iran has provided safe haven and safe passage to a number of Taliban and al Qaeda top leadership figures who fled the American assault in Afghanistan after 9/11, the possibility that Iran would share Weapons of Mass Destruction (WMD) know-how, materiel, or technology with them was considered speculative.

This report, however, identified a group of Pakistani scientists, allegedly working in Iran's nuclear weapons program, who have been "advising al-Qaida on how to weaponize fissionable materials it has now obtained." Clearly, such cooperation could not have occurred without the authority of Iran's top leadership. This is the nightmare scenario about which President George W. Bush and others have warned repeatedly: a nexus between a rogue regime, its terrorist associates, and nuclear weapons.[74]

The question of whether Iran actually would use a nuclear or other weapon of mass destruction was partially answered by a pair of *fatwas*, issued by the Shiite and Sunni camps. A February 2006 *fatwa* issued by extremist clerics in Qom stated that "Shari'a does not forbid the use of nuclear weapons."[75] This statement echoes the May

2003 *fatwa* issued by a prominent Saudi cleric, Sheikh al Fahd, who granted Osama bin Laden and other Islamist terrorists permission to use WMD, thus providing moral justification for use of nuclear and other WMD against enemies.[76]

Within the upper ranks of both Shiite Revolutionary circles and the international Sunni *jihad*, much time and effort is expended on just such ideological and theological issues in genuine attempts to align attack activities with traditions of Islamic jurisprudence.

The more likely scenario is that Iran is using a nuclear weapons capability as an insurance policy to cover its aggressive moves in the conventional weapons arena. As Michael Rubin, an expert on Iran at the American Enterprise Institute noted in a recent interview, "The real threat isn't that Iran will drop a nuclear weapon on Washington, but rather that with a nuclear deterrent, its leadership will become so overconfident that it will lash out with conventional terrorism." [77]

The biggest challenge for both the United States and Israel is how to judge the real status of Iran's nuclear weapons program. The ultimate goal is not preventing a nuclear-armed Iran from launching, but rather ensuring that this extremist regime does not reach nuclear weapons status in the first place. Accurate, actionable intelligence is the *sine qua non* of this challenge, but as the chairman of the U.S. House Intelligence Committee, Rep. Peter Hoekstra (R-Michigan), acknowledged in late April 2006, mixed messages surround Iran's nuclear capabilities; with American intelligence capabilities unable to provide a clear picture of the situation, he admitted, "we really don't know" how close Tehran is to developing a nuclear weapon.[78]

Dissonance at the top levels of American leadership about Iran, its objectives, and most importantly, its nuclear weapons program, transmit a message of disarray and hesitation to Tehran. National Intelligence Director John Negroponte said in early April 2006 that Iran, while determined to acquire a nuclear weapon, remained as many as 10 years away from having the material it needs to build one. But, a week before, Secretary of State Condoleezza Rice had brushed aside suggestions that Iran was far from nuclear weaponry and said the world believes Iran already has the capacity and the technology that lead to nuclear weapons.

Secretary of State Condoleezza Rice, 4 Aug 2006
Photo Credit Jeff Hutchens/ Getty Images

CONCLUSION

Iran's 1979 Revolution launched the Shiite campaign of Islamist conflict with the West; the Sunnis had begun the modern iteration of their own conflict with the West in the formation of the Muslim Brotherhood in the 1920s. The 70-year reign of communism across a vast swathe of Eurasia and the protracted global stand-off of the Cold War prevented both Sunni and Shiite Islamism from emerging as a power while the two superpowers vied for domination.

The clamp of a bipolar world began to loosen with the slow-motion collapse of the Soviet Union and culminated in its defeat in Afghanistan in 1989. With the retreat of the United States in the face of attacks and losses in Tehran (fall of the Shah in 1978), Beirut (embassy and marine barracks bombings in 1983 and 1984), and Mogadishu (killing of 18 U.S. soldiers in 1993), Islamism experienced a resurgence of belief and confidence worldwide. A virulently militant form of Islam first re-emerged across the Sunni Muslim world, inspired by the inflammatory philosophy of the Egyptian Sayyed Qutb, the Pakistani Mawlana Sayyid Abu A'la Mawdudi, and earlier writers dating back to Ibn Tamiyyah and Muhammad ibn Abd-al-Wahhab.[79]

In the case of Iran, its leadership cohort came of age in the street protests that brought down the Shah, who was viewed as an American puppet, and was then hardened in the crucible of war with Iraq, which was backed militarily by the United States. The experience of the Iran-Iraq War (1980-1988) defines the strategic outlook of this regime's generation of leaders, an outlook that perceives conflict with the United States as inevitable and acquisition of a nuclear deterrent as the only way to preserve the regime's hold on power.[80]

Constant friction between Iran and the United States since the Revolution on a range of issues have kept alive the mutual hostility and perception of threat for both Iran and the United States. These issues include Tehran's support for terrorist groups dedicated to the destruction of Israel; its development of chemical, biological, and nuclear weapons programs; and its blatant interference in the emerging democratic process in Iraq.

The Khamenei-Ahmadinejad regime remains obsessed with the United States and heavily preoccupied with the American presence on its borders: in Afghanistan, Iraq, and the Persian Gulf. The United States—as a symbol of individual liberty, equality of opportunity, separation of religion and state, democracy, freewheeling capitalism and open markets—remains the principal obstacle to achievement of the clerical regime's Revolutionary objectives. To Ahmadinejad and his cohort of survivors from the Iran-Iraq War, the United States appears to be leading a global conspiracy designed to prevent Iran from dominating the Middle East. Indeed, the United States does intend to stop Iran from imposing its ideology on the region.

Although the American military dispensed with two serious threats to Iranian sovereignty when it defeated the Taliban in Afghanistan and overthrew the Saddam Hussein regime in Iraq, it is now dawning on the Iranian leadership that U.S. President George W. Bush genuinely is dedicated to encouraging the spread of democracy across the Middle East.

The regime has historically pursued its objectives indirectly: Proxy terrorist groups such as Hezbollah, Hamas, and Palestinian Islamic Jihad mounted attacks against Israel; the Islamic Revolutionary Guards Corps *Qods Force* ran training camps for a hodge-podge of international terrorist groups that carried hatred and destruction to a checklist of battlefields, from Bosnia to Chechnya and North Africa.[81]

Whether or not the clerical regime actually believes it can prevail in a diplomatic or military face-off with the United States is moot, as it may have concluded that such a confrontation is inevitable, or perhaps even desirable.

> *The Iranian nation will not forgive the USA and will not compromise with it.*
> — Supreme Leader Khamenei

With its Revolution fizzling and its *Velayat-e Faqih* ideology failing to take root externally, the regime's own grip on power is increasingly unstable. A foreign adventure to divert domestic and world attention from issues the regime would rather avoid may have seemed the best of all available alternatives. The summer 2006 Hezbollah war in Lebanon may have been used also as a test run for Iran's command and control and logistics and supply capabilities as well as to probe

Iranian Soldiers Practice Military Maneuvers during Three Day Exercise, "Zolfaghar Blow," to Test New Tactics and Maneuvers Against Potential Enemies, 19 August 2006

Photo Credit Stinger, AFP/Getty Images

the defenses of an apparently weakened Israel and gauge the reaction of the international community.

In addition, the Iranian regime decided during the late 1990s to accelerate its nuclear weapons program in the belief that nuclear weapons could provide greater leverage in relations with the United States while simultaneously allowing it to pursue hegemony within the Persian Gulf. The American kid-glove approach to North Korea, which claims to have nuclear weapons, contrasted sharply with the fate that befell non-nuclear Iraq.

Iran's apparent eagerness to broadcast its progress with its nuclear program, even to the point of seeming to invite a pre-emptive military strike from either Israel or the United States, seems a puzzling miscalculation for a regime that some believe is characterized by nuanced subtlety. They suggest that years of carefully staged diplomatic initiatives, crafted to portray Iran to the international community as "sober, judicious, and aggrieved" while pushing quietly and inexorably towards mastery of nuclear technology, seem to have been jettisoned rather abruptly in favor of a far more confrontational foreign policy.[82]

> *The united Iranian nation [will] resist to fully utilize nuclear know-how and [will] not give up one iota of its nuclear rights.*
>
> — President Ahmadinejad
> 1 September 2006

The Iranian regime poses a direct challenge and a threat to U.S. national security interests as well as to those of the Middle East region as a whole. This threat is essentially a geostrategic threat that emanates from Tehran's hegemonic and ideological objectives in the Persian Gulf, Caucasus, and Central Asia. The radical Islamist ideology of *Velayat-e Faqih* is bankrupt, both domestically inside Iran and externally among other Shiite populations, but a hard core of Islamic Revolutionary Guards Corps, *Bassij* members, and radical clerics remain committed to its values and have chosen to use it as the underpinning of their expansionist goals.

> ...in each generation there are those that rise up seeking our destruction. But since Hitler, there has not risen such a bitter enemy as Iran's president, Ahmadinejad, who openly declares his desire to annihilate us and his development of nuclear weapons in order to carry out this desire
>
> — MK Benjamin Netanyahu[83]

The aggressiveness of the Iranian leadership's pronouncements during the Ahmadinejad presidency increased steadily in the period from August 2005 into 2006. Like Benjamin Netanyahu, this study takes what Ahmadinejad says as

valid statements of regime intent.

Following the Hezbollah attack on Israel in July 2006, the United States and Israel understood that such statements as the following one from Hassan Abbassi, Ahmadinejad's chief strategy advisor, cannot be dismissed as mere talk when they come from a country like Iran that is driving for a nuclear weapons capability, maintains close relations with a range of terrorist organizations, and trumpets its hegemonic ambitions.

> We have a strategy drawn up for the destruction of Anglo-Saxon civilization...we must make use of everything we have at hand to strike at this front by means of our suicide operations or by means of our missiles. There are 29 sensitive sites in the U.S. and in the West. We have already spied on these sites and we know how we are going to attack them.
>
> — Hassan Abbassi[84]

Iran's hegemonic ambitions for the Middle East region and beyond could not be clearer than in the following words from Ahmadinejad:

> We must believe in the fact that Islam is not confined to geographical borders, ethnic groups and nations. It's a universal ideology that leads

the world to justice. We don't shy away from declaring that Islam is ready to rule the world. We must prepare ourselves to rule the world.[85]

The Iranian nation has the potential to quickly become an unrivalled world power by obtaining modern technology.[86]

— President Ahmadinejad

Given the lack of urgency with which the International Atomic Energy Agency (IAEA) had dealt with Iran's nuclear program prior to August 2002, the public revelations in that month by the Iranian opposition group, the National Council of Resistance of Iran (NCRI), served as a bombshell. Whether or not American or other Western intelligence services possessed accurate classified information about Iran's nuclear status before then, the one international agency responsible for monitoring such programs, the IAEA, apparently did not have actionable intelligence with which to press Iran on the basis of its signatory status to the Nuclear Non-Proliferation Treaty (NPT).

Regime overconfidence is evidenced by repeated dismissive statements by Ahmadinejad and others indicating their belief that the United States is ideologically and militarily exhausted.

...today we have the wave of Islamic awakening, and the gradual collapse of the hegemony of the West, which is the reason why the occupiers do not feel at ease within the occupied land.

— President Ahmadinejad
20 February 2006

The timing of Hezbollah's summer 2006 attack on Israel, whether a miscalculation or not, indicates a perception on Tehran's part that it is on a winning streak and that the United States, Israel, and European powers are vulnerable. The vehemence toward Israel that exploded in July 2006 indicates Iran's acknowledgement of the potentially serious threat that Israel poses to its continued grip on power. It may also represent an Iranian perception of Shiite invincibility within the Islamic world, a perception that encourages its leadership to attempt seizure of the leading role in the confrontation with Israel.

From a geopolitical standpoint, the Iranian regime fears for its ability to stay in power, believes it is entitled to a grander role in the region and within Islam, and is seized with an ideological fervor that infuses its political calculations. Philip Zelikow, Counselor at the U.S. Department of State is clear on this point: "The fallacy in a lot of the arguments about security assurances . . . is the assumption that the agenda of the current government in Iran is fundamentally entirely defensive... Unfortunately, we're engaged in a process with a regime that is dictatorial in its practices and revolutionary in its aims, with an agenda for destabilizing neighbors and the broader Middle East."[87]

Israel is a state whose existence Tehran cannot tolerate without jeopardizing its own survival. Israel represents all that threatens the radical clerics' rule, but it is especially a proximate reminder of the values of the United States, whose protection Israel enjoys, and whose determination to democratize the Middle East poses a clear and present danger to the mullahs' own vision for the future. Leadership of the overall Muslim confrontation with Israel is also an objective in its own right, success of which would confer on Persian Shiites a much-coveted pre-eminence within the Islamic world.

> Regional states and those who are fair understand Iran's viewpoint. However if any country or power threatens Iran, the armed forces will deal with them decisively and powerfully.
>
> — Defense Minister Mostafa Mohammad Najjar; 21 April 2006

Israel is acutely aware of Iran's intentions to "wipe it off the face of the map," and its own existential threshold for national self-defense constitutes one of the most critical elements of the volatile situation Iran has created.

> Whether you like it or not, the Zionist regime is on the road to being eliminated.
>
> — President Ahmadinejad
> 14 April 2006

In an April 2006 interview, Israel's outgoing Minister of Defense, Shaul Mofaz, said, "Of all the threats we face, Iran is the biggest. The world must not wait. It must do everything necessary on a diplomatic level in order to stop its nuclear activity." He added, "Since Hitler we have not faced such a threat."[88]

In light of Iran's move to turn belligerent words into military deeds, it is more urgent than ever that appropriate policy options be formulated to ensure that both the United States and Israel are prepared to deal with the likelihood that additional aggression by Iran and its terrorist proxies may be forthcoming. The Iranian impression of American, European, and Israeli weakness was reinforced by Hezbollah's showing against the previously indomitable Israel Defense Forces. It must be expected that Iran's charged leadership soon will move to initiate new crises. That the Iranian regime is driving urgently to acquire a nuclear weapons capability only compounds the threat posed by its perception that it is on a winning streak. The United States must take seriously the Iranian regime's rhetoric and actions, because they are based ultimately on a perception of threat to Iran's extremist ideology.

ENDNOTES

[1] "Iran wants 'religious empire' in Middle East: Israel" *Agence France Presse*, 10 August 2006.

[2] Ole R. Holsti; Richard A. Brody; Robert C. North, "Measuring Affect and Action in International Reaction Models: Empirical Materials from the 1962 Cuban Crisis." *Journal of Peace Research*, Vol. 1, No. 3/4, 1964.

[3] *Ibid.*

[4] Robert North, *Content Analysis: A Handbook with Applications for the Study of International Crisis*, (Evanston: Northwestern University Press, 1963)

[5] Edward Azar, "Conflict Escalation and Conflict Reduction in an International Crisis: Suez, 1956." *Journal of Conflict Resolution* 16 (June, 1972): 183-201.

[6] "The Iranian Game." *Stratfor*, 24 April 2003; "Foggy Wars: The U.S.-Iranian Confrontation." *Stratfor*, 9 August 2004.

[7] "U.S. airlifts disaster aid into Iran." *CNN*, 30 December 2003.

[8] Olivier Roy, *The Failure of Political Islam*, (Cambridge, Massachusetts: Harvard University Press: 1994) 175.

[9] Excerpt from a Friday sermon in Tehran by Iranian Guardian Council Secretary Ayatollah Ahmad Jannati. The sermon aired on Iranian Channel 1 on 4 August 2006 and was reported by the Middle East Media Research Institute (MEMRI) in its *Special Dispatch Series*, No. 1237, 9 August 2006.

[10] Annette Young, "Iran's Jews face growing climate of fear." *Scotsman*, 7 May 2006.

[11] Sohrab Sobhani, "The Pragmatic Entente: Israeli-Iranian Relations, 1948-1988." Ph.D. dissertation presented to the Department of Government at Georgetown University in February 1989.

[12] "The Jews of Iran." *The Jewish Virtual Library*; available from http://www.jewishvirtuallibrary.org/jsource/anti-semitism/iranjews.html

[13] Sohrab Sobhani, "The Pragmatic Entente: Israeli-Iranian Relations, 1948-1988." Ph.D. dissertation presented to the Department of Government at Georgetown University in February 1989.

[14] Dilip Hiro, *The Iranian Labyrinth* (New York: Nation Books, 2005).

[15] "Iran," Institute for Jewish Policy Research (JPR); available from http://www.axt.org.uk/antisem/archive/archive1/iran/iran.htm

[16] Middle East Media Research Institute, *Special Dispatch Series*, No. 1244, 11 August 2006.

[17] It is assumed that systematic error cross-sectionally is constant across time and does not bias the inferences made based upon time series in this study.

[18] George Antonius, *The Arab Awakening : the story of the Arab National Movement* (London : Kegan Paul, 2000).

[19] George Friedman, "The 'Cedar Revolution' in Lebanon has encountered its antithesis, Hezbollah." *Stratfor*, 15 March 2005.

[20] MIPT Terrorism Knowledge Data Base; available from http://www.tkb.org/Group.jsp?groupID=3101 Lara Deeb, "Hizballah: A Primer." *Middle East Report Online*, 31 July 2006.

[21] Ahmad Nazar Hamzeh, *In the Path of Hizbullah* (New York: Syracuse University Press, 2004).

[22] *Ibid.*

[23] Lara Deeb, "Hizballah: A Primer." *Middle East Report Online*, 31 July 2006.

[24] Ahmad Nazar Hamzeh, *In the Path of Hizbullah* (New York: Syracuse University Press, 2004) 112.

[25] "Hezbollah Attacked Diplomatic Target (Mar. 17, 1992, Argentina)." MIPT Terrorism Knowledge Database

[26] Ahmad Nazar Hamzeh, *In the Path of Hizbullah* (New York: Syracuse University Press, 2004) 34.

[27] Mehdi Khalaji, "Iran's Shadow Government in Lebanon." *The Washington Institute*, Policy Watch #1124, 19 July 2006.

[28] Stratfor Intel Summary, 23 August 2006.

[29] "Iranians Upset at Government's Financial Aid to Hezbollah in Lebanon." *Asharq Al-Awsat* 21 August 2006.

[30] Mehdi Khalaji, "Iran's Shadow Government in Lebanon." *The Washington Institute*, Policy Watch #1124, 19 July 2006.

[31] "Israel: Hizbullah sponsors Palestinian militancy." *Agence France Presse*, 18 May 2004.

[32] Robin Hughes, "Iran and Syria sign mutual assistance accord." *Jane's Defense Weekly*, 21 December 2005; "Report: Syria agrees to hide Iran nukes." *World Tribune*, 20 December 2005.

[33] Farhad Pouladi, "Iran, Syria Sign Defense Agreement." *Middle East Online*, 15 June 2006.

[34] "Ahmadinejad Meets Radical Palestinian Chiefs in Syria." *Agence France Presse*, 20 January 2006.

[35] "EU Says Latest Nuclear Talks with Iran 'Disappointing.'" *AFX News Ltd.*, 11 July 2006.

[36] "Iranian Nuclear Negotiator Talks with Syrian Leaders." *DPA*, 12 July 2006.

[37] Alireza Jafarzadeh, "Iran's End Game." FoxNews.com, 21 July 2006; available from http://www.foxnews.com/story/0,2933,204920,00.html

[38] Nick Parker, "Iranians' Lebanon Battle." *The Sun*, 26 July 2006.

[39] Bill Gertz, "Hezbollah Leader Said to be Hiding in Iranian Embassy." *Washington Times*, 28 July 2006.

[40] Rosemary Righter, "When Terror Becomes Error." *The Times*, 26 July 2006; Brian Murphy, "Iranian Envoy, Hezbollah Leader Meet." Associated Press, 27 July 2006.

[41] Toby Harnden, "Iran admits it gave Hezbollah missiles to strike all Israel." *The Daily Telegraph*, 6 August 2006.

[42] "Iran press: Hezbollah Commander Says Lebanon 'Permanently Indebted' to Iran." *BBC*, 8 August 2006.

[43] "Hamas." MIPT Terrorism Knowledge Database; available from http://www.tkb.org/Group.jsp?groupID=49

[44] *Ibid*.

[45] In early 2006, the London-based al-Hayat newspaper carried this figure.

[46] Anna Mahjar-Barducci, "Fatal Attraction: the Hamas-Iran alliance." *Daily Star* (Lebanon), 8 May 2006.

[47] "Hamas." Council on Foreign Relations, 14 June 2006; available from http://www.cfr.org/publication/8968/

[48] Anna Mahjar-Barducci, "Fatal Attraction: the Hamas-Iran alliance." *Daily Star* (Lebanon), 8 May 2006.

[49] "Jordan Says It Arrested 20 Hamas Activists." *AP*, 11 May 2006.

[50] "Iran Awards Hamas Government 300 Light and Heavy Vehicles." *AP*, 12 May 2006.

[51] Palestinian Islamic Jihad, MIPT Terrorism Data Base; available from http://www.tkb.org/Group.jsp?groupID=82

[52] Matthew Levitt, "Sponsoring Terrorism: Syria and Islamic Jihad." *Middle East Intelligence Bulletin*, November-December 2002.

[53] "Profile of the Palestinian Islamic Jihad." Intelligence and Terrorism Information Center at the Center for Special Studies (C.S.S), 25 February 2005.

[54] Matthew Levitt, "Sponsoring Terrorism: Syria and Islamic Jihad." *Middle East Intelligence Bulletin*, November-December 2002.

[55] *Ibid*.

[56] "Profile of the Palestinian Islamic Jihad." Intelligence and Terrorism Information Center at the Center for Special Studies (C.S.S), 25 February 2005.

[57] "Palestinian Islamic Jihad: Seeking Relevancy, Falling Back on Militancy." *Stratfor*, 3 August 2005.

[58] "Iran Breaks Seals at Nuclear Site." *BBC* 10 January 2006; available from http://news.bbc.co.uk/2/hi/middle_east/4597738.stm

[59] "Iranian Regime Executing Plans to Start Uranium Enrichment at the Natanz Site." Statement by Alireza Jafarzadeh, Strategic Policy Consulting, Inc., Washington, DC, 10 January 2006; available from http://spcwashington.com/index.php?option=com_content&task=view&id=174&Itemid=26

[60] "Arak." *GlobalSecurity.org*, 31 August 2006. available from http://www.globalsecurity.org/wmd/world/iran/arak.htm

[61] "ISIS Imagery Brief: Kalaye Electric." *Institute for Science and International Security*, 31 March 2005; available from http://www.isis-online.org/publications/iran/kalayeelectric.html

[62] "ISIS Imagery Brief: Destruction at Iranian Site Raises New Questions About Iran's Nuclear Activities." *Institute for Science and International Security*, 17 June 2004; available from http://www.isis-online.org/publications/iran/lavizanshian.html

[63] "Supervision of Military Organs on Mullahs' Nuclear Weapons Program." Press Conference by Mohammad Mohaddessin, Chairman of the Foreign Affairs Committee of the National Council of Resistance of Iran, Brussels, Belgium, 28 April 2004; available from http://www.iranwatch.org/privateviews/NCRI/perspex-ncri-militarynuclear-042804.htm

[64] Paul Brannan and David Albright, "ISIS Imagery Brief: Activities at the Esfahan and Natanz Nuclear Sites in Iran." *Institute for Science and International Security*, 14 April 2006; available from http://www.isis-online.org/publications/iran/newactivities.pdf

[65] "Iran Expanding Its Nuclear Weapons Program Underground and into Military Sites." Statement by Alireza Jafarzadeh, Washington, DC, 16 September 2005. Available from http://spcwashington.com/index.php?option=com_content&task=view&id=124&Itemid=26

[66] Philip Sherwell, "Iran's 'nuclear university' conceals research." *The Telegraph*, 16 April 2006; available from http://www.telegraph.co.uk/news/main.jhtml?xml=/news/2006/04/16/wiran16.xml

[67] "Disclosing a Major Secret Nuclear Site under the Ministry of Defense." *GlobalSecurity.org*, 17 November 2004; available from http://www.globalsecurity.org/wmd/library/report/2004/new-nuke-info.htm

[68] "Iran regime secretly producing P2 centrifuges." *GlobalSecurity.org*, 24 August 2006; available from http://www.globalsecurity.org/wmd/library/news/iran/2006/iran-060824-ncri01.htm

[69] Jafarzadeh, Alireza, *The Iran Threat: President Ahmadinejad and the Coming Nuclear Crisis* (New York: Palgrave Macmillan, 2007) 125-126.

[70] *Kayhan*, 23 July 2005.

[71] Middle East Newsline (MENL), 3 August 2005.

[72] Ze'ev Schiff, "Iran buys surface-to-surface missiles capable of hitting Europe." *Haaretz*, 27 April 2006.

[73] "Iran Acquires Ballistic Missiles from DPRK." *Jane's Defense Weekly*, 4 January 2006.

[74] Gordon Thomas, "Brit MI6 confirms bin Laden nukes." *WorldNetDaily.com*, 7 May 2006; David Albright, Kathryn Beuhler, and Holly Higgins, "Bin Laden and the Bomb." *Bulletin of the Atomic Scientists*, January/February 2002.

[75] Middle East Media Research Institute (MEMRI), Special Dispatch Series Number 1096, 16 February 2006.

[76] "Osama bin Laden's Mandate for Nuclear Terror." *JINSA Online*, 10 December 2004.

[77] Kathryn Jean Lopez, "Dealing with Iran." *National Review Online*, 25 April 2006; available from http://www.nationalreview.com/script/printpage.p?ref=/interrogatory/rubin200604250606.asp

[78] "Rep. says Iran's Nuke Capability Unknown." *Washington Post*, 23 April 2006.

[79] Sayyed Qutb was an Egyptian author associated with the Muslim Brotherhood. Mawlana Sayyid Abu A'la Mawdudi founded Jamaat-e-Islami and had a large impact on the writings of Qutb. Ibn Tamiyyah (1268-1328) established the duty to wage jihad against non-believers. Muhammad ibn Abd-al-Wahhab (1703-1792) fathered the conservative Wahhabist movement in Saudi Arabia.
  - Richard P. Mitchell, *The Society of the Muslim Brothers* (U.S.: Oxford University Press, 1993)

[80] Ray Takeyh, "Diplomacy will not end Iran's nuclear programme." Council on Foreign Relations, 21 December 2005.

[81] Con Coughlin, "Teheran 'secretly trains' Chechens to fight in Russia." *Sunday Telegraph*, 27 November 2005; available from
http://www.telegraph.co.uk/news/main.jhtml?xml=/news/2005/11/27/wchech27.xml ;
  - "Qods (Jerusalem) Force." *Federation of American Scientists*, 21 August 1998; available from http://www.fas.org/irp/world/iran/qods/index.html ;
  - Richard J. Aldrich, "America used Islamists to arm the Bosnian Muslims." *Guardian*, 22 April 2002; available from
  http://www.guardian.co.uk/comment/story/0,3604,688310,00.html

[82] Victor Davis Hanson, "Has Ahmadinejad Miscalculated?" *National Review Online*, 7 April 2006.

[83] Ilan Marciano, "Netanyahu: Switch from unilateral to mutual steps." *Ynetnews.com*, 14 August 2006.

[84] Hassan Abbassi, head of the Iranian Center for Security Doctrines Research of the Islamic Revolutionary Guards Corps (IRGC).

[85] "Iran leader: 'Islam to rule the world.'" *WorldNetDaily.com*, 10 January 2006. Ahmadinejad reportedly was speaking to a group of Iranian religious students in the holy city of Qom.

[86] Iranian Official News Agency, 7 May 2006. Ahmadinejad was quoted speaking to a group of commanders of Iran's paramilitary Bassiji force in Tehran and widely understood to be referring to the acquisition of nuclear weapons capabilities.

[87] Daniel Dombey, "Bush Advisor Dismisses Call for Talks with Iran." *Financial Times*, 24 April 2006.

[88] "Iran 'worst threat to Jews since Hitler.'" *News Telegraph*, 24 April 2006.

CHAPTER 3

What the Nature
of Regime Means
for Policy Options

INTRODUCTION

This study set out to explain what motivated the escalating projection of hostility that defines the Iranian regime under the Supreme Leader Khamenei and his president, Mahmoud Ahmadinejad. Since 1979, the Iranian regime has been making threatening statements targeting the United States, but the regime has become more hostile in the months since Ahmadinejad became Iran's president in August 2005. Although the quantitative study ends in 2005, Appendix A includes 82 regime statements, about half of which are from Ahmadinejad, made since he took office.

There are two significant findings of the quantitative study of regime statements from 1979-2005: 1) There is a disconnection between Iranian perception of threat and expression of hostility toward the United States, on the one hand, and events, on the other hand; 2) there is a surprising dearth of Iranian statements indicating perception of threat from Israel.

These statistical results led to the conclusion that the Iranian regime generally responded to perceptions of threat from the United States by projecting a return expression of hostility. However, both of these variables fluctuated independently of events on the ground, leading to the hypothesis that a third factor explained the correlation. The study hypothesizes that the regime's radical ideology is responsible for what might be a spurious correlation between perception of threat and expression of hostility.

Regarding the Iran-United States dynamic, the research shows that the Iranian leadership over a period of 27 years perceived the United States as a significant threat to the survival of the clerical regime. The arrival into the region of large numbers of U.S. military forces following the attacks of 9/11 was the most tangible evidence of American resolve to counter the ideology of radical Islam. Despite the differences and even rivalry that separate Shiite Iran's *Velayat-e Faqih* from the Salafist-Wahhabi thinking of al Qaeda, Tehran's clerical leadership concluded that President George W. Bush's intentions to expand democracy in the Middle East posed a credible challenge to its own regional objectives, both geopolitical and ideological.[1]

During the same period of time (1979-2005), evidence suggests that the Iranian regime also perceived little or no threat from the State of Israel. Because Israel represents for the Iranian regime an outpost of Western civilization in the Middle East, however, and is a close regional ally of the United States, Israel received a full measure of the regime's expression of hostility statements.

Based on both quantitative and qualitative assessments of statements, the study concludes that Iran's hostility toward Israel was a result of two factors: proxy hostility, displaced from the real target of its fear and wrath—the United States; and genuine hatred of Jews.

President Ahmadinejad and the clerical regime single out Jews for much harsher treatment:

> They have invented a myth that Jews were massacred and place this above God, religions and the prophets.

— President Ahmadinejad
14 December 2005

In March 2006, an Iranian newspaper held a contest seeking the best holocaust-themed cartoons. One entry depicted Jews using the "myth" of the holocaust to create a military state in Palestine.

In the wake of the summer 2006 Hezbollah War, Israel's civilian and military leaderships are more than ever acutely aware of their status as Iran's target. Prime Minister Ehud Olmert, speaking at a weekly Cabinet meeting in late April 2006, named Iran as Israel's

most serious threat, saying, "From the point of view of seriousness, this tops the State of Israel's list; it is potentially an existential threat." [2] Outgoing Israeli Defense Minister Shaul Mofaz agreed: "Of all the threats we face, Iran is the biggest."[3] Also recall the statement by Benjamin Netanyahu in Chapter 2 comparing Ahmadinejad with Hitler as a threat to annihilate the Jews.

Indeed, Iran consistently has sponsored terrorist organizations that have carried out numerous attacks against Jews and Israel. In this regard, on 18 July 1994, at Iran's direction, Hezbollah bombed the Argentine Israelite Mutual Association (Jewish Community Center) building in Buenos Aires, killing 21 persons.

A candid appraisal of Israel's performance against Hezbollah after the summer 2006 hostilities could not avoid the conclusion that Israel's failure to destroy Hezbollah had cost it dearly. Israel's tremendous psychological advantage was gone and with it a good part of deterrence credibility. As opposition leader Netanyahu said, there were "failures in identifying the threat, in managing the war, and in comforting the home front." He also said that Israel must learn its lessons and correct its mistakes. "We were asleep and we received a wake-up call." [4]

Whenever U.S. facilities or personnel have been perceived as vulnerable to attack, Iranian proxies have struck. The April 1983 suicide bombing of the American Embassy and October 1983 truck bombing of the Marine Barracks in Beirut by Hezbollah underline that perception. In addition, Iran's active involvement in providing explosives, logistics, training, weapons, and direct militia support to terrorist units fighting Coalition forces in Iraq since the launch of Operation Iraqi Freedom in March 2003 reinforces terrorist belief in American vulnerability and raises the issue of the possible deterrence of Iran.

Because of the ideological imperative driving Iranian security policy, deterrence by threat, either by the United States or Israel, is not likely to succeed. Rather, at issue is deterrence by denial and/or brute force. Deterrence via denial focuses on closing windows of vulnerability not with threats but with locks. Construction of bomb shelters, distributing gas masks, and creation of anti-ballistic missile defenses illustrate deterrence by denial.

Were Israel to seek to deter Iran by threat, the Jewish State would be bound to fail. Driven by ideology, the Iranian regime does not preside over a normal state that makes cost-benefit calculations required for deterrence to hold. Instead, Iran has the institutions of such a state, but its leadership is motivated by a religious doctrine that clouds perceptions of threat and expresses hostility irrespective of the environment. As a result, Israel needs to pursue a policy of deterrence by denial while the United States adopts a policy of empowering the Iranian people to bring about regime change in Iran.

In considering policy options, the issue addressed in this study is the extent to which Iran seeks nuclear weapons, supports terrorism, and acts to destroy Israel in response to perceived external and/or internal threats relative to a hostile ideology that requires expansion to survive. The answers to this query should significantly affect the formulation of American and Israeli national policies, with added urgency as Israel's vulnerability has become a perceived opportunity for Iran to press its demands for regional hegemony.

Appropriate policies, including the credible threat of military strikes against the regime and regime change, would be expected to exert a modifying influence on Iranian leadership behavior. Of course, even normal states may be so absolutely committed to a foreign policy objective, such as regional hegemony or acquisition of nuclear weapons, that even the most credible and dire of threats affect them only fleetingly, and even then only in the context of evasive tactics, designed merely to buy time in which to achieve the strategic goal of nuclear-weapons status.

Because ideology is so important a motivating factor in Iran's decision-making no conceivable combination of containment, deterrent threats, or positive incentives would induce the regime to cease its quest for nuclear-arms status, support for terrorist groups, or destruction of Israel. Given the apocalyptic, messianic character of statements made by Iran's President Ahmadinejad and other figures within or close to the clerical leadership, Iran is on a collision course with the West in general and Israel in particular.

Ahmadinejad's fervent belief in the mystical elements of Shiite Twelver Islam suggests that he believes in the imminent return of the Disappeared Twelfth Imam (the *Mahdi*). Based on an analysis of his statements, one hypothesis is that he believes his role demands contributing to an outbreak of chaos in the Middle East sufficient to usher in Armageddon and the Day of Judgment.

At first glance, the Hezbollah War of the summer of 2006 appeared to represent near-reckless geostrategic brinkmanship by Tehran; however, given Hezbollah's

performance in that conflict, it seems more likely that Iran calculated correctly that resort to armed conflict at this time could advance its efforts to reshape the balance of power in the region to its advantage and to further its ideological goals. As stated, moreover, even a regime driven to hostility by ideology can be capable of such calculations. In any event, because the Iranian regime intends to acquire a nuclear weapons capability at any cost but its own survival, then it is precisely regime change via the Iranian people, not from outside forces, which the West must enable.

The 2006 Hezbollah War has shown hostile Shiite and Sunni state and non-state actors alike that Israel has an Achilles heel—a civilian population exposed to missile attack. But unlike the heroic warrior of Greek mythology who had a seemingly innocuous vulnerability, one unimmunized heel, Israel's exposure is a gaping hole over its territory into which rockets can fall. Against comparatively normal states like Egypt, exposure of Israel's civilian population does not preclude deterrence because there is mutual exposure. But ideologically-driven terrorist substitutes for Iran lack comparable exposed civilian populations; indeed, the proxies hide within their own civilian populations and those of a host state and dare Israel to target these noncombatants.

The bottom line is that Iran, Syria, and the spectrum of transnational Islamist terrorist groups have been incentivized to renew a stepped-up program of attacks against Israeli targets inside and outside of Israel.[5] And if the Iranian regime and its proxies attack American and Israeli targets despite military inferiority, the regime and its substitutes would only pursue their ideological goals more aggressively behind a shield of Iranian nuclear weapons.[6]

The nature of the regime in Tehran and character of its nonstate partners makes it unlikely that diplomacy will succeed. Nevertheless, diplomatic initiatives should be tried to enhance the legitimacy of the eventual regime change option and to increase the perception that military force is being used to further just war ends, should force have to be employed. Because a just war can only be waged as a last resort, all non-violent options, such as diplomacy, must be exhausted before the use of force can be justified.[7]

POLICY 1:
THE DIPLOMATIC OPTION

The focus of diplomacy should be efforts to halt Iran's nuclear program, to end its support for terrorist groups,

and its subversion of Iraq. Most of current international diplomacy focuses on the nuclear program; and though Iran's support for terrorist groups and subversion of Iraq are barely topics of international discussion, they should also be subject to negotiation.

Nuclear Program
Tehran wants to make its nuclear program a bilateral diplomatic issue with the United States for increased status abroad and enhanced legitimacy at home. The graphic containing Iranians holding hands to form a human chain supposedly in support of the "right" of Iran to recommence activity at a uranium conversion facility at Isfahan gives the impression of support among the Iranian population in general and among young people specifically for the Government of Iran to convert uranium into gas, a crucial phase of the nuclear fuel cycle, in which that gas becomes the feedstock to enrichment. But, in fact, there is evidence that economic concerns are at the top of the agenda for Iranians, and not Iran's expensive quest for nuclear status.

Although Iran claims to seek only peaceful nuclear power to generate energy, it sometimes invokes Israel so as to generate regional Muslim support in general, and Sunni Arab support in

Iranian Students Form Human Chain around the Uranium Conversion Facility at Isfahan, Iran Supporting Iran's Decision to Recommence Plant Activity; One Student Demonstrates "Down With Israel," 16 August 2005.
Photo Credit Atta Kenare, AFP/Getty Images

particular. But for the most part, the issue of a nuclear-armed Iran is of immense concern to Arab governments in the region. Yet many Arab governments are reluctant to speak out against Tehran's march toward nuclear weapons status because they are intimidated.

In sharp contrast to South Africa, Ukraine, and Libya, which abandoned their nuclear programs in exchange for cooperation with the international community, Iran has resisted the efforts of the European Union, the UN Security Council, and the International Atomic Energy Agency.

The Government of the United States for about three years has supported intensive efforts by the EU3—the United Kingdom, France and Germany—to negotiate with the Iranian regime its full compliance with the transparency requirements of the Non-Proliferation Treaty, to which Iran remains a signatory. Because Iran conducted suspect nuclear activities without revealing them to the International Atomic Energy Agency, it forfeited the right to conduct activities like conversion of uranium to gas and enriching such gas with centrifuge machines, irrespective of whether such actions are peaceful or not.

The United States and the EU3 supported a Russian initiative that called for the enrichment of uranium outside Iran to ensure that Tehran's nuclear program was exclusively for civilian purposes. But like all other diplomatic initiatives, Tehran used the diplomacy as a time to make progress on the nuclear front, taking full advantage of benefits of being a State party to the Non-Proliferation Treaty, such as receiving nuclear technology from nuclear weapons states. There is doubt that a signatory to the Treaty has an unrestricted right to retain benefits acquired as a signatory unless it is in compliance with other features of the Treaty.

Article IV of the Non-Proliferation Treaty purports to establish for parties to the Treaty rights to receive or develop nuclear technology for peaceful purposes. But Article IV should be read in conjunction with restrictions explicit in Articles I and II, and these features constrain Article IV. These three articles should be read together in such a way that assistance or activities ostensibly peaceful in nature do not as a practical matter lead to proliferation of nuclear weapons. [8]

Applied to Iran, its claim to an absolute right under the terms of the Non-Proliferation Treaty to engage in enrichment of uranium and separation of plutonium "is refuted by a close examination of the language and the history of the NPT." [9]

The United States Government also has expressed its commitment to a concerted diplomatic effort at halting Iran's nuclear weapons work and was instrumental in achieving the March 2006 decision by the International Atomic Energy Agency Board of Governors to refer Iran to the UN Security Council. And in that month, the Council President called upon Iran to halt all uranium enrichment activity. [10] These efforts failed when Iran decided to restart nuclear enrichment activities at its Natanz facility, and were followed by Iran's April 2006 announcement it had succeeded in enriching uranium.

On 31 July 2006, the United Nations Security Council passed a resolution giving Iran until 31 August to suspend uranium enrichment or face the threat of diplomatic and economic sanctions, a deadline that came and went by with hardly any notice. [11] Iran has missed so many deadlines that it would be rather odd if it were to comply on time or even late. The situation at the UN Security Council is reminiscent of the Aesop fable in which a committee of mice decide they would be well-served by placing a bell around the neck of the cat who preys on them. However, no single mouse can muster the courage to "bell the cat." Similarly, the UN Security Council has been unable to impose any but the weakest penalties for Iranian noncompliance.

Although failing to say so publicly, the European Union and the United States may have come to the realization during late 2006 that some form of coercive diplomacy was needed to bring Iran into compliance with the demands of the International Atomic Energy Agency and the United Nations Security Council. Even if the Council ultimately does not support punitive sanctions, such measures by a coalition of the willing (EU and the United States) would impose negative consequences on Tehran. The European Community still remains Iran's largest trading partner, despite Tehran's overtures to Russia and China.

Not all diplomatic measures need be economic. If Iran continues to refuse to halt its nuclear enrichment activities, there are more coercive measures that may be applied by United Nations member states alone or in concert with others. Among these would include accelerating the pressure on Tehran concerning its abysmal human rights record, limiting the circulation of Iranian diplomats within host countries, aggressively rolling up Iranian intelligence networks in Europe and the United States, developing a multilateral program of radio and television broadcasting to Iran, and even covert operations aimed at delaying its nuclear program by sabotaging key Iranian nuclear facilities.

Diplomatic engagement with Iran to date is not working and probably will not ever succeed, if not stiffened with more stringent measures, such as those taken under consideration by the UN Security Council in May 2006. Such measures would begin exacting penalties from Iran if it does not meet Council demands that it return to compliance with its obligations under the Non-Proliferation Treaty and, most importantly, cease all nuclear enrichment activities immediately.

At the top of the list of penalties are economic sanctions, which will not succeed unless applied in concerted fashion by all of Iran's major Western trading partners. Such sanctions could target Iran's oil trade, both its exports and refined imports, and might include a ban on airline travel, prohibition of a range of financial transactions, refusal of bilateral or multilateral economic assistance, and limitations on general trade.

Increased funding and strong congressional backing for radio and satellite television broadcasts into Iran would send the message that Washington wants to reach out to the Iranian people. Public statements of support from American officials in favor of imprisoned and exiled Iranian political leaders, labor leaders, and media figures would be an encouraging sign of support for the people.

The U.S. State Department can send a strong message of disapproval to the regime in Tehran by refusing to issue visas to its United Nations representatives that would permit them to travel beyond the immediate radius surrounding New York City (as occasionally has been done).

American intelligence services have many covert tactics that can be used to penalize a nation, including propaganda campaigns, incitement of factional conflicts inside the Iranian regime, harassment, surveillance, and offensive recruitment operations against Iranian representatives abroad.

Department of Homeland Security Border and Customs agents could step up scrutiny of incoming Iranian UN mission diplomats, their families, vehicles, and household goods. Local authorities, too,

such as the New York Police Department, might focus more attention on traffic and parking infractions by Iranian diplomats assigned to the United Nations.

In the same vein, the activities of Iran's diplomatic representation in the Embassy of Pakistan in Washington, as well as at the regime's UN mission in New York, should continue to be closely observed by the appropriate domestic intelligence and other agencies for possible unlawful activities that may include espionage, threat, or unlawful lobbying with Members of Congress.

Also relevant is a threat of action by an international tribunal for Iranian leadership crimes. It might charge the leaders with support for transnational terrorism and human rights abuses. This threat might be made tangible by bringing a legal case against Supreme Leader Khamenei, the already-indicted former president Hashemi Rafsanjani, and President (and former interrogator, torturer, executioner, and *Bassiji*) Mahmoud Ahmadinejad.

Despite a laundry list of diplomatic coercive initiatives to go with positive incentive packages, none is likely to be successful in view of the commitment of the Tehran regime to become a nuclear weapons state, the nature of the regime's quest for regional hegemonic status, and the vision of the clerical rulers to export their ideology to other Islamic states, all of which would be furthered if Iran were to acquire nuclear weapons.

Iranian Subversion of Post-Saddam Iraq

Thousands of Iranian-sponsored clerics crossed into Iraq from Iran since the cessation of major combat in May 2003.[12] Many of the clerics carry books, compact discs, and audiotapes that promote militant Islam. Moreover, according to Iranian dissident sources, the Revolutionary Guards *Qods* (Jerusalem) *Force* is establishing armed underground cells across the Shiite southern region of Iraq, often using the Iranian Red Crescent as a front. Such sources also contend that the Jerusalem Force has established medical centers and local charities in Najaf, Baghdad, Hillah, Basra, and al-Amarah to gain support from the local population.

Even as Tehran began to send Iranian operatives into postwar Iraq, members of Hezbollah infiltrated the country as well. Because most of Hezbollah's members are Arab, they may constitute an even more effective Iranian proxy in Iraq than Iranian agents trained in Arabic.

According to Iranian dissident sources (and confirmed in part by interviews

with U.S. intelligence sources), Tehran tasked Hezbollah with sending agents and clerics across a major portion of southern Iraq. Indeed, once major combat operations came to an end, Hezbollah "holy warriors" crossed into the country not only from Syria, but from Iran as well. Initially, these operatives numbered nearly 100, but this relatively small figure belies their potential impact on behalf of Tehran.

Hezbollah has established charitable organizations in Iraq in order to create a favorable environment for recruiting, a tactic that the organization had previously tested in southern Lebanon with Iranian assistance. Moreover, according to Mohammed al-Alawi, Hezbollah's chief spokesman in Iraq, the organization's agents act as local police forces in many southern cities (e.g., Nasiriya, Ummara), ignoring an official U.S. ban on militias. Overall, Tehran seems to be using Hezbollah to supplement its own penetration of local Iraqi governing offices and judiciaries.

In addition, Iranian dissident sources report that Tehran has used Hezbollah to smuggle Iraqis living in Iran back into their native country. A significant number of Iraqis have dual nationalities and have resided in Iran for many years; some have even served as Revolutionary Guards commanders. Hezbollah can help conceal their long association with Iran; indeed, some of these individuals have apparently joined Iraqi police forces since the end of major combat.

Such dissident sources also contend that Hezbollah is casing coalition assembly centers in Iraq and tracking the timing and order of movements by various coalition vehicles including tanks, armored personnel carriers, and motorcades (this assertion has yet to be confirmed by U.S. intelligence officials). Hezbollah agents are reportedly videotaping various locations in two-person teams, often using public transportation such as taxis. Footage of targets is sometimes concealed between banal imagery (e.g., wedding festivities) in order to avoid detection by coalition forces. Such reports echo Hezbollah's own public statements, voiced as early as mid-April 2003, regarding its willingness to attack U.S. forces in Iraq and its increasing ability to do so.[13]

In addition to covert intelligence operations, Iran supplies roadside bomb technology to militias in Iraq. There have been more U.S. casualties caused by roadside bombs in July of 2006 than in any other month of the Iraq War, which represents more than a 55% increase in the number of roadside explosive devices in Iraq from January to July 2006.[14]

Not only are roadside bombs becoming more prolific, they are becoming more lethal. According to publicly available casualty reports from the Pentagon, roadside bombs, or Improvised Explosive Devices (IEDs), have contributed to more than 925 American deaths in the period 2003-2006. From 2004 to 2005, the number of roadside bomb attacks doubled, and may more than double again in 2006. Roadside bombs have therefore become the leading cause of Coalition deaths in Iraq.

The most frightening aspect of the rise in roadside bomb attacks is that many of these devices are not being manufactured in basements in Iraq; both British and American officers have confirmed signs of Iran's signature bomb technologies in devices across Iraq. Lead intelligence reveals that Iranian ordnance factories produced during 2006 an advanced form of roadside bomb incorporating new technology, called Explosively Formed Projectiles (EFPs), to satisfy secret, coded orders placed by the Iranian regime's Islamic Revolutionary Guards Corps.

The Corps then transfers this advanced form of roadside bomb to Iraqi insurgents. The production of these explosively formed projectiles is particularly troublesome because they are more advanced than regular roadside bombs—the new versions can penetrate thicker armor, are more difficult to detect, and have proven more lethal to Coalition forces in Iraq than traditional roadside bombs.

The ordnance factories are located in the Lavizan neighborhood of northern Tehran where weapons production occurs at three independent industrial sectors called Sattari, Sayad Shirazi, and Shiroodi. The Sattari Industry specializes in making various types of anti-tank mines and bombs, and then turns these into roadside bombs. At the explicit request of the Iran Policy Committee (IPC), Iranian dissidents from the National Council of Resistance of Iran (NCRI) collected this intelligence and provided it to the IPC for release.[15]

In addition to flooding Iraq with roadside bomb technology, Iran seeks to dominate Iraq politically.

On one hand, if Baghdad cooperates with Tehran, Iraq is likely to become a weak appendage of the Islamist (militant) regime in Iran. Three times the population and four times the geographical size, Iran overwhelms its neighbor.

On the other hand, if Baghdad confronts Tehran, Iraq is likely to suffer from Iran's enhanced support for insurgency and sectarian violence in Iraq. Given the bullying of Iran, it is no surprise to find that Iraq complies with Iran. During

July 2006, Iraqi Prime Minister Maliki threatened to expel the main Iranian opposition group, the *Mujahedeen-e Khalq*, from Iraq, consistent with Iran's demands, and had cut off oil supplies to Camp Ashraf, Iraq, where the group has its headquarters.

The way Iraqi Prime Minister Maliki treats the main Iranian opposition in Iraq is a bellwether of Baghdad's independence from Tehran. If the Iranian regime sees Baghdad bending, Iraq is likely to become pliable on a whole range of issues, and the Iranian regime will become even more intransigent vis-à-vis the international community.[16]

Iraqi citizens and prominent Iraqi organizations, figures, tribal leaders, and lawyers organized an anti-Tehran campaign with the cooperation of the *Mujahedeen-e Khalq* at Camp Ashraf. In June 2006 a petition published in the New York Times and signed by 5.2 million Iraqis declared support for the MEK and emphasized the group's political refugee status in Iraq.

Regarding Iran's shipment of roadside bombs to Iraq, Arab neighbors like Saudi Arabia and Jordan need to take the initiative in getting a UN Security Council Resolution that calls on Tehran to cease the supply of militias with arms. Without

5.2 Million Iraqis Declare Solidarity with the PMOI; Camp Ashraf, Iraq, 2006

an Arab initiative, the diplomacy of the United States and the United Kingdom is unlikely to induce Iranian compliance.

The National Council of Resistance of Iran, which revealed the nuclear intelligence that led to IAEA inspections in Iran, reported to the Iran Policy Committee the shipment to Iraq of improvised explosives devices made in Tehran for use against Coalition Forces.[17]

Despite the roadside bomb technology and efforts by the Iranian regime to subvert Iraq, public diplomatic efforts to coerce Iran to cease such destabilizing activities are virtually nonexistent. Consistent with the failure to use diplomatic tools to induce Iran to cease

subverting Iraq, there also is a lack of diplomatic effort to compel Iran to cease arming Hezbollah in Lebanon.

State Sponsorship of International Terrorism: Hezbollah and Hamas

Diplomacy is mainly confined to calling for disarmament of Hezbollah, deploying international forces to monitor the borders between Lebanon and Syria, as well as to place such forces in the southern Lebanon stronghold of Hezbollah. But the source of the Hezbollah rockets pays no price for transferring these missiles into what is becoming a "Shiite crescent," ranging from Iraq toward Lebanon, where Hezbollah seeks Shiite control. Teeming with radicalism, this Shiite crescent is the

Russian made Sagger Anti-tank Missiles and Mortars Smuggled on the Karine-A
Photo Credit Sven Nackstrand, AFP/Getty Images

destination of the Iranian regime's export of the Iranian Revolution, and the core of a desired empire.

While the Shiite crescent bends southward en route from Tehran to Beirut, another crescent bends northward from Tehran to Damascus down the Beirut-Damascus Highway to southern Lebanon, supplying rockets and other armaments to Hezbollah. While revolutionary ideas flow via the southern crescent, arms flow across the northern route. Tehran was largely responsible for the rearmament of Hezbollah during the period of time between Israel's unilateral withdrawal from Lebanon in 2000 and the commencement of war in 2006.

Israeli and international observers found Iranian weapons and Revolutionary Guards members in southern Lebanon. Indeed, there also are press reports of Iranian weapons found in the possession of Hamas terrorists in Jordan.[18] Even before Hamas came to power in Palestine during January 2006, Iran engaged in arms transfers to the Palestine Liberation Organization. In January 2002, the Israel Defense Forces seized a Palestinian Authority cargo ship, the *Karine A*, loaded with 50 tons of weapons; Israeli officials claimed with good reason that these weapons were supplied by Iran and were destined for Palestine.[19]

Diplomatic efforts regarding terrorist groups in Lebanon and Palestine have only addressed Iran tangentially.

- UN Security Council Resolution (UNSCR) 1559, passed in September 2004, calls for the disarmament of all militias in Lebanon and the withdrawal of all foreign forces, but it does not mention Iran, the main source of arms for Hezbollah in Lebanon.[20]

- Security Council Resolution 1680, of May 2006, singled out Syria and strongly encouraged the country to withdraw all its forces from Lebanon, yet still did not address Iran.[21]

- Security Council Resolution 1701, which ended the July-August 2006 war between Israel and Hezbollah, reiterated the earlier call for disarmament of all militias in Lebanon, but still the Resolution failed to name the most egregious culprit, Iran.[22]

There is a need for a new resolution under Chapter VII, making it mandatory for Iran and Syria to cease their supply of rockets to southern Lebanon. Promises by president's Ahmadinejad and Bashar Assad to UN Secretary General Kofi Annan to comply with Resolution 1701 are meaningless, unenforceable, and unverifiable.

In the context of failing diplomacy in attempts to halt Iran's pursuit of nuclear weapons, provision of improvised explosive devices to militias in Iraq, and supply of rockets to Lebanese and Palestinian terrorist groups, discussion of military options grows louder.

POLICY 2: THE MILITARY OPTIONS

Just as most of the diplomatic attention goes to Iran's nuclear weapons progress, the debate about potential military strikes focuses on nuclear sites. As President Bush and other key administration figures repeatedly have warned, the option of military action remains on the table. The United States and/or Israel and other countries could significantly damage Iran's nuclear program, despite Iran's recent arms purchases and upgrading of its military capabilities. The timing of military action depends on where the "red line" is drawn that determines an unacceptable stage of progress toward obtaining a nuclear weapon.

For American national policy, the political calculus is delicate. A unilateral pre-emptive or preventive strike by Israel against Iran is more likely to destabilize the broader Middle East region than would a U.S. unilateral or multilateral military strike. The tacit or explicit concurrence (or active alignment) of Iran's Muslim and Arab neighbors in a pre-emptive or preventive strike against the regime's nuclear weapons infrastructure

Iraqi Soldiers Guard Fort Tarik, Wasit Province – east of Baghdad – on Iraq-Iran Border;
Iraqi Government Concerned Over Iranian Border-Force Build-up, 7 May 2006.
Photo Credit Wathiq Khuzaie/Getty Images

would greatly enhance the chances for success in such an operation, with the least collateral damage.[23]

Pentagon planners, too, have been hard at work preparing the complex planning required for such an operation. Seymour Hersh described the early stages of such planning for an attack against Iran in a widely-noted piece in *The New Yorker* in January 2005; James Fallows published an equally notable article in *The Atlantic Monthly* in December 2004 that described in great detail a Pentagon-style war game simulating preparations for a U.S. assault on Iran. Hersh followed up in April 2006 with another speculative piece in *The New Yorker*, which added the startling element of tactical nuclear

weapons ("bunker buster" bombs) to the Pentagon's purported planning scenario.[24]

Western militaries and the Israel Defense Forces have the force structure; command, control, and communication (C3); and the ability to sustain those capabilities in the Persian Gulf theater of operations. But the barriers to combined usage are high for a western coalition effort, as it would require prior political and operational agreements among allies, and with various host nations for basing, operations, and overflight rights before deployment.

The Iranian regime has few external political allies, and none that would need to be consulted before launching an offensive operation against Israel or U.S. assets in the Gulf region. Tehran may coordinate with Syria as it did in July 2006 operations with Hezbollah, especially if the attack were to be launched against Israel or U.S. forces inside Iraq. Such coordination is likely because of third party agreements with transnational terrorist groups that would be leveraged into any such assault. In addition, Iran and Syria already cooperate with each other in support of Hezbollah, Hamas, and Palestinian Islamic Jihad.

Given requests from Iranian regime leaders, these three proxy groups could be called into action to attack Israel or U.S. assets in the Middle East. The Iranian clerics have most likely integrated such third party forces into their planning as they view Hezbollah "as an extension of their state... [and] operational teams could be deployed without a long period of preparation," said Ambassador Henry A. Crumpton, who served as the State Department's coordinator for counterterrorism during 2006.[25]

Due to the location of Iran's proxy groups and their entrenched communications, logistics, and training/support networks in Lebanon, the Iranian regime has significantly better positioning of credible and usable threat forces and has more immediate options available

than do the United States and Israel. This third party capability also will be an issue with the Western powers, as the Islamic Revolutionary Guards Corps *Qods Force* has operatives and cells in many western nations. After the July-August 2006 military conflict with Israeli forces, intelligence reports suggest that the Hezbollah military force has been significantly degraded, but there are also reports that Iran and Syria have moved quickly to re-stock expended weapons.[26]

Israeli Military Options: Conventional Methods

The main conventional threats that Israel brings to bear in an attempt to destroy or set back the Iranian nuclear weapons program are air strikes, cruise missiles, and ground/direct contact missions using small groups of infiltrated special operations and/or clandestine operational forces, such as those operated by Mossad, Israel's external intelligence agency. Israel likely would launch a combination of these actions, as any single component would not be sufficient to cover the 100 to 200 sites where the Iranian regime conducts nuclear activities.

Given remarks by leadership figures proclaiming that Iran has joined the nuclear club of nations, there is a premium on intelligence regarding the location of high value targets.[27] The

Israelis would likely attempt to narrow their target selection to well under 100 targets to ensure they had sufficient assets to cover them with a high probability of kill. The exact number of critical sites associated with Iran's nuclear weapons program remains unknown. Some believe that it could take up to 1,000 air sorties (bombing runs) and cruise missile strikes, as well as post-damage assessment repeat strikes to ensure destruction of the entire nuclear program. Other analysts, however, believe that destruction of the entire program is just not possible.[28]

As inspectors are unsure of the exact number of sites or locations in Iran where nuclear weapons research is being conducted, plans for a thousand sortie effort do not take into account sites that are yet to be discovered. That such unknown sites exist is a near certainty, given the deception and concealment programs of the Iranian regime. In addition there is physical proof of unknown sites, including traces of Highly-Enriched Uranium discovered by International Atomic Energy Agency (IAEA) inspectors: "There are unexplained traces of enriched uranium that suggest there are more experiments in sites that are as yet unlocated." [29]

These discoveries and Iranian declaration

of uranium enrichment to the 4.8 percent level have removed doubt about their technical ability, but left unsaid is where such work is accomplished, how wide the knowledge base is for future continued refinement to higher grades, and just how many sites are actually in operation.

Any plan that anticipates completely destroying Iran's nuclear fuel cycle capability would require a high sortie count, and not a single strike or short series of closely coupled strike waves over several days. Only a multinational effort or one conducted by the United States could generate that level of sorties. Acting alone, an Israeli conventional strike would only have the effect of delaying Iran's nuclear weapons program, not destroying it. In such a scenario, most of Iran's nuclear research sites would be unaffected and unless those with the knowledge were killed, the program could be back in operation shortly after the attacks with greater intensity and dedication to success.

For such a single or closely coordinated attack by Israel to be successful it would have to benefit from extremely good intelligence. More specifically, that kind of intelligence would have to lead to precisely-located Desired Munitions Impact Points, and every weapon would have to be delivered with absolute

Israeli Special Operations Forces in Anti-Terrorist Training, 8 June 2005
Photo Credit Shaul Schwarz/Getty Images

precision and function properly.

Such impact points would be located in target areas drawn from a short list of known main activity sites, such as Natanz, Isfahan, and Bushehr. Additional impact points would include factories known to manufacture centrifuge machines, critical chemical elements, and other key components of the nuclear fuel cycle. Israeli intelligence is likely to have located small sites that are known through years of intelligence work on the ground in Iran.

Israeli Special Operations Forces (SOF) and other covert/clandestine forces could be used to target key leadership, scientific, and facilities nodes, either for direct action by such forces, or to designate them for

other strike weapons systems.

The use of ground forces to put "eyes on" certain targets would be a near imperative for a strike launched by a small force, such as that which Israel possesses. A pilot in an F-15I aircraft would take off from Israel prepared to strike primary, secondary, and perhaps tertiary targets. Some of the targets might be time sensitive or relocatable, requiring near constant surveillance in the hours and minutes preceding the strike. The "eyes on" the target provided by ground observers would better enable the airborne shooters the flexibility necessary to select their secondary target if the primary were not available, or in a situation in which established rules of engagement or conditions do not allow a successful engagement of the primary aim point.

Out-of-the-Box Scenario

A possibility that has been informally discussed in defense and intelligence circles and thus deserves some mention is that the threat of an Israeli air strike may be used as a forcing function to press Washington into action on its own. Consider this scenario: The United States perceives a strong potential for Israel to strike with a force limited by Israel's capabilities. Based upon that force strength, Washington calculates that the additional negative reaction to an Israeli strike against a Muslim-majority country would be overwhelming. The United States might determine there would be more risk than if the U.S. military were to conduct the strike itself. Given that the Israeli force structure would not permit nearly as extensive a series of strikes as U.S. military capabilities could, the effectiveness and outcome of an Israeli strike would be questionable indeed.

In the final analysis, it is possible that instead, the United States would choose to conduct the strikes, both to maximize their potential for success and to minimize the potential for negative response from other Middle East and Muslim countries. Moreover, Washington would probably be blamed for complicity in any Israeli strike or be identified as the instigator, regardless of the actual level of U.S. participation.

Therefore, Washington might conclude that American national security objectives would be better served were it to share in Israeli-developed intelligence but take ownership of such strikes from start to finish. If the U.S. Government told the Government of Israel that such strikes were going to be launched, the Israelis would want to share their targeting and intelligence information, as it would be in their interests for the strikes to achieve success. Such an arrangement would also allow the Israeli military the flexibility to turn the brunt of their forces defensively against Hezbollah, Palestinian Islamic Jihad, and other terrorist allies of Iran that are based closer to Israeli territory. These Iranian clients would be activated regardless of the presence of the United Nations Peacekeeping Force present under UN Security Council Resolution 1701. In fact, one cannot discount the potential for such a UN force to be held as virtual hostages should Iran and Israel engage in hostilities.

Israeli Nuclear Options

The main effective unconventional capability available for Israel against Iran is a nuclear strike using Israel's Jericho

II/III or ship/submarine-launched cruise missiles armed with nuclear warheads. According to Jane's Information Group, "Israel is understood to hold up to 300 nuclear warheads of various types - more than the UK has in its arsenal. The bulk of these warheads are available for about 100 Jericho II and Jericho III missiles. Warheads are understood to be available for free-fall bombs and for 155 or 203 mm artillery projectiles."[30]

Nuclear-armed Jericho missiles could eliminate most of the known nuclear weapons sites within Iran and do so within hours. The nuclear option is Israel's only way to destroy completely the Natanz "A" and "B" sites, which are extremely hardened. The Natanz Fuel Enrichment Plant complex, according to the National Council of Resistance of Iran, boasts two 25,000-meter halls, built eight meters deep into the ground and protected by a concrete wall 2.5 meters thick, itself protected by another concrete wall.[31]

A policy study conducted by a group of American and Israeli experts, led by Professor Louis Rene Beres of Purdue University, resulted in issuance during 2003 of the Final Report of Project Daniel. This analysis, a summary of which appears as Appendix C in this book, addresses Israel's national defense policy with special reference to the role of its undeclared nuclear weapons arsenal in a strategy that includes deterrence as well as the right to a defensive pre-emptive first strike.

As Israel faces an extremist regime in Tehran that spews anti-Semitic hatred and repeated genocidal intentions, its national decision-makers must formulate policy that can defend Israel's existence. Israel does not have the luxury to conclude that Iranian rhetoric is for domestic consumption only, or that it never will be transformed into action. The right to a pre-emptive self-defense option much like that described in the United States 2002 National Security Strategy and a doctrine of deterrence based on making explicit its nuclear weapons first- and second-strike capabilities form the core of the Project Daniel recommendations.

Moreover, the authors of Project Daniel recommended that Israel's nuclear capability be openly described as aimed at "countervalue" targets, e.g. 15 or so heavily populated cities scattered around the Middle East. Potential enemies of the State of Israel should know in advance that should a nuclear or even a biological weapons attack be unleashed against Israel it would be met automatically with a nuclear response targeted against the civilian populations of 15 pre-identified Middle Eastern cities.

Put simply, the Project Daniel statement makes clear that after such a direct threat to its existence, Israel would not investigate to determine which of its potential hostile neighbors launched, condoned, or participated in the attack. Israel would instead take out all of their potential enemies' main cities. Doing so would place the onus on the neighbors to have a vested interest in the well-being of Israel and to counsel others in the neighborhood to make sure such an attack against Israel does not occur. Back channel private communications and public statements of the governments of Jordan, Egypt, and Saudi Arabia condemning Hezbollah as the aggressor and chastising Iran for its part in the 2006 war in Lebanon stand as examples of Arab concern that Iran be deterred from igniting war with Israel.[32]

For Israel and the United States, Iranian capabilities in the context of its nuclear weapons program matter more than Tehran's intentions following the acquisition of a nuclear weapon and delivery system. In such a situation, a policy of nuclear deterrence and maintenance of a second strike capability are irrelevant, for it is not first use of nuclear (or certain biological) weapons that Israel must prevent, but rather the acquisition by Iran of a nuclear weapon

that must be prevented.

Although Israel is assessed by most intelligence analysts to possess both a chemical and biological weapons program, it is highly unlikely that such weapons would be selected for use in any Israeli attack scenario designed to set back or destroy Iran's nuclear weapons program. Chemical weapons are "area denial" armaments; their main utility is to force defending ground troops to dress in protective gear, which results in limitations to their mobility and degradation of their ability to fight. Moreover, the effects of these weapons tend to dissipate relatively quickly. Biological weapons have persistent effects and could cause mass casualties but would also lack effectiveness over wide geographical areas.

Iranian Force Structure and Military Options

The Iranian military is divided into two main groupings: regular or conventional military forces comprised of the Army, Navy/Marines, and Air Force; and a second group of forces under the Islamic Revolutionary Guards Corps, which also is referred to as the *Pasdaran* (Guards).

The regular Iranian military forces are considered to be mostly defensive. The Revolutionary Guards through their asymmetric capabilities and control of all of Iran's Scud missiles, most of its chemical and biological weapons, and production of all weapons of mass destruction, are the offensive forces that could attack Israel. Additionally, the Revolutionary Guards could leverage military mutual defense agreements with Syria to bring that country into the fray, in the event of an Israeli attack on Iran.

The Revolutionary Guards serves as "guards of the Islamic revolution" and as such is under the direct command of the clerical leadership in the country. The Islamic Revolutionary Guards Corps is far more ideologically focused than are the regular armed forces. The Guards has a ground force, a naval arm, and also operates an air component. It also has two additional groupings: the *Qods Force* and the *Bassij*. The Guards adds about 120,000 men to the ranks of Iran's overall military force structure. Roughly 100,000 are ground forces, including many conscripts.[33]

Most of the discussion below is centered on what the Revolutionary Guards brings to bear in a military response/attack and what the conventional forces bring to the table in the defense of the Iranian homeland. The Guards naval component is an attack/suicide force but would also be used to harass commercial shipping,

attack naval assets in the Gulf, and sow naval mines.

Iranian conventional naval, ground, and air forces appear to be primarily designed to provide a credible deterrent against attack by neighboring countries and also to serve as a coercive threat to the countries on Iran's borders and, to some extent, those across the Gulf. Although Iran's military forces are quite capable of defending the homeland from attack by the other countries in the region, they would come up well short should they be forced to deal with a modern military like those fielded by the Western nations. Iran's biggest weakness is in the air defense network and in the quantity, quality, and readiness of its Air Force.

In a power projection role, the Iranian Air Force would have a very difficult time maintaining the necessary level of air superiority required to cover a cross-Gulf attack by limited amphibious forces. As for its defensive capability, very little is known about how Iran would deploy its air defenses. The surface-to-air missile systems that Iran possesses are a hodge-podge of everything from early U.S. I-HAWK to Russian SA-2/5/6 designs to Chinese-made variants.[34]

There appears to be no Iranian central command and control system; in any case, it would be very difficult to network these various weapons systems together into an integrated system that would provide the type of coverage of a modern Integrated Air Defense System. Also, given the relatively small number of total air defense systems compared to the physical size of the country, what does exist is thinly scattered. It is reasonable to conclude that the limited defenses would be clustered and most dense around targets the regime holds dear. Iran appears to be aware of its shortcomings in this regard and has been working with the Russian government to bolster air defenses. The Russian Chief of the General Staff said that Russia would honor its commitments to supply military equipment to Iran, including 29 Tor MI, mobile air defense systems, in the framework of bilateral cooperation, "...carried out in the framework of the law and taking into account international obligations." [35]

At the end of 2005, Russia concluded a $700-million contract for delivery of 29 Tor MI air defense systems to Iran. The Tor-MI is a fifth-generation integrated mobile air defense system designed for operation at medium, low, and very low altitudes against fixed/rotary wing aircraft, Unmanned Aerial Vehicles (UAVs), guided missiles, and other high-precision weapons.[36] The delivery of these systems will probably occur during 2006-2007.

Although individuals in the Iranian armed forces can be expected to fight fiercely—especially if they were defending their homeland—the forces are generally poorly-equipped, and the material readiness of that equipment is itself poor, due to a lack of spare parts and few upgrades due to embargoes over the last decades. Much of the western equipment purchased during the Shah's regime has gone without system updates and there have been few replacement parts as well.

Iran's indigenous manufacturing capability is mostly limited to ammunition, helicopters, and light aircraft. The regime has, however, focused on building rockets and missiles. These efforts have resulted in some successes. Most sophisticated equipment is purchased from Russia, China, and North Korea. An unknown element is what indigenous modifications have been made to Western equipment that could "surprise" U.S. threat detection and warning systems.

In addition to the conventional force structure, the Islamic Revolutionary Guards Corps serves as an adjunct ground force element for the conventional army. The Corps also provides the unconventional forces for ground and maritime operations and an internal

Iranian Soldiers Test New Weapons and Tactics During Military Maneuvers, "Zolfaghar Blow," in Sistan-Baluchestan Province Near the Pakistani Border, 19 August 2006
Photo Credit Stringer, AFP/Getty Images

airlift capability to move its forces quickly around the country or to insert themselves rapidly into an offensive operation near the borders or immediately across contiguous frontiers. Revolutionary Guards forces could be used to augment conventional forces or in independent operations as they have their own command structure that leads directly to the Supreme Leader.

The Revolutionary Guards provides training to an international terrorist network in its domestic camps as well as international unconventional training and operational forces through the *Qods Force*. The domestic reserve and internal population monitoring and

militia structure are provided through its *Bassij* force elements. The Revolutionary Guards "...also operates all of Iran's Scuds, controls most of its chemical and biological weapons, and provides the military leadership for missile production and the production of all weapons of mass destruction." [37]

The command and control structure for any potential nuclear missile capability or its long range missile forces are not well understood. Based on the mission and elite nature of the Revolutionary Guards, the control of these weapons could be decentralized and thus a traditional decapitation option may be less than effective. The Revolutionary Guards is the force that is most trusted to remain "ideologically pure," and thus expected to remain in direct support of the Revolution under all contingencies. Under routine circumstances, it is under the orders of the clerical leadership, and although it has been placed under an integrated command with Iran's regular armed forces at the General Staff level, the Guards retains an independent command chain below this level and generally continues to exercise as an independent force.[38]

There is also a new and completely irregular force named the *Special Unit of Martyr Seekers in the Revolutionary Guards IRAN*. These are battalions of suicide bombers whose mission is to strike at British and American targets if Iran's nuclear sites were attacked. According to Iranian officials, 55,000 trained suicide bombers are ready for action. During the 2006 war with Israel, several Iranian spokesmen stated that some of these suicide bombers had been deployed to Lebanon to assist Hezbollah.

The main force of *Martyrs* was first seen during March 2006 when members marched in a military parade, dressed in olive-green uniforms with explosive packs around their waists and detonators held high. Hassan Abbasi, head of the Centre for Doctrinal Strategic Studies in the Revolutionary Guards, said in

a speech that 29 western targets had been identified: "We are ready to attack American and British sensitive points if they attack Iran's nuclear facilities." He added that some of them were "quite close" to the Iranian border in Iraq.[39]

Iran also has invested in significant domestic development and foreign purchase of theater-range and medium-range ballistic missiles and cruise missiles. The Shahab-3 ballistic missile, with a range of about 1,300 km, has become operational. The Shahab-3 is but the first in a family of missiles that are now in various stages of research, development, and production in Iran. This family includes missiles with ranges of 1,500 km, 1,700 km, 2,000 km, 2,200 km, and 3,500 km.

Israel is the publicly-stated destination of these missiles. Such targeting is not only declared in speeches of Iran's top leadership but also inscribed on the fuselages of the missiles. Additionally, multiple press reports state that Iran has acquired 18 BM25 land mobile missiles with launchers from North Korea that can strike targets in Europe. In the past, the BM25 has been produced in two models, one with a range of 2,500 km and the other with a range of 3,500 km.[40]

These missiles also reach parts of Russia,

China, India, and Central Europe. Some of them are powered by solid fuel, which means that they are ready for launching at any point in time. The preparatory stage for such a launch is very brief, and therefore the warning time is very short. At the same time, Iran is developing ideas for deceptive weaponry, such as transferable warheads. Iran's ballistic missile development is racing ahead in much the same way as its uranium enrichment, formulating missiles that could be fitted with the nuclear, chemical, or biological weapons as well as the conventional warheads that most of them were designed to carry.

Iranian Nuclear Options

There is speculation that Iran may already have nuclear weapons capability or at least be on the threshold of having such capability. This conjecture is fueled by a statement allegedly made on 8 March 2006 in a closed session of the International Atomic Energy Agency. According to a press report, U.S. Ambassador Gregory Schulte, the U.S. envoy to the IAEA, stated that Iran now has the materials to make up to ten nuclear weapons.[42] Even if this were true, there still is no clear understanding of how Iran would use, control, or store them. Russian sources have stated that Iran should have the capability within

five years, with some saying as few as six months.

One can only speculate whether or not Iran would employ such weapons, if the regime were to be attacked, and what their targets would be. Popular thinking on the matter is that Iran would use any such attack as a pretext for a retaliatory strike on Israel. The Iranians would have to weigh the type of strike and the weapons used since the Israelis are believed to have the nuclear capability to destroy high value targets in Iran. The other question that arises is how Iran would use any of its enriched uranium short of a high yield mode e.g. would they consider arming terrorist third parties with the capability to deliver a "dirty bomb?"

Iran provided 69 Zelzal-2 launchers and an unspecified number of other launchers to Hezbollah prior to the July 2006 war. The Israel Air Force made the destruction of these weapons a major priority, and within the first days of air operations estimated that 70% of the launchers were destroyed. Hezbollah, taken aback by the pounding of their strategic missile capability, quickly relocated and hid the remaining launchers, which saw little action during the conflict. These weapons may have been sent to Hezbollah as the "surprise" weapon that would be capable of reaching almost anywhere in Israel from anywhere in Lebanon. In brief, since the Shahab-3 was not used during the 2006 war in Lebanon, Iran may have been authorizing a closely-located third party to strike back strategically if the need arose, such as a response to an Israeli strike on Iran's nuclear program.[43]

United States Military Options

Washington brings the greatest force potential to any military contingencies with Iran. The U.S. Navy could blockade most of the Persian Gulf with surface ships and submarines. Aircraft carrier strike and fighter assets augmented by the carrier-based E-2C Airborne Early Warning and control assets could be used to strike targets in Iran. These strikes would be conducted in combination with U.S. and overseas-based U.S. Air Force B-1, B-2, and F-117 stealth bombers. Such a massive and combined force would overwhelm the Iranian Air Force and the country's main air defenses then they would over the next several days and weeks roam throughout to destroy almost any Iranian target.

The strikes on the nuclear facilities and the Iranian air defenses would not necessarily have to be sequential. Rather, there might be a mix of efforts to destroy as many of the defenses as possible while striking at the very high value nuclear facilities. If some of the Gulf nations were to agree to host U.S. Air Force tactical air operations, then the number of air assets would rise dramatically. This possibility would give the United States the ability to achieve air superiority over Iran within a week and with some effort, air supremacy over portions of the country.

Navy surface ships and submarines would participate in strike operations ashore through the use of their TOMAHAWK cruise missiles. Additionally, U.S. Air Force Airborne Warning and Control Systems, other command and control platforms, and air refueling tankers could participate from outside the Gulf, if necessary, should host nation political considerations make land-basing strike assets in the Gulf nations unworkable. The difficult part of strike operations for the United States remains finding those targets in the first place. The Rules of Engagement would have to be such that desired targets could be accessed. Given that several of the key targets have been constructed underground in residential neighborhoods, likely Rules of Engagement would make targeting them problematic.

U.S. Special Operations Forces and CIA operatives could provide targeting as described earlier in the Israeli options portion of this chapter. Press reports indicate that the United States has had Special Operations Forces on the ground in Iran for some time.[44] The Department of Defense has refused to confirm or deny such operations, and the White House characterized one report as "riddled with inaccuracies." It seems likely that there are covert and clandestine operations ongoing in Iran, because such operations would be prudent given the history of relations and potential for greater hostilities between the two countries.

U.S. Nuclear Options

Although senior leadership in the United States has been intentionally vague about conditions under which nuclear weapons would be used, they would not likely be employed unless Iranian forces were to use weapons of mass destruction against U.S. forces. If American weapons were to be used in Iran, it is likely that targets would be deeply buried facilities at Natanz; but it is not likely that other population centers would be on the target list for nuclear weapons.

U.S. Regional Defensive Capability

Another aspect that should be considered is the ability of U.S. forces to defend not only American facilities and troop concentrations in the Middle East but also some of the territories and likely targets

of its allies. The U.S. Navy would have Ticonderoga class Cruisers and Arleigh Burke class destroyers with their Aegis weapons systems and Standard Missiles available in the Gulf south of Iran and in the eastern Mediterranean to destroy any Iranian-launched ballistic missiles. Also, Patriot batteries in Israel and Iraq would be used for terminal engagements. Patriot missile attacks would be in addition to those Israeli efforts for defense, such as the new Arrow anti-ballistic missile system.

This description of military options is intended to describe systems available, but does not assess the appropriateness of using them; military alternatives that are feasible are not necessarily desirable. In light of failing diplomacy and problematic nature of military action, there is a need to create political options on the ground in Iran that strengthen diplomacy while keeping military options on the table.

POLICY 3: REGIME CHANGE

The regime change option has two main variants dealing with force: nonviolent and violent. The nonviolent alternative implies that the regime is bound to fall eventually on its own, and the best strategy is to sit and wait for the natural course of events to transpire.

Broadcasting into Iran from Los Angeles

radio and television channels might facilitate the process of nonviolent regime change. Because of the strength of the Iranian regime and resolve to do what is necessary to survive as a clerical regime, nonviolent alternatives appear to be a classic case of wishful thinking.

The violent alternative implies either military invasion by external powers to aid opposition groups, funding such opposition to help them bring down the regime, and/or removing from the foreign terrorist organizations list the principal Iranian opposition groups.

An overview of the options for preventing Iran's Islamist leadership from acquiring a nuclear weapons capability was the subject of a March 2006 article in *The New Yorker* by Connie Bruck, in which she surveys the spectrum of Iranian opposition groups intent on effecting regime change in Tehran.[45] Among these opposition figures is the Shah of Iran's heir, Reza Pahlavi, who announced in late April 2006 that he was organizing a movement to overthrow the Islamic regime in Tehran by means of massive civil disobedience and replace it with a democratic government.[46] Because the regime in Tehran barely takes notice of the existence of the monarchists, it appears as if the regime does not perceive much of a threat from this opposition

group. The Iran Policy Committee finds that the regime-based websites pay attention to the National Council of Resistance of Iran and related groups 350 percent more than all other opposition groups combined.[47]

Other dissidents, exiles, and groups run the gamut from former Islamic Revolutionary Guards Corps member Mohsen Sazegara, who favors a constitutional referendum to change the government, to student leaders such as Amir Abbas Fakhravar, and the Iranian Solidarity Council (formed in May 2006). The Iranian Solidarity Council supports United Nations Security Council action to impose smart sanctions and an embargo against the regime and calls on the Iranian military and members of the *Bassij* forces to abandon the regime and support the people.

The oldest, strongest, and best-organized of the democratic Iranian opposition is the *Mujahedeen-e Khalq* and its associated groups under the umbrella of the National Council of Resistance of Iran (NCRI). They await a chance to launch a regime change movement from exile in Ashraf City, Iraq and Paris in combination with their network in Iran. These groups are the most likely to succeed in speeding up the regime change clock.

Protestors Chant "Stop Tehran's Nukes, UN Sanctions Now!" outside UN Headquarters in New York City as Iran Faces UN Deadline to Cease Uranium Enrichment, 31 Aug 2006

Photo Credit Sylwia Kapuscinski/ Getty Images

While far from united in their backgrounds and approaches to regime change, what all of these opposition figures and movements hold in common is a mounting unwillingness to tolerate any longer the repressive Islamist fascist rule of Tehran's clerical regime and a growing determination to take action instead of waiting either for the regime to acquire a nuclear weapons capability or to implode from within.

The anti-regime movement entered a new phase after the brutal suppression of the 1999 student democratic movement destroyed all illusions about the "reformist" nature of the Khatami presidency. The six-day uprising, mostly led by the *Mujahedeen-e Khalq* and related organizations, spread to 19 Iranian cities, shook the regime to its foundations, and effectively ended the population's false expectations that reform could come from within.

Yet another chapter in brutality, terrorism, and nuclear adventurism opened in August 2005, with the takeover of Iran's presidency by Mahmoud Ahmadinejad. The following year witnessed a sequence of demonstrations; protests; uprisings; assassinations of regime intelligence, military, and security personnel; and acts of sabotage against regime targets across Iran. The regime responded with helicopter gunships deployed to fire on protesters, martial law and curfews, as well as a spate of new repressive measures, including arrests, detentions, jailings, torture, and executions.

Constant unrest occurred on the periphery of the country, populated largely by the nearly fifty percent of Iranians who are not Persian, but rather from ethnic minorities like Azeris, Arabs, Baluchis, or Kurds. Even in the capital, Tehran, angry young Iranians seized upon any gathering that offered the opportunity to protest against an increasingly hated regime: Soccer matches at large city stadiums and even the regime's own demonstrations organized to show national support for its nuclear program were turned spontaneously into furious outbursts against the regime for its mishandling of the economy and repressive measures against a youthful population yearning to partake of the modern culture enjoyed in the rest of the world.

The ancient Zoroastrian celebration of *Nowruz*, a timeless commemoration of the coming of spring each March, turned into a street festival of defiance against the disapproval of Shiite mullahs who long have sought to suppress the festivities, during which Iranians pour into the streets for a night of revelry and fire jumping.

Mysterious explosions, bombings, and reports of unidentified surveillance aircraft over Iranian air space added to an atmosphere of building suspense. In December 2005, gunmen ambushed the motorcade of Iranian president Ahmadinejad in the city of Zabol in the southeastern province of Baluchistan. Although the whereabouts of Ahmadinejad at the time of the attack remain in question, his driver and a bodyguard were killed in the attack.[48]

Then, in early January 2006, a plane carrying eleven top Revolutionary Guards leaders went down near the Iraqi border, killing General Ahmad Kazemi, the commander of the Guards ground forces, and Brigadier-General Nabiollah Shahmoradi, who was deputy commander for intelligence. While Iranian officials blamed bad weather and dilapidated engines for the crash, other sources (such as the Stratfor intelligence analysis company) noted that there were other possible explanations, including foul play, for the incident.[49]

The Iranian people are reaching a point of frustration with the failures and oppression of the Tehran regime. Although many are complacent given the small likelihood of success, many are more and more willing to take action to bring about change. Despite the grim reality of security service retaliation that faces every potential dissident, Iranians across the social spectrum are overcoming their fear and finding the courage to stand up to the authorities.

Among the international community, as diplomatic patience wears thin in the wake of three years of failed European and International Atomic Energy Agency efforts at negotiations with Iran, the threat of military strikes against Iran's nuclear weapons program gathers momentum across Western capitals, at the UN, and especially among academics, officials, and pundits in Washington.

With the war drums beating louder and louder, observers are calling for other measures short of military action to support Iranians who are ready to take a stand for freedom and against repression. Empowering the democratic Iranian opposition to take control of its own liberation is a far more attractive option for preventing Tehran's radical clerics from obtaining nuclear weapons than military strikes; empowering the people is also feasible and would strengthen diplomatic efforts of the EU-3, the IAEA, and the UN Security Council.

A complementary alternative is for U.S.

funding of broadcasts into Iran. Consider a March 2006 announcement by the U.S. Department of State that between $75 and 85 million will be allotted to broadcasting in the Farsi language targeted at the Iranian population. In this regard, the U.S. Government has taken a first tentative step toward reaching out to the Iranian people. Iranians have indicated growing antipathy to a repressive regime that has degraded their economy through corruption and squandering of oil income on military expenditures. The regime also crushes free speech, association, and expression; it imposes religious strictures on a society that is well-educated, cosmopolitan, and yearns for the opportunity to enter a modern, globalized, international community.

In the almost three decades since the Iranian Revolution, successive American administrations have considered the possibility of encouraging the creation of a democratic and free Iran, but none has focused directly on the Iranian opposition as an instrument of regime change. Rather, Washington has placed its bet on so-called reformers within the Iranian clerical establishment at the expense of exiles, expatriates, and dissidents.

The hopes that Iran's reform movement alone could effect democratic change

have been dashed with the failure of President Khatami and the rise of his successor, President Ahmadinejad, who upon assuming office purged Government ministries and re-staffed them with former members of the Revolutionary Guards. Starting with the smashing of the 1999 student movement, the Tehran regime has cracked down severely on Iranian civil society organizations, the press, and intellectuals as well as clerics who are active participants in the reform movement. At the same time, the deterioration of the Iranian economy (despite the high price of oil) and the young age of the largest segment of its population are internal pressure points on the regime to produce in the social and economic fields.

As the diplomatic process enters a new phase, the United States along with its allies should encourage the open discussion among Iranians both internally and abroad about the future political direction of their country. To this end, the United States and willing allies should provide material, financial, and technical assistance to all groups and organizations that seek a democratic Iran. To further the movement toward democracy, the West should convene a summit of Iranian opposition leaders and groups, including the leadership of the National Council of

WHAT MAKES TEHRAN TICK: ISLAMIST IDEOLOGY AND HEGEMONIC INTERESTS

Resistance of Iran, to develop an action plan for the future of Iran. Practical steps like creating an emergency fund for the families of political prisoners, striking workers, and dissidents should be given an immediate priority. Fortunately, the main Iranian opposition coalition—the National Council of Resistance of Iran and the *Mujahedeen-e Khalq*—have such a strong base among exiles, expatriates, and dissidents that they neither desire nor request American funding.[50] Those organizations that lobby hardest for American funding are those with the least support within the Iranian population within and outside the country.

Indeed, there is a great difference between the Iraqi National Congress and the National Council of Resistance of Iran. The Iraqi opposition group was created by United States funding, had no base in Iraq, and provided false intelligence about supposed weapons of mass destruction in Iraq. The principal Iranian opposition organization, the Mujahedeen-e Khalq, came into existence before the Iranian Revolution that overthrew the Shah of Iran, has strong support within Iran and in Iraq, as well as in dissident communities within the United States, and has provided lead intelligence that has been validated by independent sources, such as the

International Atomic Energy Agency and national intelligence services.

Destabilization

Application of diplomatic measures, even the most coercive, might not alter the regime's behavior on those issues of paramount concern to the international community, such as state support for terrorism, pursuit of nuclear weapons, and subversion of Iraq. If not, then Washington should be prepared to embrace a new option, short of direct military action, but which might have the best chance for success.

The middle option would open a campaign of destabilization, whose aim would be to weaken the grip of the ruling regime over the Iranian people sufficiently that Iranian opposition groups inside the country and abroad are empowered to change the regime. To the extent that any or all of the foregoing diplomatic measures, coercive or not, are deemed useful, their application should be sustained during a destabilization phase.

This next stage of an American-led campaign to compel conformity to international norms of behavior should include explicit official encouragement to Iranian opposition groups. This is an option that has never actually been on the table and has not been explored sufficiently; this option relies on the Iranian opposition to take the lead role in coordinating a campaign for regime change and establishing representative institutions.

A critical step for the United States to take in signaling its seriousness about regime change in Tehran and that it stands with the Iranian people in their struggle for freedom is to remove the *Mujahedeen-e Khalq* (MEK) and its associated umbrella parliamentary organization in exile, the National Council of Resistance of Iran (NCRI), from the Department of State's list of Foreign Terrorist Organizations (FTO).

Fortunately, there is considerable movement away from keeping the NCRI and related organizations on the FTO list. A comparison of the Department of State rationale used in 2004 with that used in 2005 reveals progress on the road to removal. The Department removed from the 2005 list terms used to describe these organizations in unflattering tones during prior years. One of the most important accusations concerns whether the MEK killed Americans. State finally acknowledges that a "...Marxist element of the MEK murdered several of the Shah's U.S. security advisers prior to the Islamic Revolution, and the group helped guard [helped protect] the U.S. Embassy after Islamic students seized it in 1979."

The NCRI scored a significant legal victory in June 2006 when the French Court of Appeals removed all restrictions on movement of the group's leadership, including the National Council's president-elect Maryam Rajavi, which had been imposed following a 2003 French police raid on the group's compound outside of Paris. Additionally, as of late 2006, initiatives are underway in Belgium, the United Kingdom, and European Parliament to remove the MEK from respective terrorist lists.

The *Mujahedeen-e Khalq*, whose approximately 3,500 members reside under the protection of the U.S. military in Ashraf City in northern Iraq, is the largest, best-organized, and most disciplined Iranian opposition group. The MEK, having been granted the civilian status of "protected persons" under the Fourth Geneva Convention in 2004, is poised to work on behalf of a democratic Iran. Its removal from the FTO list would enable *Mujahedeen-e Khalq* representatives to expand their organization, broadcasting, fund-raising and recruitment activities. A renewed threat of eviction by the Iraqi government and sabotage to Ashraf City water and fuel supply lines in 2006 underlined the tenuous nature of the situation of the *Mujahedeen-e Khalq* and highlighted the urgency of ending

Supporters of the Mujahedeen-e Khalq Protest in Washington DC against Iran's Nuclear Weapon Intransigence; Protestors Wave Posters of Maryam Rajavi, 19 November 2004
Photo Credit Matthew Cavanaugh/Getty Images

restrictions on the group's ability to move about freely and protect itself.

Together, the *Mujahedeen-e Khalq* and National Council of Resistance of Iran represent the most credible threat to the continued survival of the extremist regime in Tehran. This threat was empirically documented by an earlier study by the Iran Policy Committee. It compared public attention paid by the clerical regime to its various opposition groups, and the Committee found through tallying the quantity of regime statements directed at such groups that the regime devoted the content of fully 350 percent more statements to the MEK than to all other groups combined.

The astounding number of individuals who have joined the MEK and gone on to give their lives to its cause is compelling evidence of the support the group has among the Iranian population. The opposition has lost nearly 120,000 members to execution by the regime, 21,676 of whom have been documented in a text depicting photographs, family histories, and manner of execution. The vast majority of these were MEK members.[51] In February 2006, Tehran executed MEK member, Hojjat Zamani after six years of imprisonment in Tehran's notorious Evin prison, and in September 2006, Valliollah Feyz-Mahdavi,

an MEK member lost life in Gohardasht prison after five years of imprisonment.[52]

Moreover, the steady stream of intelligence revelations since 2002, many of which have been verified, by the *Mujahedeen-e Khalq* and National Council of Resistance of Iran from their sources inside Iran's nuclear weapons program, demonstrate in a most graphic way the extent of a dissident support network inside Iran.

Delisting Serves U.S. National Security Interests

On the basis of a systematic analysis of options, the National Council of Resistance of Iran and the MEK should be delisted from the Foreign Terrorist Organizations list first and foremost because it would serve U.S. national security interests. This book and earlier books and White Papers have described in extensive detail the nature and urgency of the threats posed by the aggressive clerical regime in Tehran, which has reached the verge of a nuclear weapons capability and so alarmed the international community that the issue has been brought to the UN Security Council for action.

Goals of the United States for greater democracy, economic development, and equal opportunity for all the people of the Middle East meet a particular focus and challenge in Iran. Empowerment of the Iranian people, who long to achieve these goals for themselves, would result in obvious benefits to themselves and provide a symbol of hope to their neighbors. Removing the MEK from the FTO list is the first step. That first step will trigger a number of positive outcomes.

Delisting would reinforce the sincerity of President Bush's promise that America stands with the people of Iran in their struggle to liberate themselves and send a strong message to the Iranian people that America is on their side. Additionally, it would signal the unified resolution of the U.S. administration to support a policy of regime change in Tehran, thereby putting the clerical rulers on notice that a new option is now on the table, and that America is not limited to a problematic military option or the foundering diplomatic option. The Iranian regime would know that it faces an enabled and determined opposition on its borders; this will shift the attitude of the Ahmadinejad presidency from an offensive mode to a defensive one.

As noted above, it appeared by late-2006 that a number of European parliamentary bodies, including those of the UK, Belgium, and the European Parliament itself, might beat the United States to the delisting of the MEK from terrorist lists. U.S. delisting would bolster the negotiating position of all official parties attempting to deal with Iran, improving the chances of eliciting better cooperation from Tehran, since, as it has been shown, Tehran is less cooperative when it senses weakness in its foes. Conversely, the very real threat of an empowered MEK and NCRI might make it more responsive. Even more importantly, in the longer term, friends and allies would appreciate that the United States is taking the lead in demanding that Iran honor its obligations to the international community on nuclear issues. The likelihood is that they would follow this lead.

Delisting would improve the ability of the National Council of Resistance and *Mujahedeen-e Khalq* to collect high quality intelligence about Iran's nuclear program by encouraging additional intelligence sources inside Iran to provide information. The outcome would certainly inhibit Tehran's efforts to move ahead with its nuclear weapons program. Also in the intelligence arena, delisting would serve to support an expansion of the *Mujahedeen-e Khalq* intelligence network inside Iran on a variety of important collection requirements, including information about Iran's terrorist network throughout the Middle East, its support for terrorist groups in Iraq, and a detailed understanding of the political situation in Iran, including leadership issues and popular sentiment. By creating doubt in the minds and commitment of lower level regime officials, moreover, the likelihood of defections to the camp of regime opponents would rise.

In terms of the Iranian people themselves, enabling the *Mujahedeen-e Khalq* would help to energize the majority who are either undecided "fence-sitters" or heretofore have been uncommitted in the absence of an active policy in favor of regime change. Allowing the MEK to assume a role among leaders of pro-democracy groups in Iran shifts the financial and organizational responsibility for regime change from external entities to the Iranian people themselves and empowers the *Mujahedeen-e Khalq* and other opposition groups to play their rightful role in organizing anti-government demonstrations and other political activity among women, students, merchants, and other groups naturally interested in regime change.

The majority of Iranian clerics, who are not associated with the regime, and who are sympathetic to the secular Islamic ideas about government of the *Mujahedeen-e Khalq*, would be encouraged to take a more positive

attitude toward the United States: Many leaders come from families of prominent Ayatollahs.

The ability to raise funds would also greatly assist the MEK to mount expanded satellite television and radio broadcasting into Iran and to develop an integrated publication and information program not only inside Iran, but abroad as well.

The effects of delisting on U.S. and Coalition efforts to support secure democratic development in Iraq can hardly be overstated. For Iran's Revolutionary Guards, Ministry of Intelligence and Security, and other security services to be thrown on the defensive would force them to scale back their large-scale assistance to terrorist and insurgent forces inside Iraq (as well as those perpetrating terrorist attacks against Israel).

Other pro-Iranian groups, such as the *Supreme Council for the Islamic Revolution in Iraq (SCIRI)* and its armed militia wing, the Badr Organization, would have to adopt a lower profile in southern Iraq, permitting the forces of integration and moderation to advance. Iraqi Shiite militias would find their scope for ethnic-based attacks, reprisals, and neighborhood cleansing operations more circumscribed if their principal sponsor in Tehran were threatened; by the same token, Iraqi Shiite militias would find their scope for ethnic-based attacks, reprisals, and neighborhood cleansing operations more circumscribed if their principal sponsor in Tehran were threatened; similarly, Iraqi Sunnis would be able to take a more assertive role in the political process, thus helping to tamp down forces attempting to incite sectarian warfare among Iraq's ethnic groups.

Additionally, empowerment of the *Mujahedeen-e Khalq* would allow it to operate as a legitimate opposition group in Iraq, thereby providing a cultural, political, and religious counter-weight to the rising tide of Islamist extremism there, much of which is funded and sponsored by Tehran. This positive effect would aid the United States efforts to strengthen the position of moderate forces overall in Iraq, sending a signal to radical Iranian proxy groups in Iraq that their efforts are not welcome.

Regionally, and especially among the Gulf States, the signal would go out that small, weak neighboring countries do not have to put up with Tehran's bullying pressures and destabilization operations.

In the United States, delisting would allow the *Mujahedeen-e Khalq* and its associated larger coalition, the National Council of Resistance of Iran, to open offices, organize the American-Iranian community in line with U.S. Government efforts to spread democracy in the Middle East, and to establish a representative government in Iran. Once the *Mujahedeen-e Khalq* is no longer an officially-designated "terrorist organization," the United States could turn to a decision about whether to return the *Mujahedeen-e Khalq* weapons, confiscated at the outset of Operation Iraqi Freedom, which would relieve the American military of its current responsibility for the protection of camps and personnel where the *Mujahedeen-e Khalq* reside in Iraq.

CONCLUSIONS

Recall the title of this study, "What Makes Tehran Tick." That title arises from Iran's challenging behavior: As Tehran has pressed forward to a proxy confrontation with Israel and ever closer to outright confrontation with the international community, rather than seeking to avoid a clash, Iran becomes even more aggressive in its rhetoric and its actions. Three questions flow from this puzzle and guide the above analysis regarding Iran:

1) What is the nature of the Iranian regime? 2) What difference does its character make? 3) And what is the international community prepared to do

about the Iranian regime?

Because the regime is Islamist fascist in nature, it expresses hostility, but barely bothers to justify such hostility as a result of claims of perceived threats to it. In this regard, revolutionary ideology, religious claims, and regional hegemonic aspirations undergird both expression of hostility and perception of threat.

Given the nature of the regime as well as its capability and intent to acquire the bomb, there are three broad options in play: diplomacy, military action, and regime change. Because diplomacy and military action do not eliminate the outcome of an Islamist Iran with nuclear weapons, they are not as attractive as regime change.

The nature of the regime in Iran is that of a rising regional power with expansionist objectives. Already having demonstrated its willingness to activate its terrorist proxy, Hezbollah, to attack Israel directly, and suffered no consequences for such action, Iran in the aftermath of the Israeli-Hezbollah War of 2006 undoubtedly feels emboldened and validated. This is a dangerous state of affairs, specifically for Israel, whose prior status as regional superpower has been considerably eroded.

Iran, through Hezbollah, has shown for the first time that it is possible to fight

Israel and lose neither existentially nor psychologically in the eyes of the Muslim world. Such a state with nuclear arms is an unacceptable outcome. Diplomacy is irrelevant to the problem of the nature of the regime. Diplomacy accepts the regime as legitimate and seeks to find compromise solutions. But the West should not compromise its principles and security by negotiating endlessly with an Islamist fascist regime intent on getting the bomb.

Military action against nuclear sites also fails to deal with the nature of the regime. Strikes, moreover, only delay the bomb, at best. And at worst, such strikes may delay the onset of regime change. An Iraq-like ground invasion is a nonstarter, and Tehran knows that Iran is not Iraq.

Diplomacy implies a grand bargain where the West would offer a package of economic, political, and security concessions to Iran in the hope that the regime would abandon its quest for the bomb. Military action by Israel and/or the United States suggests surgical airstrikes against Iran's nuclear facilities at a minimum or an Iraqi-style invasion targeting regime assets. The third option consists of empowering the Iranian people through their opposition groups to bring about regime change before the regime gets the bomb.

There are essentially two kinds of diplomacy—coercive diplomacy or a grand bargain of mutual concessions. The problem with coercive diplomacy is the tension among nations that want to dissuade Iran from going down the fast track to get the bomb while still benefiting from trade with Iran. The grand bargain is also problematic. It implies that there is a package of benefits that would persuade Iran to give up its quest for nuclear status, when Iran has rejected such proposals out of hand.

The diplomatic option is already far advanced, and planning for the military option is also proceeding at a rapid pace. The third option of regime change, however, is underdeveloped and has received far less attention than the other two options. While Iran's nuclear program is in development, the international community has a narrow window of time to prepare its options for preventing or dealing with a nuclear Iran.

When diplomacy runs its course, it is imperative that the regime change option be fully developed so that the United States is not left with only a choice between military action and doing nothing to prevent the leadership in Iran from acquiring nuclear weapons.

Diplomats and military planners battle against time before Tehran has the expertise and technology to get the bomb. But Iran's radical President Mahmoud Ahmadinejad shortened the time for Iran to join the nuclear club. Given Iran's extensive underground and scattered nuclear sites, military action can slow but not stop bombmaking.

As diplomacy stalls and costly military alternatives begin to appear inevitable, one emerging option is to speed up the regime change pursuit to slow the nuclear one: Force the clerical rulers from power before they get the bomb. How? Unleash the main Iranian opposition—the *Mujahedeen-e Khalq*. It has support in Iran and a sizable force in Iraq.

Without MEK help, satellite assets would be even less effective in monitoring Iran's increasingly sophisticated, rapidly expanding, and effectively hidden underground nuclear program. Still, the main Iranian opposition operates on half-throttle because terrorist designation by the United States:

1) limits *Mujahedeen-e Khalq* ability to collect intelligence on regime nuclear sites and terrorist networks; 2) shuts down broadcasting from the United States to Iran, while State requests $75 million for such broadcasting; 3) forces the FBI to arrest Iranian-Americans suspected of

Mujahedeen-e Khalq fundraising, diverting scarce Bureau resources from investigating regime violations of U.S. sanctions and intelligence operations in America.

To speed up regime change, end the MEK terrorist designation. Delisting would slow down the nuclear clock by facilitating the work of the most significant intelligence asset on Iranian nuclear programs. Removal of the MEK adds another whirling dervish to the dance of coercive diplomacy, designed to prevent a nuclear-armed Islamist Iran.

The bottom line is that only regime change by empowering the Iranian people via their pro-democracy opposition groups can meet the challenge of what to do with an Islamist state intent on securing nuclear weapon status. Unlike other members of the world's nuclear club, Iran is an Islamist fascist state ruled by fanatical clerics whose calculations of national interest seem ever more likely to set them on a collision course with Israel, the United States, and the international community.

ENDNOTES

[1] *Velayat-e Faqih* (Rule of the Supreme Religious Jurisprudent) is a system of government developed by Ayatollah Khomeini in which the senior religious leader in the country exercises ultimate political authority. Salafism, also referred to as Wahhabism, is a conservative Sunni Islamic sect originating in Saudi Arabia that emulates the religious practices of the companions of the Prophet Muhammad.

[2] Herb Keinon, "Olmert Lays Convergence Groundwork." , 24 April 2006.

[3] "Iran 'worst threat to Jews since Hitler.'" *Telegraph*, 24 April 2006.

[4] Julie Stahl, "What Went Wrong and How Can it be Fixed? Israelis Ask." *CNS News.com*, 15 August 2006.

[5] Anthony H. Cordesman, "Preliminary 'Lessons' of the Israeli-Hezbollah War." *Center for Strategic and International Studies* (CSIS), 18 August 2006.

[6] Edward N. Luttwak, "Three Reasons Not to Bomb Iran—Yet." *Commentary*, May 2006.

[7] One just war condition establishes war as a last resort. If there were other practical and effective means of stopping the aggressor, they must be used first. "Alternatives include one-to-one diplomacy; international pressure; economic sanctions; and such tools as blockades, quarantines, covert actions, and small-scale raids that do not amount to a full-scale war effort. It is not necessary to employ all such methods before going to war. It is sufficient if rigorous consideration reveals them to be impractical or ineffective."
Catholic Answers, "Just War Doctrine." *Answer Guide*; available from http://www.catholic.com/library/Just_war_Doctrine_1.asp

[8] Eldon Greenberg, "The NPT and Plutonium: Application of NPT Prohibitions to 'Civilian' Nuclear Equipment, Technology and Materials Associated with Reprocessing and Plutonium Use." Nuclear Control Institute, 1993; available from http://www.nci.org/03NCI/12/NPTandPlutonium.pdf

[9] "Press Release." Nuclear Control Institute, 3 May 2005; available from http://nci.org/

[10] "Security Council, in Presidential Statement, Underlines Importance of Iran's Re-Establishing Full, Sustained Suspension of Uranium-Enrichment Activities." UN Department of Public Information, 29 March 2006; available from http://www.un.org/News/Press/docs/2006/sc8679.doc.htm

[11] Security Council Demands Iran Suspend Uranium Enrichment by 31 August, or Face Possible Economic, Diplomatic Sanctions, UN Department of Public Information, 31 July 2006; available from http://www.un.org/News/Press/docs//2006/sc8792.doc.htm

[12] Raymond Tanter, "Iran's Threat to Coalition Forces in Iraq." *PolicyWatch* #827, 15 January 2004, http://washingtoninstitute.org/templateC05.php?CID=1705

[13] *Ibid.*

[14] Michael R. Gordon, Mark Mazzetti and Thom Shanker, "Insurgent Bombs Directed at G.I.'s Increase in Iraq." New York Times, 17 August 2006; Renae Merle, "Fighting Roadside Bombs." Washington Post, 29 July 2006; available from http://www.washingtonpost.com/wp-dyn/content/article/2006/07/28/AR2006072801462_pf.html

[15] Iran Policy Committee, "New Intelligence Pinpoints Iranian Regime Explosives Factories." Press Release, 27 July 2006; available from http://iranpolicy.org/

[16] Raymond Tanter, "EU-USA Inter-Parliamentary Briefing on the Iranian Threat and U.S. Options." Remarks delivered at a Congressional Briefing in Rayburn House Office Building, Washington, DC, 27 July 2006, http://iranpolicy.org/

[17] Iran Policy Committee Press Conference, 25 July 2006, http://iranpolicy.org/

[18] "Jordan Says It Arrested 20 Hamas Activists." AP, 11 May 2006.

[19] "IDF Seizes PA Weapons Ship." *Jewish Virtual Library*, 2006; available from http://www.jewishvirtuallibrary.org/jsource/Peace/paship.html

[20] "Security Council Declares Support for Free, Fair Presidential Election in Lebanon; Calls for Withdrawal of Foreign Forces There." UN Department of Public Information, 9 February 2004; available from http://www.un.org/News/Press/docs/2004/sc8181.doc.htm

[21] "Security Council Strongly Encourages Syria to Respond to Lebanon's Request to Delineate Border, Establish Diplomatic Relations." UN Department of Public Information, 17 May 2006; available from http://www.un.org/News/Press/docs/2006/sc8723.doc.htm

[22] "Security Council Calls for End to Hostilities Between Hizbollah, Israel, Unanimously Adopting Resolution 1701 (2006)." UN Department of Public Information, 11 August 2006; available from http://www.un.org/News/Press/docs/2006/sc8808.doc.htm

[23] Lt. Gen. Thomas McInerney (Ret.), "Target Iran." *Weekly Standard*, 24 April 2006.

[24] Seymour M. Hersh, "The Secret Iran Plans." *The New Yorker*, 17 April 2006, 30-37; Seymour M. Hersh, "The Coming Wars." *The New Yorker*, 24 and 31 January 2005, 40-47; James Fallows, "Will Iran Be Next?" *The Atlantic*, December 2004, 99-110.

[25] Dana Priest, "Attacking Iran May Trigger Terrorism: U.S. Experts Wary of Military Action Over Nuclear Program." *Washington Post*, 2 April 2006.

26 "Iran Suspected of Attempts to Rearm Hezbollah Since Cease-Fire." Fox News, 17 August 2006; available from http://www.foxnews.com/story/0,2933,209071,00.html

[27] Christian Oliver, "Iran says it joins nuclear technology club." *Reuters*, 11 April 2006.

[28] David E. Sanger, "Why Not A Strike On Iran?" *New York Times*, 22 January 2006.

[29] "Special Report: Iran's nuclear programme, When Soft Talk Has to Stop." *The Economist* 12 January 2006.

[30] Harold Hough, "Could Israel's nuclear assets survive a pre-emptive strike?" *Jane's Intelligence Review*, 9 January 2006; available from http://www.janes.com/regional_news/africa_middle_east/news/jir/jir990901_1_n.shtml

[31] "Natanz Kashan." *GlobalSecurity.org*, 2006; available from http://www.globalsecurity.org/wmd/world/iran/natanz.htm

[32] Interview between Captain Chuck Nash and a Senior Israeli military official, 27 July 2006.

[33] Anthony Cordesman, *Iran's Developing Military Capabilities* (Washington, DC: CSIS Press, 2005).

[34] *Ibid.*

[35] "Russia Defends Iran Missile Sale." *Agence France-Presse* 5 December 2005.

[36] "Russia will deliver air defense systems to Iran - top general." Free Republic, 20 April 2006; available from http://www.freerepublic.com/focus/f-news/1618116/posts

[37] Anthony Cordesman, *Iran's Developing Military Capabilities* (Washington, DC: CSIS Press, 2005).

[38] *Ibid.*

[39] Marie Colvin, Michael Smith and Sarah Baxter, "Iran suicide bombers 'ready to hit Britain.'" The Sunday Times, 16 April 2006; available from http://www.timesonline.co.uk/newspaper/0,,176-2136638,00.html

[40] Uzi Rubin, "The Global Range of Iran's Ballistic Missile Program." *Jerusalem Issue Brief*, Vol. 5, No. 26, 20 June 2006.

[41] Alex Fishman, "Air Force Chief Views Israel Preparedness for Iranian Threat, Hezbollah, Qassams." Yedi'ot Aharonot 18 April 2006.

[42] Gregory L. Schulte, U.S. Department of State, Remarks at the European Policy Centre, Brussels, Belgium, 22 March 2006. Available from; http://usinfo.state.gov/is/Archive/2006/Mar/24-427575.html

[43] Interview between Captain Chuck Nash and a Senior Israeli military official, 27 July 2006.

[44] "US special forces 'inside Iran.'" BBC, 17 January 2005; available from http://news.bbc.co.uk/1/hi/world/americas/4180087.stm

[45] Connie Bruck, "Next Stop Iran." *The New Yorker*, 6 March 2006; Iran Policy Committee, *Appeasing the Ayatollahs and Suppressing Democracy*, (Washington DC: Iran Policy Committee, 2006).

[46] "Shah of Iran's Heir Plans Overthrow of Regime." *Human Events Online*, 1 May 2006.

[47] Iran Policy Committee, *Appeasing the Ayatollahs and Suppressing Democracy*, (Washington DC: Iran Policy Committee, 2006).

[48] "Assassination Attempt on Iran's Ahmadinejad?" *World Net Daily.com*, 17 December 2005.

[49] "Tehran Insider Tells of US Black Ops." *Asia Times Online*, 25 April 2006.

[50] Iran Policy Committee, *Appeasing the Ayatollahs and Suppressing Democracy*, (Washington DC: Iran Policy Committee, 2006).

[51] People's Mojahedin Organization of Iran, *List of Names and Particulars of 21,676 Victims of Political Executions in Iran: A partial list of 120,000 political execution under mullahs' regime, 2004.*

[52] "Iran 'murders' political prisoner." Iran Focus, 7 September 2006; available from http://www.iranfocus.com/modules/news/article.php?storyid=8527

APPENDIX DOCUMENTS

APPENDIX A: IRANIAN REGIME STATEMENTS

1) Iranian Regime Perception of Threat Statements

2) Iranian Regime Expression of Hostility Statements

3) 2005–2006 Iranian Regime Statements Regarding the United States and Israel

APPENDIX B: HEZBOLLAH AND HAMAS STATEMENTS

1) Hezbollah Statements Regarding the United States and Israel

2) Hamas Statements Regarding the United States and Israel

APPENDIX C: ISRAEL'S STRATEGIC FUTURE: A REPORT ON PROJECT DANIEL

Prepared for the Iran Policy Committee by Professor Louis Rene Beres, Chair of Project Daniel

APPENDIX D: INTERNATIONAL ATOMIC ENERGY AGENCY AND IRAN NUCLEAR SITES

1) IAEA Inspectors and Iran Clash Over Frequency of Inspections of Underground Facilities

2) Construction Activities at Arak 40 MW Heavy Water Reactor

APPENDIX E: IRAN POLICY COMMITTEE BIOGRAPHIES

APPENDIX A: IRANIAN REGIME STATEMENTS

Below are sample statements reflecting Iranian regime perception of threat emanating from the United States and Israel. Following this is a comparable selection of statements reflecting regime hostility toward the United States and Israel. This is only a small selection of over 2,400 total statements collected for the period 1979-2005. These statements were collected by searching the Foreign Broadcast Information Service (available in microfiche and via World News Connection) and BBC Worldwide Monitoring (via Lexis-Nexis). Search parameters were "Iran and United States" and "Iran and Israel." Searches were conducted for three two-week periods each year surrounding specific dates: Embassy Takeover Day (4 November), Jerusalem Day (the last Friday of the Muslim holy month of Ramadan), and May Day (1 May). The collected statements were sorted according to perception of threat and expression of hostility.

Iranian Regime Perception of Threat Statements

Actor	Statement	Date	Expression of
Pani-Sadr (P)	While the Israeli [indistinct] hatch plots for a coup d'etat in Iran and for its implementation, we should draw up the plan for the liberation of the Arabs and the world from this aggressive, fascist government, which is an American puppet.	1980	threat
Khomeyni	And they [US, Israel, everyone] are all united to exploit us, exploit Muslims and the people of Asia and Africa.	1980	threat
Khomeyni	But today, when Israel has attacked an Arab country and is dragging Muslims through blood and dust, what excuse is there for their deadly silence?	1982	threat
Khamene'I	God willing, it will conclude the war victoriously- is that very day when the Islamic revolution will move toward the Zionists and utterly extirpate this cancer.	1984	threat
Khamene'I	The Zionists themselves most certainly were interested in directing Iraq toward our borders and setting Iraqis at the throat of the revolutionary state of Iran.	1984	threat
Khamene'I	And all those people who help Iraq are partners with Iraq in warmongering	1984	threat
Montazeri	They [Zionists and Americans] hope to compensate for the Israeli military defeat by creating civil and religious war among Muslim forces	1985	threat
Musavi	We consider Saddam's invasion (of the Islamic Republic) as having been an invasion against us by the United States	1985	threat
Khamene'I	"We shall regard any aggressive American presence in the Persian Gulf as war against our nation	1986	threat
Larijani	For the United States, this would mean that it will not achieve its prime goal, to bring us to our knees.	1987	threat
TDS	The smallest spark could bring the whole region down in flames at any moment	1990	threat
Rafsanjani	Israel is thinking about expansion	1991	threat
Khamene'I	The arrogant world powers [...] are now the biggest threat to humanity.	1991	threat
Salehabadi (Majles)	The United States intends to dominate all the oil resources of the region and overthrow the independent countries of the region that do not accept the domination	1991	threat
	massacres, murders, and wars which America, Israel, and Saddam are imposing on the Muslim nations	1993	threat
Khamene'I	The usurping government has elevated savagery and brutality to their highest levels and has proven that it is prepared to commit any crime to serve its expansionist and dangerous objectives	1993	threat

Iranian Regime Expression of Hostility Statements

Author	Statement	Perception of Threat or Expression of Hostility	Date
Musavi	Islam cannot be in line with America	Expression of Hostility	1982
Revolution Guards Program	The Islamic Republic's great aim of bringing down the regime of Saddam is to reach Israel and to silence forever this archenemy of the Muslims and this US jugular vein.	Expression of Hostility	1982
Musavi	An American and Saudi Islam would not be a real Islam; such an Islam would be in line with ideology of Satan.	Expression of Hostility	1982
Khomeini	While once again declaring our support for the deprived Palestinian nation and southern Lebanon, we call upon all oil-producing countries to use this weapon to bring the world-devouring America and criminal Zionism to their knees.	Expression of Hostility	1982
val Moslemin (FPS)	As long as the United States of America continues its domineering and ill intentioned policies towards nations, in the name of Islam and the Islamic Revolution we cannot have relations with it	Expression of Hostility	1984
Khamenei	We urgently call on all Islamic governments and responsible authorities in Islamic governments and responsible authorities in Islamic countries to hold Jerusalem Day dear so as to enable and encourage their people- God willing- to observe Jerusalem Day most gloriously as a crushing fist aimed at the United States and Zionism!	Expression of Hostility	1984
Rafsanjani	Israel, a usurper in which a group of Zionists, backed by the political and economic	Expression of Hostility	1984
Ayatollah Montezeri	Death to America means death to colonialism and oppression	Expression of Hostility	1986
Musavi-Ardabili (FPS)	In other words, anything America says we reject	Expression of Hostility	1987
Khamenei	There is no doubt that the long-lasting wish of the United States and its allies has been to confront the Islamic revolution	Expression of Hostility	1987
Voice of the Front	The heroic Iranian nation is ready to teach another lesson to the arch Satan through martyrdom-seeking operations	Expression of Hostility	1987
Rafsanjani	our revolutionary people will demonstrate the revolutionary wrath of the nation and the disgust of the Muslims toward the tyrannical, bullying, hegemonistic methods used by Americans	Expression of Hostility	1987
Voice of the Front	The United States is identified as the enemy of mankind and not just a political-military adversary	Expression of Hostility	1987

Below are statements collected for August 2005-August 2006, as this period was not covered in the quantitative study. The Islamic Republic News Agency website archives were browsed for leadership statements regarding the United States and Israel.

2005-2006 Iranian Regime Statements Regarding the United States and Israel

Actor	Statement	Date	Citation
President Ahmadinejad	Any historian, commentator or scientist who doubts that is taken to prison or gets condemned. Although we don't accept this claim, if we suppose it is true, if the Europeans are honest they should give some of their provinces in Europe—like in Germany, Austria or other countries—to the Zionists and the Zionists can establish their state in Europe. You offer part of Europe and we	8/10/2005	IRNA
President Ahmadinejad	The Islamic Republic never seeks weapons of mass destruction and with respect to the needs of Islamic countries, we are ready to transfer nuclear know-how to these countries	9/15/2005	IRNA
President Ahmadinejad	This Committee should also be asked to investigate as to how contrary to the NPT - material, technology and equipment for nuclear weapons were transferred to the Zionist regime, and to propose practical measures for the establishment of a nuclear-weapons-free zone in the Middle East.	9/17/2005	IRNA
President Ahmadinejad	The palestinian issue has not ended. It would end when a government belonging to the Palestinian people takes over, the homeless return home and a free election is held to form a government representing all people	10/26/2005	IRNA
Ahmadinejad	Israel must be wiped off the map	10/26/2005	IRNA
Ahmadinejad	The establishment of the Zionist regime was a move by the world oppressor against the Islamic world	10/26/2005	IRNA
Ahmadinejad	Anyone who signs a treaty which recognises the entity of Israel means he has signed the surrender of the Muslim world	10/26/2005	IRNA
Ahmadinejad	here is no doubt that the new wave (of attacks) in Palestine will soon wipe off this disgraceful blot (Israel) from the face of the Islamic world.	10/26/2005	IRNA
President Ahmadinejad	The oppressed Palestinians are martyred by Zionists, their properties are looted, their houses are bombarded and they are assassinated but the Zionists expect that no one should object them	10/28/2005	IRNA
President Ahmadinejad	The Qods occupying regime must be eliminated from the surface of earth.	10/30/2005	IRNA
President Ahmadinejad	I, in my recent speech, said those who do this (recognize Israel), actually stand up to Islamic Ummah and this is an unforgivable crime. Islamic states must not recognize a fake regime, which makes no secret of its terrorist nature.	10/30/2005	IRNA
President Ahmadinejad	I have no doubt that the new wave that has started in Palestine, and we witness it in the Islamic world too, will eliminate this disgraceful stain from the Islamic world. But we must be aware of tricks	10/30/2005	IRNA

APPENDIX B: HEZBOLLAH STATEMENTS

Below are sample statements reflecting Hezbollah leadership views of the United States and Israel. These statements were collected by searching the major international news wires (AP, Reuters, AFP, and DPA) and BBC Worldwide Monitoring via Lexis-Nexis. Search parameters were "Hezbollah and United States" and "Hezbollah and Israel."

Hezbollah Statements Regarding the United States and Israel

Speaker	Quote	Date
Nasrallah	Faced with this, we find ourselves looking at a new phenomenon - no, not a phenomenon, an example - of Western hypocrisy in its slogans. It is hypocrisy. It can be described as double standards, as we have got used to saying in the Arab region. In other words, they treat us one way and others in a different way.	2/4/2006
Nasrallah	We cannot allow the Israelis to shed the blood of anyone in Lebanon. The resistance will remain ready to respond to and punish the assassins and criminals in any position, regardless of the sacrifices.	2/4/2006
Nasrallah	hose who say that there is Iranian interference in Lebanon should show evidence." He says: "Such talk does not serve Lebanon or the Lebanese but serves Iran's enemies, and Iran's enemies are America and Israel.	2/4/2006
Nasrallah	Hezbollah in Lebanon and Hezbollah leadership in Lebanon is an independent leadership that makes its decision with its full free will.	2/4/2006
Nasrallah	He urges those who make charges against it "to stop being part of the US campaign against Iran in its nuclear file". He adds: "The issue of the United States, Europe, Iran, and the nuclear file is bigger than Lebanon with all its leaders and political parties. Everyone should know their size, respect their size, and behave accordingly."	2/4/2006
Nasrallah	The entire world should give Hamas a chance. The Palestinians - in all their factions, trends, and directions, especially the brothers in Fatah - should give Hamas this chance. The world, which speaks of freedom, democracy, elections, and the [peaceful] transfer of authority, must respect the will of the Palestinian electorate. This is where US and Western hypocrisy emerges anew. This is where the double- standards exist. The US and Western hypocrisy was clear in dealing with the outcome of the elections.	2/4/2006
Nasrallah	In some places, they [Americans] try to overturn elections through hidden and covert methods, and in other places through declared and political means. If they could and if it were not for fear of exposure and scandal, they would have used uglier methods to overturn elections.	2/4/2006
Nasrallah	According to information and indicators, America interfered in the Iraqi elections. He [Bush] says we want free and honest elections. He warns Iran, Syria and the countries of the region of interfering in Iraq when he himself is interfering in Iraq. They interfered with the elections law, with the elections list, the alliances, and the media. There are reports that the US Administration spent 1 billion US dollars to support its agents in the Iraqi elections but it failed because the Iraqi people have proven that they listen to their religious and national leaders and not to the language of suspicious money coming from abroad with the intention of confiscating their freedom.	2/4/2006

Below are sample statements reflecting Hamas leadership views of the United States and Israel. These statements were collected by searching the major international news wires (AP, Reuters, AFP, and DPA) and BBC Worldwide Monitoring via Lexis-Nexis. Search parameters were "Hamas and United States" and "Hamas and Israel."

Hamas Statements Regarding the United States and Israel

Speaker	Quote	Date	Source
Hamas Leaflet	"The terrorist Israeli government understands only the language of bayonets."	4-Jan-93	AFP
Hamas Leaflet	"The Israeli occupying forces kill innocent civilians, women and children."	4-Jan-93	AFP
Hamas Leaflet	"The Jihad (Holy war) against Israeli soldiers and border police is legitimate ... and recognised under the United Nations charter."	4-Jan-93	AFP
Imad Al-Azami	"Our ties with Iran have no relation with the export of revolution, it's only to try to liberate our land. Our relations with any country or organization are for that goal"	5-Feb-93	AP
Official Statement	"If the Israeli government seeks to widen the circle of conflict and decides to hit Hamas personalities or political and media offices abroad, the Qassam brigades will consider this a start of a new war in which Israeli blood and interests and Jewish communities around the world are open for our strikes."	17-Apr-94	Reuters
Official Statement	"We will respond to every attack by a stronger one,"	17-Apr-94	Reuters
Official Statement	"The government of Israel realizes more than anyone that the Islamic Resistance Movement has strong and long arms all over the world and we so far have been committed to the rules of the game in the battle arena."	17-Apr-94	Reuters
Official Statement	"if the Israeli government wants to break the game's rules then the Jewish people and government will be the first to pay for it and they will be the first to have their faces slapped."	17-Apr-94	Reuters
Hamas Pamphlet	"Hamas can never participate in the autonomy, which came as a result of an agreement signed in Cairo and neglects Jerusalem, gives legitimacy to Jewish settlements in Gaza and ignores 4 million Palestinians who live in the Diaspora,"	13-Jun-94	UPI
Official Statement	"The decision, which has an American form and a Zionist content, was issued as a great service to the Zionists, who are fighting Muslims under the cover of combating fundamentalist terrorism."	5-May-95	BBC
Official Statement	"The US administration's insistence on maintaining its biased policy in favour of Zionist military superiority and on accusing Islam of terrorism would inflame Arab and Islamic sentiments against the United States."	5-May-95	BBC
Razi Mohammad	"The Israelis don't want peace."	30-May-96	AFP
Razi Mohammad	"The election of Netanyahu is a declaration of war against Palestinians and the Arabs"	30-May-96	AFP
Mahmoud Zahar	"Israel will gain nothing from more prisoners, and America will gain nothing by gaining a new enemy -- Hamas,"	30-Jan-97	NY Times
Mahmoud Zahar	"Up to this minute, we do not consider America the enemy, but if they are going to send Mr. Abu Marzook to Israel, this will be seen as if they are serving the Israeli aims directly, and that will result in a more dangerous situation."	30-Jan-97	NY Times
Mahmoud Zahar	"We are afraid that somebody will try to punish America by sending a lesson that if you going to serve Israel's interests, you have to expect attacks on your interests in the area,"	30-Jan-97	NY Times
Sheikh Ahmed Yassin	"We are in the same boat, we have the same enemy" (referring to the Golan Heights which Israel captured from Syria in the 1967 war)	21-May-98	AFP

APPENDIX C

Nothing about Israel's recent military action against Hezbollah in southern Lebanon suggests any needed changes in the published recommendations of Project Daniel. To the contrary, as Iran used this period of surrogate warfare to accelerate its development of threatening (to Israel) nuclear weapons technologies and infrastructures, all of the arguments of Project Daniel - especially those concerning preemption, nuclear disclosure and counter-value targeting - must now be reaffirmed.

— Louis Rene Beres,
Chair of Project Daniel
4 September 2006

ISRAEL'S STRATEGIC FUTURE

A Report on PROJECT DANIEL

Prepared for the Iran Policy Committee

By Professor Louis Rene Beres, Chair of Project Daniel

INTRODUCTION

ISRAEL'S STRATEGIC FUTURE: THE FINAL REPORT OF PROJECT DANIEL was completed in mid-January 2003 — several months before the start of Operation Iraqi Freedom - and transmitted by hand to Prime Minister Sharon. The underlying rationale of "Daniel" was the presumption that Israel urgently needs a coherent plan for dealing with authentically existential threats, and that we ("The Group") were well-positioned intellectually and professionally to design such a plan. We began with an overriding concern for the possible fusion of certain WMD-capacity with irrational adversaries. Project Daniel concluded, however, that the primary threats to Israel's physical survival were actually more likely to arise among enemies that were not irrational. With this in mind, we proceeded to consider a broad variety of complex issues concerning deterrence, defense, preemption and warfighting.

Combining legal with strategic analyses, The Group linked the concept of "anticipatory self-defense" to various preemption scenarios and to The National Security Strategy of the United States of America (September 20, 2002). We also examined closely the prospects for expanded strategic cooperation between Washington and Jerusalem, with particular reference to maintaining Israel's "qualitative edge" and to associated issues of necessary funding. Project Daniel looked very closely at a recommended "paradigm shift" to deal with various "low intensity" and long-range WMD threats to Israel, and also considered the specific circumstances under which Israel should purposefully end its current posture of "nuclear ambiguity." Overall, The Group urged continuing constructive support to the United States-led War Against Terror (WAT) and stipulated that Israel combine a strengthening of multilayered active defenses with a credible, secure and decisive nuclear deterrent. This recognizable retaliatory (second-strike) force is to be fashioned with the capacity to destroy some 10 - 20 high-value targets scattered widely over pertinent enemy states in the Middle East - an objective entirely consistent with our explicit assumption that the main goal of Israel's nuclear forces must always be deterrence *ex ante*, not revenge *ex post*.

The Group recognized a very basic asymmetry between Israel and the Arab/Iranian world concerning, *inter alia*, the desirability of peace; the absence of democracy; the acceptability of terror as a legitimate weapon and the overwhelming demographic advantage of the Arab/Iranian world. With this in mind, ISRAEL'S STRATEGIC FUTURE concluded that non-conventional exchanges between Israel and adversary states must always be scrupulously avoided and that Israel must do whatever is needed to maintain its conventional supremacy in the region. Facing a growing anarchy in world affairs and an increasing isolation in the world community, Israel is strongly encouraged by Project Daniel to incorporate The Group's considered recommendations into codified IDF doctrine, and to systematically expand Israeli strategic

studies into a more disciplined field of inquiry. In the end, Israel's survival will depend largely upon policies of its own making, and these policies will be best-informed by The Group's proposed steps regarding deterrence; defense; warfighting and preemption options. Today, with the steadily advancing nuclear threat from Iran, the preemption option has become even more compelling.

ISRAEL, SUN-TZU AND THE ART OF WAR

Although The Group's collaborative analyses drew upon very contemporary strategic thinking, we were also mindful of certain much-earlier investigations of war, power and survival. One such still-relevant investigation can be found in Sun-Tzu's THE ART OF WAR. The following brief section of this paper uses Sun-Tzu to elucidate The Group's main ideas and recommendations.

Sun-Tzu's THE ART OF WAR, written sometime in the fifth century BCE, synthesized a coherent set of principles designed to produce military victory and minimize the chances of military defeat. Examined together with ISRAEL'S STRATEGIC FUTURE, the Final Report of Project Daniel, the full corpus of this work should now be studied closely by all who wish to strengthen Israel's military posture and its associated order of battle. At a time when the leaders of particular Arab/Islamic states might soon combine irrationality with weapons of mass destruction, the members of Project Daniel were markedly determined to augment current facts and figures with dialectical reasoning, imagination and creativity.

Israel, we reported, must continue its "imperative to seek peace through negotiation and diplomatic processes wherever possible." Indeed, we continued: "This imperative, codified at the United Nations Charter and in multiple authoritative sources of international law, shall always remain the guiding orientation of Israel's foreign policy." What are Sun-Tzu's principles concerning negotiation and diplomacy? Political initiatives and agreements may be useful, he instructs, but purposeful military preparations should never be neglected. The primary objective of every state should be to weaken enemies without actually engaging in armed combat. This objective links the ideal of "complete victory" to a "strategy for planning offensives." In Chapter Four, "Military Disposition," Sun-Tzu tells his readers: "One who cannot be victorious assumes a defensive posture; one who can be victorious attacks....Those who excel at defense bury themselves away below the lowest depths of Earth. Those who excel at offense move from above the greatest heights of Heaven."

Project Daniel took note. Today, with steadily more menacing Iranian nuclearization, the whole world - informed by the insights of this Iran Policy Committee White Paper - should take note. Recognizing the dangers of relying too heavily upon active defenses such as anti-ballistic missile systems, a reliance whereby Israel would likely bury itself away "below the lowest depths of Earth," Project Daniel boldly advises that Israel take certain prompt initiatives in removing existential threats. These initiatives include striking first (preemption) against enemy WMD development, manufacturing, storage, control and deployment centers - a recommendation fully consistent with longstanding international law regarding "anticipatory self defense" and also with the current defense policy of the United States.

If, for any reason, the doctrine of preemption should fail to prevent an enemy Arab state or Iran from acquiring nuclear weapons, the Daniel group advises that Israel cease immediately its current policy of nuclear ambiguity, and proceed at once to a position of open nuclear deterrence. Additional to this change in policy, we recommend that Israel make it perfectly clear to the enemy nuclear state that it would suffer prompt and maximum-yield nuclear "countervalue" reprisals for any level of nuclear aggression undertaken against Israel.

Under certain circumstances, our team

continues, similar forms of Israeli nuclear deterrence should be directed against enemy states that threaten existential harms with biological weapons.

What exactly are "existential harms?" Taken literally, an existential threat implies harms that portend a complete annihilation or disappearance of the state. We feel, however, that certain more limited forms of both conventional and unconventional attack against large Israeli civilian concentrations could also constitute an existential threat. In part our calculation here is based upon Israel's small size, its very high population density and its particular concentrations of national infrastructure. If the Government of Israel follows the advice of Project Daniel, prospective aggressors would understand in advance that launching certain kinds of attack would result in their own cities turning to vapor and ash.

Following Sun-Tzu, the clear purpose of our recommendation is to achieve a complete Israeli "victory" without engaging in actual hostilities. In the exact words of our Report, ISRAEL'S STRATEGIC FUTURE: "The overriding priority of Israel's nuclear deterrent force must always be that it preserves the country's security without ever having to be fired against any target."

To preserve itself against any existential threats, some of which may stem from terrorist organizations as well as from states, Israel should

learn from Sun-Tzu's repeated emphasis on the "unorthodox." Drawn from the conflation of thought that crystallized as Taoism, the ancient strategist observes: "...in battle, one engages with the orthodox and gains victory through the unorthodox." In a complex passage, Sun-Tzu discusses how the orthodox may be used in unorthodox ways, while an orthodox attack may be unorthodox when it is unexpected. Taken together with the recommendations of Project Daniel, this passage could represent a subtle tool for operational planning, one that might usefully exploit an enemy state's or terrorist group's particular matrix of military expectations.

For Israel, the "unorthodox" should be fashioned not only ON the battlefield, but also BEFORE the battle. To prevent the most dangerous forms of battle, which would be expressions of all-out unconventional warfare called "counterforce" engagements, Israel should now examine a number of promising strategic postures. These postures could even focus upon a reasoned shift from an image of "orthodox" rationality to one of somewhat "unorthodox" irrationality, although Project Daniel does confine itself to prescriptions for certain defensive first-strikes using conventional weapons and massive countervalue (countercity) nuclear reprisals.

Everyone who studies Israeli nuclear

strategy has heard about the so-called "Samson Option." This is generally thought to be a last resort strategy wherein Israel's nuclear weapons are used not for prevention of war or even for war-waging, but simply as a last spasm of vengeance against a despised enemy state that had launched massive (probably unconventional) countercity and/or counterforce attacks against Israel. In this view, Israel's leaders, faced with national extinction, would decide that although the Jewish State could not survive, it would "die" only together with its destroyers.

How does the "Samson Option" appear to the Arab/Iranian side? Israel, it would seem, may resort to nuclear weapons, but only in reprisal, and only in response to overwhelmingly destructive first-strike attacks. Correspondingly, anything less than an overwhelmingly destructive first-strike would elicit a measured and proportionate Israeli military response. Moreover, by striking first, the Arab/Iranian enemy knows that it could have an advantage in "escalation dominance." These calculations would follow from the more or less informed enemy view that Israel will never embrace the "unorthodox" on the strategic level, that its actions will likely always be reactions, and that these reactions will always be limited.

But what if Israel were to fine-tune its "Samson Option?" What if it did this in conjunction with certain doctrinal changes in its longstanding policy of nuclear ambiguity? By taking the bomb out of the "basement" and by indicating, simultaneously, that its now declared nuclear weapons were not limited to existential scenarios, Israel might go a long way to enhancing its national security. It would do this by displaying an apparent departure from perfect rationality; in essence, by expressing the rationality of threatened irrationality. Whether or not such a display would be an example of "pretended irrationality" or of an authentic willingness to act irrationally would be anyone's guess. It goes without saying that such an example of "unorthodox" behavior by Israel could actually incite enemy first-strikes in certain circumstances, or at least hasten the onset of such strikes that may already be planned, but there are ways for Israel in which Sun-Tzu's "unorthodox" could be made to appear "orthodox."

HOW A NUCLEAR WAR MIGHT BEGIN BETWEEN ISRAEL AND ITS ENEMIES

Israel remains the openly-declared national and religious object of Arab/Islamic genocide. This term is used in the literal and jurisprudential sense - not merely as a figure of speech. No other country is in a similar predicament. What is Israel to do? How might Israel's possible actions or inactions affect the likelihood of a regional nuclear war in the Middle East? And in what precise ways might a nuclear war actually begin between Israel and certain of its enemies?

Israel's nuclear weapons, unacknowledged and unthreatening, exist only to prevent certain forms of enemy aggression. This deterrent force would never be used except in defensive reprisal for certain massive enemy first-strikes, especially for Arab and/or Iranian attacks involving nuclear and/or biological weapons. For a limited time, Israel's enemies are not yet nuclear. Even if this should change, Israel's nuclear weapons could continue to reduce the risks of unconventional war as long as the pertinent enemy states were (1) to remain rational; and (2) to remain convinced that Israel would retaliate massively if attacked with nuclear and/or certain biological weapons of mass destruction.

But there are many complex problems to identify if a bellicose enemy state were allowed to acquire nuclear weapons, problems that belie the seemingly agreeable notion of stable nuclear deterrence. Whether for reasons of miscalculation, accident, unauthorized capacity to fire, outright irrationality or the presumed imperatives of "Jihad," such a state could opt to launch a nuclear first-strike against Israel in spite of the latter's nuclear posture. Here, Israel

would certainly respond, to the extent possible, with a nuclear retaliatory strike. Although nothing is publicly known about Israel's precise targeting doctrine, such a reprisal might surely be launched against the aggressor's capital city or against a similarly high-value urban target. There would be no assurances, in response to this sort of aggression, that Israel would limit itself to striking back against exclusively military targets or even to the individual enemy state from which the aggression was launched.

What if enemy first-strikes were to involve "only" chemical and/or biological weapons? Here Israel might still launch a reasonably proportionate nuclear reprisal, but this would depend largely upon Israel's calculated expectations of follow-on aggression and on its associated determinations of comparative damage-limitation. Should Israel absorb a massive conventional first-strike, a nuclear retaliation could still not be ruled out altogether. This is especially the case if: (1) the aggressor were perceived to hold nuclear or other weapons of mass destruction in reserve; and/or (2) Israel's leaders were to believe that non-nuclear retaliations could not prevent national annihilation. As indicated earlier in this paper, Project Daniel determined that the threshold of existential harms must be far lower than wholesale physical devastation.

Faced with imminent and existential attacks, Israel - properly taking its cue from THE NATIONAL SECURITY STRATEGY OF THE UNITED STATES OF AMERICA - could decide to preempt enemy aggression with conventional forces. Announced on September 20, 2002, this Bush-era American strategy affirms the growing reasonableness of anticipatory self-defense under international law. If Israel were to draw upon such authoritative expressions of current U.S. policy, the targeted state's response would determine Israel's subsequent moves. If this response were in any way nuclear, Israel would assuredly undertake nuclear counter-retaliation. If this enemy retaliation were to involve certain chemical and/or biological weapons, Israel might also determine to take a quantum escalatory initiative.

If the enemy state's response to an Israeli preemption were limited to hard-target conventional strikes, it is highly improbable that Israel would resort to nuclear counter-retaliation. On the other hand, if the enemy state's conventional retaliation were an all-out strike directed toward Israel's civilian populations as well as to Israeli military targets - an existential strike, for all intents and purposes - an Israeli nuclear counter-retaliation could not be ruled out. Such a counter-retaliation could be ruled out only if the enemy state's conventional retaliations were entirely proportionate to Israel's preemption; confined entirely to Israeli military targets; circumscribed by the legal limits of "military necessity"; and accompanied by explicit and verifiable assurances of no further escalation.

It is exceedingly unlikely, but not entirely inconceivable, that Israel would ever decide to preempt enemy state aggression with a nuclear defensive strike. While circumstances could surely arise where such a defensive strike would be completely rational and also completely acceptable under international law (such a policy HAS been embraced by the United States in Joint Publication 3-12, DOCTRINE FOR JOINT NUCLEAR OPERATIONS, 15 March 2005), it is improbable that Israel would ever permit itself to reach such dire circumstances. An Israeli nuclear preemption could be expected only if: (1) Israel's state enemies had unexpectedly acquired nuclear or other unconventional weapons presumed capable of destroying the tiny Jewish State; (2) these enemy states had made explicit that their intentions paralleled their capabilities; (3) these states were authoritatively believed ready to begin a countdown-to-launch; AND (4) Israel believed that non-nuclear preemptions could not possibly achieve the minimum needed levels of damage-limitation - that is, levels consistent with its own national survival.

Should nuclear weapons ever be introduced into a conflict between

Israel and the many countries that wish to destroy it, some form of nuclear war fighting could ensue. This would be the case so long as: (a) enemy state first-strikes against Israel would not destroy the Jewish State's second-strike nuclear capability; (b) enemy state retaliations for Israeli conventional preemption would not destroy Israel's nuclear counter-retaliatory capability; (c) Israeli preemptive strikes involving nuclear weapons would not destroy enemy state second-strike nuclear capabilities; and (d) Israeli retaliation for enemy state conventional first-strikes would not destroy enemy state nuclear counter-retaliatory capability. From the standpoint of protecting its security and survival, this means that Israel must now take proper steps to ensure the likelihood of (a) and (b) above, and the unlikelihood of (c) and (d).

Both Israeli nuclear and non-nuclear preemptions of enemy unconventional aggressions could lead to nuclear exchanges. This would depend, in part, upon the effectiveness and breadth of Israeli targeting, the surviving number of enemy nuclear weapons, and the willingness of enemy leaders to risk Israeli nuclear counter-retaliations. In any event, the likelihood of nuclear exchanges would obviously be greatest where potential Arab and/or Iranian aggressors were allowed to deploy ever-larger numbers of unconventional weapons without eliciting appropriate Israeli and/or American preemptions.

Should such deployment be allowed to take place, Israel might effectively forfeit the non-nuclear preemption option. Here its only alternatives to nuclear preemption could be a no-longer viable conventional preemption or simply waiting to be attacked itself. It follows that the risks of an Israeli nuclear preemption, of nuclear exchanges with an enemy state, AND of enemy nuclear first-strikes could all be reduced by certain timely Israeli and/or American non-nuclear preemptions. These preemptions would be directed at critical military targets and/or at pertinent regimes. As explained by Project Daniel, the latter option could include dedicated elimination of enemy leadership elites and/or certain enemy scientists.

ISRAEL'S POLICY OF NUCLEAR AMBIGUITY

We have seen some of the precise ways in which a nuclear war might actually begin between Israel and its enemies. From the standpoint of preventing such a war, it is essential that Israel now protect itself with suitable policies of preemption, defense and deterrence. This last set of policies, moreover, will depend substantially upon whether Israel continues to keep its bomb in the "basement," or whether it decides to change from a formal nuclear posture of "deliberate ambiguity" to one of selected and partial disclosure.

In one respect, the issue is already somewhat moot. Shortly after coming to power as Prime Minister, Shimon Peres took the unprecedented step of openly acknowledging Israel's nuclear capability. Responding to press questions about the Oslo "peace process" and the probable extent of Israeli concessions, Peres remarked that he would be "delighted" to "give up the Atom" if the entire region would only embrace a comprehensive security plan. Although this remark was certainly not an intended expression of changed nuclear policy, it did raise the question of a more tangible Israeli shift away from nuclear ambiguity.

The nuclear disclosure issue is far more than a simple "yes" or "no." Obviously, the basic question was already answered by Peres's "offer." What needs to be determined soon is the timing of purposeful disclosure and the extent of subtlety and detail with which Israel should communicate its nuclear capabilities and intentions to selected enemy states. This issue is central to the deliberations of Project Daniel, which concluded that Israel's bomb should remain in the basement as long as possible, but also that it should be revealed in particular contours if enemy circumstances should change in an ominous fashion.

In essence, therefore, because the Report stipulates the need for an expanded Israeli doctrine of preemption, this Project Daniel statement on nuclear ambiguity means that Israel should promptly remove the bomb from its "basement" if - for whatever reason - Israel should have failed to exploit the recommended doctrine of preemption.

The rationale for Israeli nuclear disclosure does not lie in expressing the obvious; that is, that Israel has the bomb. Instead, it lies in the informed understanding that nuclear weapons can serve Israel's security in a number of different ways, and that all of these ways could benefit the Jewish State to the extent that certain aspects of these weapons and associated strategies are disclosed. The pertinent form and extent of disclosure would be especially vital to Israeli nuclear deterrence.

To protect itself against enemy strikes, particularly those attacks that could carry existential costs, Israel must exploit every component function of its nuclear arsenal. The success of Israel's efforts will depend in large measure not only upon its chosen configuration of "counterforce" (hard-target) and "countervalue" (city-busting) operations, but also upon the extent to which this configuration is made known in advance to enemy states. Before such an enemy is deterred from launching first-strikes against Israel, or before it is deterred from launching retaliatory attacks following an Israeli preemption, it may not be enough that it simply "knows" that Israel has the Bomb. It may also need to recognize that these Israeli nuclear weapons are sufficiently invulnerable to such attacks and that they are aimed at very high-value targets. In this connection, the Final Report of Project Daniel recommends that "a recognizable retaliatory force should be fashioned with the capacity to destroy some 15 high-value targets scattered widely over pertinent enemy states in the Middle East." This "countervalue" strategy means that Israel's second-strike response to enemy aggressions involving certain biological and/or nuclear weapons would be unambiguously directed at enemy populations, not at enemy weapons or infrastructures.

It may appear, at first glance, that Israeli targeting of enemy military installations and troop concentrations ("counterforce targeting") would be both more compelling as a deterrent and also more humane. But it is entirely likely that a nuclear-armed enemy of Israel could conceivably regard any Israeli retaliatory destruction of its armed forces as "acceptable" in certain circumstances. Such an enemy might conclude that the expected benefits of annihilating "the Zionist entity" outweigh any expected retaliatory harms to its military. Here, of course, Israel's nuclear deterrent would fail, possibly with existential consequences.

It is highly unlikely, however, that any enemy state would ever calculate that the expected benefits of annihilating Israel would outweigh the expected costs of its own annihilation. Excluding an irrational enemy state - a prospect that falls by definition outside the logic of nuclear deterrence - state enemies of Israel would assuredly refrain from nuclear and/or biological attacks upon Israel that would presumptively elicit massive countervalue reprisals. This reasoning would hold only to the extent that these enemy states fully believed that Israel would make good on its threats. Israel's nuclear deterrent, once it were made open and appropriately explicit, would need to make clear to all prospective nuclear enemies the following: "Israel's nuclear weapons, dispersed, multiplied and hardened, are targeted upon your major cities. These weapons will never be used against these targets except in retaliation for certain WMD aggressions. Unless our population centers are struck first by nuclear attack or certain levels of biological attack or by combined nuclear/biological attack, we will not harm your cities."

Some readers will be disturbed by this reasoning, discovering in it perhaps some ominous hint of "Dr. Strangelove." Yet, the countervalue targeting strategy recommended by Project Daniel represents Israel's best hope for avoiding a nuclear or biological war. It is, therefore, the most humane strategy available. The Israeli alternative, an expressed counterforce targeting doctrine, would produce a markedly higher probability of nuclear or nuclear/biological war. Such a war, even if all weapons remained targeted on the other side's military forces and structures (a very optimistic assumption) would entail high levels of "collateral damage."

The very best weapons, Clausewitz wrote, are those that achieve their objectives without ever actually being used. This is especially the case with nuclear weapons; Israel's nuclear weapons can succeed only through non-use. Recognizing this, Project Daniel makes very clear in its Final Report to Prime Minister Sharon that nuclear warfighting must always be avoided by Israel.

Summing up, the Project Daniel Group recommends that Israel do whatever it must to prevent enemy nuclearization, up to and including pertinent acts of preemption. Should these measures fail, measures that would be permissible under international law as expressions of "anticipatory self-defense," the Jewish State should immediately end its posture of nuclear ambiguity with fully open declarations of countervalue targeting.

ISRAEL'S SURVIVAL AMIDST GROWING WORLDWIDE ANARCHY

In an age of Total War, Israel must always remain fully aware of those harms that would threaten its very continuance as a state. Although the Jewish State has always recognized an overriding obligation to seek peace through negotiation and diplomacy wherever possible, there are times when its commitment to peaceful settlement will not be reciprocated. Moreover, as noted earlier, there are times when the idea of an existential threat may reasonably apply to a particular level of harms that falls well below the threshold of complete national annihilation.

Examining pertinent possibilities, our Project Daniel group noted three distinct but interrelated existential threats to Israel:

1) Biological/Nuclear (BN) threats from states;

2) BN threats from terror organizations; and

3) BN threats from combined efforts of states and terror organizations.

To the extent that certain Arab states and Iran are now allowed to develop WMD capabilities, Israel may have to deal someday with an anonymous attack scenario. Here the aggressor enemy state would not identify itself, and Israeli post-attack identification would be exceedingly difficult. What is Israel to do in such a situation? The Group recommended to the Prime Minister that "Israel must identify explicitly and early on that all enemy Arab states and Iran are subject to massive Israeli reprisal in the event of a BN attack upon Israel." We recommended further that "massive" reprisals be targeted at between 10 and 20 large enemy cities ("countervalue" targeting) and that the nuclear yields of such Israeli reprisals be in very high range. Such deterrent threats by Israel would be very compelling to all rational enemies, but - at the same time - would likely have little or no effect upon irrational ones. In the case of irrational adversaries, Israel's only hope for safety will likely lie in appropriate and operationally feasible acts of preemption.

A policy of Mutual Assured Destruction (MAD) which once obtained between the United States and the Soviet Union would never work between Israel and its Arab/Iranian enemies. Rather, the Project Daniel Group recommended that Israel MUST prevent its enemies from acquiring BN status, and that any notion of BN "parity" between Israel and its enemies would be intolerable. Accordingly, The Group advised the Prime Minister that "Israel immediately adopt - as highest priority - a policy of preemption with respect to enemy existential threats." Such a policy would be based upon the more limited definition of "existential" described above, and would also enhance Israel's overall deterrence posture.

Recognizing the close partnership and overlapping interests between Israel and the United States, the Project Daniel Group strongly supports the ongoing American War Against Terror (WAT). In this connection, we have urged full cooperation and mutuality between Jerusalem and Washington regarding communication of intentions. If for any reason the United States should decide against exercising preemption options against certain developing weapons of mass destruction, Israel must reserve for itself the unhindered prerogative to undertake its own preemption options. Understood in the more formal language of international law, these operations would be an expression of "anticipatory self-defense."

Our Group began its initial deliberations with the following urgent concern: Israel faces the hazard of a suicide-bomber in macrocosm. In this scenario, an enemy Arab state or Iran would act against Israel without ordinary regard for any retaliatory consequences. In the fashion of the individual suicide bomber who acts without fear of personal consequences - indeed, who actually welcomes the most extreme personal consequence, which is death - an enemy Arab state and/or Iran would launch WMD attacks against Israel with full knowledge and expectation of overwhelming Israeli reprisals. The conclusion to be drawn from this scenario is that Israeli deterrence vis-a-vis "suicide states" would have been immobilized by enemy irrationality and that Israel's only recourse in such circumstances would have been appropriate forms of preemption.

ISRAEL'S PREEMPTION AND NUCLEAR WARFIGHTING DOCTRINE

International law has long allowed for states to initiate forceful defensive measures when there exists "imminent danger" of aggression. This rule of "anticipatory self-defense" has been expanded and reinforced by President George W. Bush's issuance of THE NATIONAL SECURITY STRATEGY OF THE UNITED STATES OF AMERICA. Released on September 20, 2002, this document asserts, inter alia, that traditional concepts of deterrence will not work against an enemy "whose avowed tactics are wanton destruction and the targeting of innocents...." As Israel is substantially less defensible and more vulnerable than the United States, its particular right to resort to anticipatory self-defense under threat of readily identifiable existential harms is beyond legal question.

Following the Bush doctrine expansion of preemption, the Group suggested to Prime Minister Sharon that such policy pertain as well to certain nuclear and/or biological WMD threats against Israel, that this policy be codified as doctrine, and that these actions be conventional in nature. Such preemption may be overt or covert, and range from "decapitation" to full-scale military operations. Further, the Group advised that decapitation may apply to both enemy leadership elites (state and non-state) and to various categories of technical experts who would be essential to the fashioning of enemy WMD arsenals, e.g., nuclear scientists. The Group reminded Prime Minister Sharon that any forcible prevention of enemy nuclear/biological deployment would be profoundly different from an Israeli preemption of an existing enemy nuclear/biological force. Attempts at preemption against an enemy that had already been allowed to go nuclear/biological may be far too risky and could even invite an existential retaliation. It was also recommended that any preemptions be carried out exclusively by conventional high-precision weapons, not only because they are likely to be more effective than nuclear weapons, but also because preemption with nuclear weapons could be wrongly interpreted as Israeli nuclear first-strikes. If unsuccessful, these preemptive strikes could elicit an enemy's "countervalue" second strike; that is, a deadly intentional attack upon Israeli civilian populations.

The Group advised emphatically that Israel should avoid non-conventional exchanges with enemy states wherever possible. It is not in Israel's interest to engage these states in WMD warfare if other options exist. ISRAEL'S STRATEGIC FUTURE does not instruct how to "win" a war in a WMD Middle-East environment. Rather, it describes what we, the members of Project Daniel, consider the necessary, realistic and optimal conditions for nonbelligerence toward Israel in the region. These conditions include a coherent and comprehensive Israeli doctrine for preemption, warfighting, deterrence and defense.

The Group advised the Prime Minister that there is no operational need for low-yield nuclear weapons geared to actual battlefield use. Overall, we recommended that the most efficient yield for Israeli deterrence and counterstrike purposes be a "countervalue" targeted warhead at a level sufficient to hit the aggressor's principal population centers and fully compromise that aggressor's national viability. We urged that Israel make absolutely every effort to avoid ever using nuclear weapons in support of conventional war operations. These weapons could create a seamless web of conventional and nuclear battlefields that Israel should scrupulously avoid.

The Group considers it gainful for Israel to plan for very selective regime-targeting in certain residual instances. With direct threats employed against individual enemy leaders and possible others, costs to Israel could be very much lower than alternative forms of warfare. At the same time, threats of regime targeting could be even more persuasive than threats to destroy enemy weapons and infrastructures, but only if the prospective victims were first made to feel sufficiently at risk.

The Group advanced a final set of suggestions concerning the lawful remedy of anticipatory self-defense. Israel must be empowered with a "Long Arm" to meet its preemption objectives. This means long-range fighter aircraft with capability to penetrate deep, heavily defended areas, and to survive. It also means air-refueling tankers; communications satellites; and long-range unmanned aerial vehicles. More generally, it means survivable precision weapons with high lethality; and also considerably refined electronic warfare and stealth capacities.

ISRAEL'S DETERRENCE AND DEFENSE DOCTRINE

The Group strongly endorsed the Prime Minister's acceptance of a broad concept of defensive first-strikes, but just as strongly advised against using his undisclosed nuclear arsenal for anything but essential deterrence. This means that enemy states must begin to understand that certain forms of aggression against Israel will assuredly elicit massive Israeli nuclear reprisals against city targets. For the moment we maintain that such an understanding can be communicated by Israel without any forms of explicit nuclear disclosure, but we also recognize that the presumed adequacy of nuclear ambiguity would change immediately if enemy nuclearization anywhere should become a reality.

Nuclear deterrence, ambiguous or partially disclosed, is essential to Israel's physical survival. If, for whatever reason, Israel should fail to prevent enemy state nuclearization, it will have to refashion its nuclear deterrent to conform to vastly more dangerous regional and world conditions. But even if this should require purposeful disclosure of its nuclear assets and doctrine, such revelation would have to be limited solely to what would be needed to convince Israel's enemies of both its capacity and its resolve. More particularly, this would mean revealing only those aspects needed to identify the survivability and penetration-capability of Israel's nuclear forces and the political will to launch these massive forces in retaliation for certain forms of enemy state aggression.

The Group advised the Prime Minister that Israel must always do whatever it can to ensure a secure and recognizable second-strike nuclear capability. Once nuclear ambiguity was brought to an end, nuclear disclosure would play a crucial communications role. The essence of deterrence here lies in the communication of capacity and will to those who would do Israel existential harm. Significantly, the actual

retaliatory use of nuclear weapons by Israel would signify the failure of its deterrent. Recalling the ancient Chinese military thinker Sun-Tzu, who was mentioned earlier in this paper, the very highest form of military success is achieved when one's strategic objectives can be met without any actual use of force.

To meet its "ultimate" deterrence objectives - that is, to deter the most overwhelmingly destructive enemy first-strikes - Israel must seek and achieve a visible second-strike capability to target approximately fifteen (15) enemy cities. Ranges would be to cities in Libya and Iran, and nuclear bomb yields would be at a level "sufficient to fully compromise the aggressor's viability as a functioning state." By choosing countervalue-targeted warheads in this range of maximum-destructiveness, Israel would achieve optimal deterrent effect, thereby neutralizing the overall asymmetry between the Arab states/Iran and the State of Israel. All enemy targets would be selected with the view that their destruction would promptly force the enemy aggressor to cease all nuclear/biological/chemical exchanges with Israel.

As a professor of international law, I was able to assure the Group that all of our recommendations to the Prime Minister regarding Israeli nuclear deterrence were fully consistent with authoritative international law. On July

8, 1996, the International Court of Justice at The Hague (not known for any specifically pro-Israel sympathies by any means) handed down its Advisory Opinion on THE LEGALITY OF THE THREAT OR USE OF FORCE OF NUCLEAR WEAPONS. The final paragraph concludes, inter alia:

The threat or use of nuclear weapons would generally be contrary to the rules of international law applicable in armed conflict, and in particular the principles and rules of humanitarian law. However, in view of the current state of international law, and of the elements of fact at its disposal, the Court cannot conclude definitively whether the threat or use of nuclear weapons would be lawful or unlawful in an extreme circumstance of self-defense, in which the very survival of a State would be at stake.

The Group advised the Prime Minister that Israel must display flexibility in its nuclear deterrence posture in order to contend with future enemy expansions of nuclear weapon assets. It may even become necessary under certain circumstances that Israel deploy a full "triad" of strategic nuclear forces. For now, however, we recommended that Israel continue to manage without nuclear missile-bearing submarines. This recommendation holds only as long as it remains highly improbable that any enemy or combination of enemies could destroy Israel's land-based and airborne-launched nuclear missiles on a first-strike attack.

Israel's nuclear deterrent must be backed up by far-reaching active defenses. With this in mind, the Group emphasized that Israel take immediate steps to operationalize an efficient, multi-layered antiballistic missile system to intercept and destroy a finite number of enemy warheads. Such interception would have to take place with the very highest possible probability of success and with a fully reliable capacity to distinguish between incoming warheads and decoys.

Israel's "Arrow" missile defense system involves various arrangements with US Boeing Corporation. The Israel Air Force (IAF), which operates the Arrow, will likely continue to meet its desired goal of deploying interceptors in inventory on schedule. Arrow managers also hope to sell their product to other carefully-selected states. This would help Israel to reinforce its qualitative edge over all adversaries. Israeli engineers are continually taking appropriate steps to ensure that Arrow will function well alongside American "Patriot" systems. The Group advised that IAF continue working energetically on all external and internal interoperability issues.

In its effort to create a multi-layered defense system, Israel may already be working on an unmanned aircraft capable of hunting-down and killing any enemy's mobile ballistic missile launchers. Israeli military officials have tried to interest the Pentagon in joining the launcher-attack project, known formally as "boost-phase launcher intercept" or BPLI. For the moment, Washington appears focused on alternative technologies. The Group advised the Prime Minister that Israel undertake BPLI with or without US support, but recognized that gaining such support would allow the project to move forward more expeditiously and with greater cost-effectiveness. Also, enlisting US support for BPLI would represent another important step toward maintaining Israel's qualitative edge.

Project Daniel underscored the importance of multi-layered active defenses for Israel, but affirmed most strongly that Israel must always prepare to act preemptively before there is any destabilizing deployment of enemy nuclear and/or certain biological weapons.

CONCLUSIONS

Looking back over this paper, we have been able to consider the broad range of Group recommendations contained in ISRAEL'S STRATEGIC FUTURE. These recommendations concern, *inter alia*, the manifest need for an expanded policy of preemption; an ongoing re-evaluation of "nuclear ambiguity;" recognizable preparations for appropriate "countervalue" reprisals in the case of certain WMD aggressions;

adaptations to a "paradigm shift" away from classical patterns of warfare; expanded cooperation with the United States in the War Against Terror and in future inter-state conflicts in the Middle East; deployment of suitable active defense systems; avoidance of nuclear warfighting wherever possible; and various ways to improve Israel's nuclear deterrence. Along the way we have also explored vital differences between rational and non-rational adversaries; changing definitions of existential harms; legal elements of "anticipatory self-defense;" possibilities for peaceful dispute settlements in the region; budgetary constraints and opportunities; maintaining Israel's qualitative edge; preparations for "regime targeting;" and implications for Israel of the growing anarchy in world affairs. ISRAEL'S STRATEGIC FUTURE must be understood as a work in progress. The geostrategic context within which Israel must fashion its future is continually evolving, and so, accordingly, must Israel's strategic doctrine. Ultimately it must be from such doctrine that the Jewish State's particular policies will have to be derived and implemented.

Since the presentation of our original document to Prime Minister Ariel Sharon on January 16, 2003, there have been a few minor "victories" in the effort to control WMD proliferation among Israel's enemies. A case in point is Libya. At the same time, the circumstances in North Korea (which has manifest ties to some of Israel's regional enemies), Iran and Pakistan remain highly volatile and dangerous. There is also evidence of expanding WMD ambitions in Egypt and Syria. At the level of terrorist groups, which are sustained by several Arab/Islamic states, new alignments are being fashioned between various Palestinian organizations and al Qaeda. The precise configurations of these alignments are complex and multifaceted, to be sure, but the net effect for Israel is unmistakably serious.

ISRAEL'S STRATEGIC FUTURE is founded on the presumption that current threats of war, terrorism and genocide derive from a very clear "clash of civilizations," and not merely from narrow geostrategic differences. Both Israel and the United States are unambiguously in the cross-hairs of a worldwide Arab/Islamic "Jihad" that is fundamentally cultural/theological in nature, and that will not concede an inch to conventional norms of "coexistence" or "peaceful settlement." This situation of ongoing danger to "unbelievers" is hardly a pleasing one for Jerusalem and Washington, but it is one that must now be acknowledged forthrightly and dealt with intelligently.

The ongoing war in Iraq has demonstrated the evident weaknesses of national intelligence agencies in providing critical warnings and in enhancing strategic stability. Israel, itself, is not without a history of serious intelligence failure, and Israel's strategic future will require an enhanced intelligence infrastructure and highly-refined "backup systems."

Facing growing isolation in the world community, it will also have to fend for itself more than ever before. In the end, Israel's survival will depend upon plans and postures of its own making, and these plans and postures will themselves require a broader and more creative pattern of strategic studies as a disciplined field of inquiry.

We learn from ECCLESIASTES (34: 1) that "Vain hopes delude the senseless, and dreams give wings to a fool's fancy." Israel's strategic future is fraught with existential risk and danger; it is essential, therefore, that friends of Israel now approach this future with utter realism and candor. A nuclear war against the Jewish State would likely be undertaken as a distinct form of genocide, and there can be no greater obligation for Israel than to ensure protection from such new crimes against humanity. It is with the incontestable and sober understanding that Holocaust can take new forms at the beginning of the 21st century that Project Daniel completed its critical work.

PARTICIPANTS IN THE PROJECT DANIEL RESEARCH AND REPORT

The Group is comprised of the following individual members:

Professor Louis Rene Beres, Chair, USA

Naaman Belkind, Former Assistant to the Israeli Deputy Minister of Defense for Special Means, Israel

Maj. Gen. (Res.), Israeli Air Force/ Professor Isaac Ben-Israel, Israel

Dr. Rand H. Fishbein, Former Professional Staff Member, US Senate Appropriations Committee, and former Special Assistant for National Security Affairs to Senator Daniel K. Inouye, USA

Dr. Adir Pridor, Lt. Col. (Ret.), Israeli Air Force; Former Head of Military Analyses, RAFAEL, Israel

Fmr. MK./Col. (Res.), Israeli Air Force, Yoash Tsiddon-Chatto, Israel

APPENDIX D: INTERNATIONAL ATOMIC ENERGY AGENCY AND IRAN NUCLEAR SITES

ISIS Imagery Brief: IAEA Inspectors and Iran Clash Over Frequency of Inspections of Underground Facilities

By David Albright and Paul Brannan
August 23, 2006
The Institute for Science and International Security (ISIS)

Iran over the weekend denied International Atomic Energy Agency inspectors access to underground facilities at the Natanz site in Iran. This latest incident stems from a clash between IAEA inspectors and Iranian officials over the frequency of inspections of the underground halls in which Iran intends to house centrifuge cascades but which currently remain empty of centrifuges. The IAEA wants monthly visits to the underground facilities which Iran refuses to permit. The design verification visits which Iran now refuses to permit are intended to ensure that what Iran is building at the underground site matches the designs that Iran has already provided to the IAEA. It is unclear whether Iran will allow the IAEA to visit the underground facilities next month.

Iran is also denying access to an inspector with centrifuge expertise who has visited Natanz and other centrifuge sites many times in the past. The current inspectors are only being granted single entry visas and denied multiple entry visas. Allowing inspectors multiple entry visas had been the accepted practice when Iran was observing the Additional Protocol. One senior diplomat in Vienna said that Iran was "nickel and diming" the IAEA.

New imagery from GeoEye shows the Natanz site in Iran. The two shaded squares cover the approximate location of two underground cascade halls. IAEA inspectors and Iran are battling over the frequency of visits to these underground facilities.

ISIS Imagery Brief: Update on Construction Activities at Arak 40 MW Heavy Water Reactor

By Paul Brannan and David Albright
April 21, 2006
Institute for Science and International Security (ISIS)

ISIS has obtained commercial satellite imagery from GeoEye that shows steady progress in the construction of the Arak reactor, a 40 megawatt-thermal heavy water reactor that is adjacent to a heavy water production plant. In a speech on 11 April 2006, Gholamreza Aghazadeh, the head of the Atomic Energy Organization of Iran, stated that the Arak reactor is expected to be finished in 2009, which is consistent with other statements made by Iranian officials. This date might be delayed if the adjacent production facility cannot produce enough heavy water. It is not yet producing at its nominal capacity.

Once fully operational, the Arak reactor can produce about nine kilograms of weapon-grade plutonium each year, or enough for about two nuclear weapons each year. Because of concerns about the potential misuse of this reactor, the IAEA's Board of Governors called on Iran to halt construction of the Arak reactor in a resolution adopted February 4, 2006.

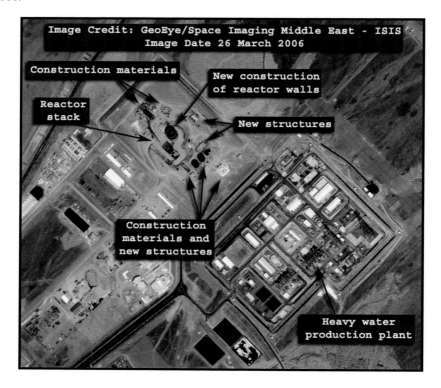

APPENDIX E: IRAN POLICY COMMITTEE BIOGRAPHIES

RAYMOND TANTER, PRESIDENT, IPC; FORMER SENIOR STAFF MEMBER, NATIONAL SECURITY COUNCIL

Raymond Tanter served at the White House as a Senior Member on the National Security Council staff, from 1981 to 1982. In 1983-1984, he was personal representative of the Secretary of Defense to arms control talks in Madrid, Helsinki, Stockholm, and Vienna. In 1967, Tanter was deputy director of behavioral sciences at the Advanced Research Projects Agency of the U.S. Department of Defense and a member of the Civilian Executive Panel, Chief of Naval Operations, 1980-1981.

In 2005, Tanter helped found the Iran Policy Committee and serves as its President. He is a member of the Council on Foreign Relations and the Committee on the Present Danger.

Professor Tanter teaches courses on terrorism and weapons proliferation at Georgetown University. He is adjunct scholar at The Washington Institute for Near East Policy and was scholar-in-residence at the Middle East Institute in Washington. He researched U.S. policy

options regarding Iran at both think tanks.

After receiving a Ph.D. from Indiana University in 1964, Professor Tanter taught at Northwestern, Stanford, the Hebrew University of Jerusalem, and the University of Michigan.

Professor Tanter was a fellow at the Hoover Institution at Stanford and the Woodrow Wilson International Center in Washington, and a Fulbright scholar, at the University of Amsterdam. In 1975, Tanter spent a month as scholar-in-residence at the American Embassy, in Tokyo, lecturing on petroleum-interruption scenarios, with special reference to the Middle East.

Among Tanter's publications is *Rogue Regimes: Terrorism and Proliferation* (New York: St. Martin's Press, 1997; revised edition Palgrave Press, 1999). Tanter also coauthored *Appeasing the Ayatollahs and Suppressing Democracy: U.S. Policy and the Iranian Opposition* (Washington, DC: Iran Policy Committee, 2006).

LT. GENERAL THOMAS MCINERNEY, USAF (RET.); CHAIRMAN, IPC ADVISORY COUNCIL

General McInerney established his own consulting firm, GRTT (Government Reform through Technology), in January 2000. Working with high-tech companies that do business with federal, state, city, and local governments, GRRT helps them introduce advanced technology into the private sector. From 1996-1999, Gen. McInerney was Chief Executive Officer and President of Business Executives for National Security (BENS), a national, nonpartisan organization of business and professional leaders headquartered in Washington.

Prior to joining BENS, Gen. McInerney was Vice President of Command and Control for Loral Defense Systems-Eagan. He joined Loral (then Unisys Electronic Systems Division) in 1994 following 35 years as a pilot, commander, and Joint Force Commander in the United States Air Force. Gen.

McInerney retired from military service as Assistant Vice Chief of Staff of the Air Force and as Director of the Defense Performance Review (DPR), reporting to the Secretary of Defense. In that capacity, Gen. McInerney led the Pentagon's "reinventing government" effort, visiting more than 100 leading-edge commercial companies to assimilate their ideas about business re-engineering.

Gen. McInerney earned a B.S. degree at the U.S. Military Academy in 1959, and a M.S. degree in international relations from George Washington University in 1972. He completed Armed Forces Staff College in 1970 and the National War College in 1973.

Gen. McInerney is a member of several boards of directors. He is a military analyst for Fox News Channel, a guest on many nationally-syndicated radio talk shows, and he has co-authored *The Endgame, Winning the War on Terror.*

JAMES AKINS, CO-CHAIRMAN, IPC; AMBASSADOR (RET.)

James Akins was U.S. ambassador to Saudi Arabia during the Nixon administration. He was a career U.S. Foreign Service officer, with postings to Naples, Paris, Strasbourg, Damascus, Beirut, Kuwait, Baghdad and the Department of State. In Kuwait he served as consul and principal officer, and in Baghdad as chief of the embassy's political section. He was assigned to the Office of Fuels and Energy in the Department of State and was later appointed director of that Office.

An internationally respected expert on Middle East and energy issues, Akins has been an active and outspoken proponent for a just resolution of the Arab-Israeli conflict and a prescient analyst of the Middle East peace process and Arab politics in general. Author Jean-Jacques Servan Schreiber has called Akins "the westerner who knows the most about the Middle East and has the closest relationship of trust with its leaders."

Ambassador Akins is a member of the Council on Foreign Relations. He graduated from the University of Akron with a degree in physics and obtained a certificate of history from the University of Strasbourg.

LT. COL. BILL COWAN, CO-CHAIRMAN, IPC; USMC (RET.), CO-FOUNDER OF wvc3

Bill Cowan is an internationally acknowledged expert in areas of terrorism, homeland security, intelligence, and military special operations. Cowan served three tours of duty in Vietnam and was awarded the Silver Star for valor in combat.

The Pentagon sent Cowan to Beirut in 1983. A military intelligence officer at the time, Cowan had the task of determining who was responsible for bombing the U.S. Embassy there. In the 1980s, he was selected to serve as one of the first members and only Marine in the Pentagon's most classified counterterrorist unit, the Intelligence Support Activity (ISA). There, Cowan served as a senior military operations officer and field operative on covert missions to the Middle East, Europe and Latin America. Following retirement from the Marine Corps in 1985, he worked two years on the staff of U.S. Sen. Warren B. Rudman as a legislative assistant and as the senator's primary staff assistant during the Iran/Contra hearings.

From 1989 through 1994, he was involved in numerous operations in the Middle East in response to terrorist incidents and the holding of Western hostages in Beirut and Kuwait. He was directly involved in the Beirut hostages drama, including international negotiations leading to their release in 1991.

In 1990, on behalf of a major New York law firm and working with former Director of Central Intelligence Bill Colby, Cowan organized and successfully conducted a series of operations resulting in the repatriation of a number of Western hostages from Iraqi-occupied Kuwait. Cowan is a FOX News Channel contributor and a co-founder of wvc3, a company providing homeland security services, support and technologies to government and commercial clients.

ALLAN GERSON, COUNSEL, IPC; AG INTERNATIONAL LAW, PLLC

Allan Gerson is Chairman of AG International Law, PLLC—and has long been involved in the struggle for accountability against sponsors and supporters of international terrorism. He brought the first suit against a foreign state (Libya) on behalf of the families of the victims of the Pan Am 103 Lockerbie bombing. He was also instrumental on passage of the 1996 AEDPA law (The Anti-Terrorism and Effective Death Penalty Act) that makes it possible today for U.S citizens to hold foreign governments accountable in U.S. courts for complicity in terrorism. His work on behalf of the families of Pan Am flight 103 is chronicled in *The Price of Terror* (New York: HarperCollins, 2001), which he co-authored with Jerry Adler of *Newsweek*.

Dr. Gerson earned his J.D. at New York University Law School, his LL.M. from Hebrew University of Jerusalem, and J.S.D in international law from Yale Law School.

He joined the U.S Justice Department in 1977 and has been the recipient of two Distinguished Performance citations. In 1979, he was the first trial lawyer to join the Justice Department's Office of Special Investigations (OSI), aimed at deporting Nazi collaborators. In 1981, Dr. Gerson became Counsel to the U.S. Ambassador to the United Nations, Jeane Kirkpatrick, and then to her successor, General Vernon Walters.

Afterwards, he served at the U.S. Department of Justice as Deputy Assistant Attorney General for Legal Counsel and Counselor for International Affairs. From 1986 to 1989 he was a senior fellow at the American Enterprise Institute, and from 1989-1995 he served as a Distinguished Professor of International Law and Transactions at George Mason University. From 1998-2000, he served as Senior Fellow for International Law and Organizations at the Council on Foreign Relations. Since 1991 he has also served in various capacities in private law practice and in 2003 was asked to join the U.S. Delegation to the United Nations Commission on Human Rights as Senior Counsel.

Gerson's other books include: *Lawyers' Ethics: Contemporary Dilemmas* (1980); *Israel, The West Bank and International Law* (1978); *The Kirkpatrick Mission: Diplomacy Without Apology* (1991); and *Privatizing Peace: From Conflict to Security* (2002).

R. BRUCE McCOLM, CHAIRMAN, IPC EMPOWERMENT COMMITTEE; PRESIDENT OF THE INSTITUTE FOR DEMOCRATIC STRATEGIES

Bruce McColm is the President of the Institute for Democratic Strategies, a non-profit organization committed to strengthening democratic processes abroad. For the past 25 years, he has been actively involved in the global movement toward democracy and has written extensively on political transitions in Latin America, Africa, and Central Europe.

McColm has served on numerous boards of directors and acts as a trustee for various private foundations and advocacy groups. McColm served as president of the International Republican Institute, where he extended the organization's capacity to provide technical assistance on economic and political reform around the world, introducing the use of information technologies to democracy programs.

Previously, McColm worked in a variety of capacities at Freedom House—a New York-based human rights organization—including the position of Executive Director from 1988 to 1993. McColm was also elected a member of the Inter-American Commission of Human Rights by the General Assembly of the Organization of American States (OAS).

McColm was educated at Williams College, Harvard University, and the University of Chicago.

CAPTAIN CHARLES T. "CHUCK" NASH, USN (RET.); CO-CHAIRMAN, IPC MILITARY COMMITTEE

Captain Nash is founder and President of Emerging Technologies International, Inc. (ETII). The company's focus is to understand military requirements and then actively search out and identify high leverage, emerging technologies that can be inserted quickly and inexpensively into tools for the U.S. military.

Capt. Nash served as Vice President, Emerging Technologies Group for Santa Barbara Applied Research, Inc., from Tkyear-Tkyear. For the previous 25 years, Capt. Nash served as an officer in the U.S. Navy, accumulating over 4,300 hours of flight time and 965 carrier landings on nine different aircraft carriers as a Naval Aviator.

He served in a variety of command positions with Naval Operations at the Pentagon and U.S. Naval Forces Europe, and has filled billets with U.S. and foreign special operations forces in Turkey, Northern Iraq and elsewhere. Capt. Nash previously served on the Defense Threat Reduction Agency (DTRA) and on the Naval Air Systems Command (NAVAIR) Expert Panel for the Supersonic Cruise Missile Advanced Concept Technology Demonstration. He sat on the Board of Visitors of the Office of Naval Research.

Capt. Nash serves on a number of boards of directors and is an advisor to the Chairman of the Board of Isothermal Systems Research, Inc., and to the President and CEO of Vision Technologies International, Inc.

Capt. Nash earned his B.S. in Aeronautics from Parks College of Aeronautical Technology, St. Louis University, and attended the National War College at Fort L. J. McNair in Washington. A Fox News Channel Military Analyst, Capt. Nash frequently appears on the network to discuss military, terrorism and aviation issues.

LT. GENERAL EDWARD ROWNY, CO-CHAIRMAN, IPC;USA (RET.)

General Rowny began his military career following graduation from the Johns Hopkins University and the U.S. Military Academy, two Masters degrees from Yale University and a Ph.D. from American University.

He fought in WW II, Korea, and Vietnam, commanding units from platoon to Corps size. Later, he served in the 1970s and 1980s as an advisor to the SALT II talks and as the chief negotiator of the START negotiations, with the rank of ambassador. As a soldier and strategic thinker, General Rowny was Deputy Chairman of the NATO Military Committee and initiated the Mutual and Balanced Forces Reduction negotiations in Vienna.

From 1985 to 1990, he was Special Advisor for Arms Control to Presidents Ronald Reagan and George H.W. Bush. In 1989, President Reagan awarded him the Presidential Citizens Medal. The citation reads that Gen. Rowny is "one of the principal architects of America's policy of peace through strength. As an arms negotiator and as a presidential advisor, he has served mightily, courageously, and nobly in the cause of peace and freedom." In 1991, Ambassador Rowny retired from government and currently consults on international affairs.

MAJOR GENERAL PAUL E. VALLELY, USA (RET.); CO-CHAIRMAN, IPC MILITARY COMMITTEE

General Vallely retired in 1991 from the U.S. Army as Deputy Commanding General, U.S. Army Pacific in Honolulu, Hawaii. Gen. Vallely graduated from the U.S. Military Academy at West Point and was commissioned in the Army in 1961, serving a distinguished career of 32 years in the Army.

He served in many overseas theaters, including Europe and the Pacific Rim countries, as well as two combat tours in Vietnam. He has served on U.S. security assistance missions pertaining to civilian-military relations in locations around the world.

Gen. Vallely is a graduate of the Infantry School, Ranger and Airborne Schools, Jumpmaster School, the Command and General Staff School, The Industrial College of the Armed Forces and the Army War College. His combat service in Vietnam included positions as infantry company commander, intelligence officer, operations officer, military advisor and aide-de-camp. He has over 15 years experience in Special Operations, Psychological and Civil-Military Operations.

Gen. Vallely was one of the first nominees for Assistant Secretary of Defense for Special Operations under President Reagan, and commanded the 351st Civil Affairs Command during the 1980s. He has served as a consultant to the Commanding General of the Special Operations Command as well as the Department of Defense Anti-Drug and Counter-Terrorist Task Forces.

Gen. Vallely is a military analyst for Fox News Channel and is a guest on many nationally-syndicated radio talk shows. He also is a guest lecturer on the War on Terror and co-authored *The Endgame, Winning the War on Terror.*

CLARE M. LOPEZ; IPC CONSULTANT

Clare Lopez is a strategic policy and intelligence expert with a focus on Middle East, homeland security, national defense, and counterterrorism issues. Lopez began her career as an operations officer with the Central Intelligence Agency (CIA), serving domestically and abroad for 20 years in a variety of assignments, acquiring extensive expertise in counterintelligence, counternarcotics, and counter-proliferation issues with a career regional focus on the former Soviet Union, Central and Eastern Europe and the Balkans.

Lopez has served in or worked in over two dozen nations worldwide, she speaks several languages, including Spanish, Bulgarian, French, German, and Russian, and currently she is studying Farsi.

Now a private consultant, Lopez has served as a Senior Scientific Researcher at Battelle Memorial Institute; a Senior Intelligence Analyst, Subject Matter Expert, and Program Manager at HawkEye Systems, LLC.;

and previously produced Technical Threat Assessments for U.S. Embassies at the Department of State, Bureau of Diplomatic Security, where she worked as a Senior Intelligence Analyst for Chugach Systems Integration.

Lopez received a B.A. in Communications and French from Notre Dame College of Ohio, and an M.A. in International Relations from the Maxwell School of Syracuse University. She completed Marine Corps Officer Candidate School (OCS) in Quantico, Virginia before declining a commission in order to join the CIA.

Lopez is a member of the Advisory Board for the Intelligence Analysis and Research program and guest lecturer at her undergraduate alma mater, Notre Dame College of Ohio. She also has been a visiting researcher and guest lecturer on counterterrorism, national defense, and international relations at Georgetown University. Lopez is a regular contributor to print and broadcast media on subjects related to Iran and the Middle East.

INDEX

PUBLICATIONS BY THE IRAN POLICY COMMITTEE INCLUDE:
Appeasing the Ayatollahs and Suppressing Democracy:
U.S. Policy and the Iranian Opposition

What Makes Tehran Tick:
Islamist Ideology and Hegemonic Interests

For ordering and all other inquiries, please contact us at

Iran Policy Committee
Alban Towers, Suite L-34
3700 Massachusetts Ave. NW
Washington, DC 20016
(202) 249-1142
www.iranpolicy.org